A DEVIL'S
TRIANGLE

A DEVIL'S TRIANGLE

Terrorism, Weapons of Mass Destruction, and Rogue States

Peter Brookes

ROWMAN & LITTLEFIELD PUBLISHERS, INC.

Lanham • Boulder • New York • Toronto • Oxford

ROWMAN & LITTLEFIELD PUBLISHERS, INC.

Published in the United States of America
by Rowman & Littlefield Publishers, Inc.
A wholly owned subsidiary of The Rowman & Littlefield Publishing Group, Inc.
4501 Forbes Boulevard, Suite 200, Lanham, Maryland 20706
www.rowmanlittlefield.com

PO Box 317
Oxford
OX2 9RU, UK

Distributed by National Book Network

British Library Cataloguing in Publication Information Available

Library of Congress Cataloging-in-Publication Data

Brookes, Peter, 1960–
   A devil's triangle : terrorism, weapons of mass destruction, and rogue states / Peter
Brookes.
      p.   cm.
   Includes bibliographical references and index.
   ISBN 0-7425-4952-6 (cloth : alk. paper)
   1. Terrorism.   I. Title.
HV6431.B77   2005
363.32′0973—dc22   2005012940

Printed in the United States of America

♾ ™ The paper used in this publication meets the minimum requirements of
American National Standard for Information Sciences—Permanence of Paper for
Printed Library Materials, ANSI/NISO Z39.48-1992.

For Tory and Cubby Brookes

CONTENTS

ACKNOWLEDGMENTS

Winston Churchill once quipped: "Writing a book is an adventure. To begin with it is a toy and an amusement, then it becomes a mistress, then it becomes a master, then it becomes a tyrant. The last phase is that just as you are about to be reconciled to your servitude, you kill the monster and fling him about the public." Perhaps, no truer words were ever spoken about the penning of a book.

Writing a book is a tremendous burden—one that is rarely borne by just the author. A great debt of gratitude goes out to my family, friends, and Heritage—and other—colleagues, who continuously steeled me for this challenge and offered endless support and advice. Excellent research support for the book came from Ji Hye Shin and Louis Deszeran. But my greatest inspiration came from Tory, Cubby, and Khris Bershers, who—never for a single moment—doubted my ability to get the job done.

INTRODUCTION

We've entered a new security environment, perhaps the most dangerous the world has ever known.

> —Secretary of Defense Donald Rumsfeld before the National
> Commission on Terrorist Attacks upon the
> United States on March 23, 2004

It is morning rush hour in Washington, DC. All seems in its usual, mun-
dane order as government bureaucrats cross the five main bridges from the
suburbs of Virginia into DC. The city subway—known simply as "the
metro" to locals—is its usual packed-to-capacity self. At one point, five people board five different metro lines heading downtown, where businesses
and key agencies of the U.S. government are located. Their watches syn-
chronized, the five terrorists place plastic bags on the floor of the subway
cars, puncture them quietly with sharpened umbrella tips, and depart the
trains. Toxic vapors emanate from the plastic bags, spreading throughout
the metro cars and onto station platforms. Within moments, 911 calls pour
into police stations from metro stops along all five commuter lines. Thousands are reported injured. The police, emergency crews, and local hospitals are overwhelmed by the chemical weapon attack.

This is not a scenario from a Hollywood docudrama or the opening from
a pulp fiction thriller. It actually happened, but not in Washington, DC. It
happened in Tokyo, Japan, on March 20, 1995, just ten short years ago.
Members of the Japanese doomsday terrorist group Aum Shinrikyo
("Supreme Truth") released the deadly nerve agent sarin into the Tokyo
subway system. By the end of the day, commuters at fifteen subway stations
on the world's busiest subway network felt the effects of the sarin gas

attack. Twelve people died, leaving over five thousand injured. Nearly one thousand people were hospitalized. Some victims remained hospitalized for years.

The same thing could happen right here in the United States—tomorrow. Even after four years of relative quiet at home since the unspeakable horrors of 9/11, we cannot become complacent about today's national security threats—not for a second.

THE NEW NATIONAL SECURITY ENVIRONMENT

The world is an increasingly dangerous place. A gathering storm of international Islamic terrorism, weapons of mass destruction (WMD) and ballistic missiles, and rogue states has replaced the Cold War nuclear balance of terror between the United States and the Soviet Union as the greatest threat to international peace and stability. These threats form a Devil's Triangle—a significantly more complex, dangerous, and unpredictable national security environment than at any time in the recent past. The potential for surprise, the blurring of war and peace, the lack of a distinct battlefield, and the sheer number of possible adversaries that threaten American interests at home and abroad is unprecedented in our history as a nation.

From al-Qaeda's blood-thirst to fundamentalist Iran's nuclear weapons program to the proliferation of North Korean deadly ballistic missiles, these seemingly random elements have the potential to unsettle global peace and stability on a broad scale for an extended period of time. The possibility of a catastrophic 9/11-like attack on the United States or its interests overseas, involving WMD, remains strong. A new national security era, marked by different, yet equally treacherous challenges, has begun. America and the free world are once again in the struggle of a lifetime.

INTERNATIONAL TERRORISM

Even four years after 9/11, terrorism continues to loom large over the international security landscape and presents one of the most serious challenges to American security. A loosely networked, but nonetheless deadly, network of Islamic terrorist groups, including al-Qaeda, Jemaah Islamiya, Hezbollah, and Hamas, span the globe, bent on changing the world order through holy wars of death, fear, and intimidation. Using the most modern technology to recruit, fund, plan, and operate, they are more sophisticated and lethal in their terrorist tradecraft than ever. They use money gathered from "deep-pocket" donors, "benevolent" Muslim charities, legitimate businesses, petty crime, and the illegal drug trade to strike undefended civilian, government, and military targets across the globe, seeking ever-increasing body counts and the toppling of governments.

Since 9/11, Muslim terrorist groups have indiscriminately spread death and destruction from the United States and Spain in the West to Indonesia and the Philippines in the East, resulting in thousands of deaths, countless injuries, mounting economic damage, and innumerable shattered lives. From Australia to the Americas, no continent is immune from their presence. The CIA concludes that al-Qaeda is still intent on finding ways to circumvent American homeland security efforts to strike the United States. Al-Qaeda's strategic horizon for its battle with America and the West stretches far into the future.

Moreover, scores of planned attacks have been prevented or preempted before they could wreak their deadly toll. Grim Reaper–like suicide bombers, undeterred by losing their own lives or, more precisely, motivated by their own deaths, have become commonplace and a significant threat to the soldier and civilian alike. Terrorism is not new, but the global menace of today's Islamic terrorism is unprecedented in mankind's history. President George W. Bush called preventing another terrorist strike on the United States, "The greatest challenge of my day," at the 2005 swearing-in of Secretary of Homeland Security Michael Chertoff.

WEAPONS OF MASS DESTRUCTION AND MISSILES

Proliferation of the world's most destructive weapons into the hands of the world's most dangerous regimes and terrorist groups is a recipe for disaster. Following terrorism, the greatest threat to American national security comes from the proliferation of nuclear weapons. Unfortunately, the end of the Cold War led to a significant increase in the availability of the materials and knowledge necessary for producing chemical, biological, radiological, and nuclear (CBRN) weapons and ballistic missiles. Nations such as Iran and North Korea are seeking these instruments of national power, prestige, and status to deter America and others from responding to their acts of intimidation, coercion, or aggression. Moreover, terrorist groups do not consider WMD a weapon of last resort, but a weapon of first use.

At least twenty countries now possess or are in the process of developing WMD and the means to deliver them. There are seven confirmed nuclear weapons states. Israel is believed to have a nuclear weapons arsenal, and North Korea's crazed leader Kim Jung Il is trying to develop—or has developed—a few as well. Iran is on the brink of a nuclear breakout, and many experts are convinced that Syria and Saudi Arabia have aspirations for the bomb. Egypt and Brazil worry some analysts. Pakistan—through the network of the rogue nuclear scientist A.Q. Khan—shared significant nuclear weapons technology with Iran, North Korea, Libya, and likely others over the last few years, possibly including al-Qaeda, devastating international nonproliferation efforts. China, India, and Pakistan are still adding to the size of their nuclear arsenals.

Iran, North Korea, Russia, and Syria all have chemical and biological weapons capability. An additional twelve countries are suspected of chemical weapons (CW) and biological weapons (BW) programs. The challenge posed by CW and BW is expected to become even more difficult in the next ten years. According to the director of the Defense Intelligence Agency, VADM Lowell Jacoby, U.S. Navy, in a hearing before the Senate Select Committee on Intelligence in February 2005, while some countries will focus on traditional CW and BW agents, "Others are likely to develop nontraditional chemical agents or use advanced biotechnology to create agents that are more difficult to detect, easier to produce, and resistant to medical procedures." On the ballistic missile front, North Korea, China, Russia, India, Pakistan, and Iran all have significant ballistic missile programs, many capable of carrying WMD. Many more nations have ballistic missiles of various ranges with conventional explosive capabilities.

ROGUE STATES

Anti-American rogue states, which support international terrorism, possess or are developing WMD and ballistic missiles, brutally repress their own people, and continue to threaten our national security and international peace and stability. Islamic fundamentalist Iran has both chemical and biological weapons and is in hot pursuit of nuclear weapons. Tehran is considered the world's most active state sponsor of terrorism, including supporting Hezbollah, Hamas, Palestinian Islamic Jihad, and, perhaps, al-

Qaeda. Its human rights record is dismal at best. The United States and Israel are its sworn enemies.

North Korea has chemical and biological weapons and may have breached the nuclear weapons threshold as well. It is the world's most active proliferator of ballistic missiles and has sold medium-range missiles to both Pakistan and Iran. Though North Korea does not appear to be an active state sponsor of terrorism, the impoverished, reclusive communist nation may be willing to sell its chemical, biological, or nuclear wares to the highest bidder. The regime is the world's most repressive. North Korea has vowed the destruction of American "imperialists" and its South Korean "puppet" government.

Syria is believed to have both a chemical and a biological weapons program, and appears to have aspirations for nuclear weapons as well. Damascus directly supports some of the world's deadliest terrorist groups, including Hezbollah, Hamas, and Palestinian Islamic Jihad. Moreover, the Syrian government is responsible for numerous human rights abuses against the Syrian people. Syria also hosts insurgents, terrorists, and foreign fighters working to destabilize Iraq.

A DEVIL'S TRIANGLE

Terrorism, WMD, and rogue regimes are enough of a threat to American interests and international peace and stability when considered in isolation from one another. A relationship between the three presents the United States and the international community with their greatest national security challenge in years. President George W. Bush characterized his concern with this possibility in his 2002 State of the Union speech:

> Today, the gravest danger in the War on Terror, the gravest danger facing America and the world now, is outlaw regimes that seek and possess nuclear, chemical, and biological weapons. These regimes could use such weapons for blackmail, terror, and mass murder. They could also give or sell those weapons to terrorist allies, who would use them without the least hesitation.

Though spoken in the days following 9/11, these words still hold true. American intelligence agencies believe that as many as two dozen terrorist groups are pursuing the development or acquisition of CBRN weapons at some level. Indeed, the threat of weapons of mass destruction placed wittingly—or unwittingly—into the hands of terrorist groups by rogue states or others acting independently, such as A.Q. Khan, could be disastrous.

It is widely assessed that al-Qaeda has been pursuing weapons of mass destruction with vigor and determination, perhaps since as early as 1993. As early as 1998, Osama bin Laden said that it was the religious duty of his al-Qaeda followers to acquire the most lethal of weapons. This belief is supported by the discovery of chemical and biological weapons work at field laboratories in Afghanistan after the fall of the Taliban in 2001.

Some believe that should these weapons fall into the hands of al-Qaeda or one of its affiliates, their use is an almost certainty. Some experts and government officials believe the likelihood of a WMD or radiological attack in the United States is inevitable. Director of Central Intelligence Porter Goss said in open testimony before the Senate Select Committee on Intelligence during a February 2005 hearing: "It may only be a matter of time before al-Qaeda or another group attempts to use chemical, biological, radiological and nuclear weapons." Sam Nunn, former chairman of the Senate Armed Services Committee, said that same year, "We are in a new arms race between terrorists' efforts to acquire nuclear, biological, and chemical weapons, and our efforts to stop them."[1]

THE CHALLENGE

The struggle against Islamic terrorism, the proliferation of weapons of mass destruction and missiles, and rogue regimes is a campaign of uncertain sacrifice and hardship. Some have even equated it to the protracted Cold War struggle with communism. And just like the Cold War, this troubling period is one in which the civilized world must prevail over intolerance, extremism, and hatred. The United States, in cooperation with international partners, must develop—and implement—a comprehensive strategy to simultaneously counter all of these threats, using all instruments of national power from diplomacy to economics to military might. America needs to be relentlessly proactive in the pursuit of its national security. Passivity and "hoping for the best" is not a sound national security strategy.

With North Korea and Iran on the nuclear boil, radical Islamists and terrorists doing their best to disrupt burgeoning democracy in the Middle East and to overthrow existing Muslim governments, and freelancing weapons merchants willing to sell their WMD plans and materials to the highest bidder, there is a need for a book that makes sense of the billowing political rhetoric, streaming television news commentary, and the barrage of newsprint on terrorism, WMD proliferation, and rogue states.

This book does that. *A Devil's Triangle* bridges a much-needed gap in current affairs literature, giving the American public and students of international affairs the first one-book guide to America's most pressing national security threats.

This book not only attempts to define and explain the challenges of the new national security environment, but also examines the key players and how they operate, the context in which they do so, how they are interconnected, and why we should care. Not satisfied just to define the problem without laying out options for solving it, *A Devil's Triangle* explores the means to emerge victorious against these pernicious national security problems.

After a change in "luck" for the Allies at El Alamein in North Africa in 1942, Winston Churchill, understanding the epic nature of the war before him, said: "Now this is not the end. It is not even the beginning of the end. It is, perhaps, the end of the beginning." This is also true for the epic struggle we face today in guarding our national security. Unfortunately, 9/11 was only the opening salvo of the battle. Iran, North Korea, or Syria could be next. Like Churchill, we must realize that this test of our character as a nation is closer to the beginning than the end. If we expect to win both the war and the peace in these struggles, it is imperative that we understand the monumental challenges that face us—and swear off complacency, which, arguably is as dangerous as our potential adversaries.

NOTES

1. "The Threat of Nuclear Terrorism," *The Week*, April 15, 2005, 13.

I

THE TERRORIST SCOURGE

Kill one, frighten 10,000.

—Chinese proverb

Carrying both Philippine and Indonesian passports, the thirty-three-year-old, baby-faced, Indonesian bomb-maker was arrested in the Philippines in January 2002 as he prepared to flee to Bangkok, Thailand. In Bangkok, this Southeast Asian Muslim was expected to continue planning for a series of bombings in Singapore against American military personnel, navy ships, and the British, Australian, and Israeli embassies. Fathur Rohman al Ghozi was a high-ranking member of the regional terrorist group Jemaah Islamiya, which had personal dealings with some of Asia's most wanted terrorists. Suspected of a series of deadly bombings in the Philippines, including a string in Manila in December 2000 that killed 22 people and injured more than 120, police discovered that al Ghozi possessed a ton of TNT, 300 detonators, and 17 M-16 assault rifles.

In addition to his membership in Jemaah Islamiya, al Ghozi served as an explosives trainer for the Moro Islamic Liberation Front (MILF), a Muslim terrorist-separatist group based on Mindanao Island in the southern Philippines. He also acted as a middleman between Jemaah Islamiya and MILF, and would facilitate the movement of other terrorists from Singapore and Malaysia who were traveling to Mindanao. Slipping effortlessly across international borders with a religious license to kill, al Ghozi is today's archetype modern terrorist.

MODERN TERRORISM

There is no doubt that today's terrorist is a different breed. The modern terrorist is not an idealistic left-winger trained in the Soviet Union and bent on nudging his homeland toward communist utopia through trash can bombings at local train stations. The modern terrorist is a "Tyrannosaurus Rex" in comparison—a cold-blooded killer with a seemingly endless appetite for violence and death. Unfortunately, the new breed is smarter, more capable, and more lethal than ever. Indeed, they are more dangerous because of their willingness, if not eagerness, to die for a religious cause that will bring eternal salvation. Like an international businessperson, the new terrorist is global in his efforts, planning, and operating across continents and time zones using cell phones, the Internet, and laptop computers to communicate with terror cells in every corner of the world. Whether it is Iraq, Afghanistan, Spain, Turkey, Uzbekistan, or Saudi Arabia, chaos and carnage are his calling cards and he or she might be coming to a neighborhood near you.

The new terrorist is much more entrepreneurial than his predecessor. In the past, terrorist groups relied more heavily on the largesse of state sponsors such as the Soviet Union, which had an axe to grind with the West. Today, through the donations of wealthy, "deep-pocket" donors, siphoning of funds from international Muslim charities, and even running legitimate businesses, modern terrorists often finance themselves. With multiple passports, forged documents, and a Byzantine list of aliases, the new terrorist slips almost effortlessly across international borders, moving from one holy war to another and calling no single country home. Akin to a multinational corporation with international franchises, terrorist groups have loosely networked themselves into a global organization. This international terrorist alliance shares ideology, intelligence, tactics, training, funding, weapons, and even personnel.

Once plucked from poor, uneducated, disaffected youth, today's terrorist groups are recruiting the middle class and the college educated for their ranks. They change and adapt their techniques and tactics to overcome technological, legal, and political barriers placed in their way. Not satisfied with the deaths of thousands on September 11, 2001, the modern terrorist is looking for new, even more efficient instruments of mass fear, death, and destruction, including the use of apocalyptic nuclear, chemical, biological, and radiological weapons. Once you think you have figured out today's terrorist, he changes modes and methods.

Burning with religious fervor and an inspired "higher calling," today's terrorists are willing to wrap themselves in pounds of explosives and go up in a blaze of "glory." Someone who passionately hates your country more than they love life itself cannot be dissuaded from taking his or her own life—and yours. They have no interest in negotiating a settlement or even a truce. For them, it is war and they will not be satisfied until the "infidel" is vanquished. More Americans will meet an unfortunate fate at the bloody hands of terrorists before the scourge is defeated. Make no mistake: The modern terrorist is more sophisticated, wily, and lethal than ever. The only thing to expect is the unexpected.

DEFINING THE SCOURGE

Most Americans do not believe that they need to be given a textbook definition of terrorism. Without a doubt, the graphic images of 9/11, forever seared into their memories, provide all the definition necessary. But an objective definition is important, since the media and even policy-makers often create misconceptions by using the term indiscriminately. Unfortunately, a single definition is hard to come by—academic research has indicated that there are over one hundred different definitions of the term "terrorism" alone.

For instance, the U.S. government defines terrorism in law (Title 22 of U.S. Code, Section 2656f(d)) as: "Premeditated, politically motivated violence perpetrated against noncombatant targets by subnational groups or clandestine agents, usually intended to influence an audience."[1] The operative phrase in that definition is the term "noncombatant." A noncombatant can include both military personnel as well as civilians. Military personnel are noncombatants when they are on-duty and unarmed or in an off-duty status. Acts of violence against military bases or armed military personnel when a state of hostilities does not exist is also considered terrorism by the U.S. government. So an attack on an American soldier on patrol in a combat zone like Iraq or Afghanistan, though reprehensible, would not necessarily be considered terrorism. An attack on an unarmed civilian is almost always terrorism.

The international community also cannot agree on a single definition of "terrorism." Because of the competing ideas of terrorism and national liberation among its 191 members, the United Nations has no official defini-

tion of the term. Although it has set a goal for defining it by 2006, the
closest it has come is the 2004 UN resolution 1566:

> Recalls that criminal acts, including against civilians, committed with the
> intent to cause death or serious bodily injury, or taking of hostages, with the
> purpose to provoke a state of terror in the general public or in a group of
> persons or particular persons, intimidate a population or compel a govern-
> ment or an international organization to do or abstain from doing an act,
> which constitute offences within the scope of and as defined in the interna-
> tional conventions and protocols relating to terrorism, are under no circum-
> stances justifiable by considerations of a political, philosophical, ideological,
> racial, ethnic, religious or other similar nature, and calls upon all States to
> prevent such acts and, if not prevented, to ensure that such acts are punished
> by penalties consistent with their grave nature.

Beyond the UN, there is still no international consensus on what constitutes terrorism. In some cases, the objection comes down to the old saying:
"one man's terrorist is another man's freedom fighter." Of course, one can
fight for his freedom, but a freedom fighter does not target innocent civilians in the pursuit of his political objectives, while a terrorist does. The lack
of a coherent, international definition does not help in fighting terrorism.

THE CONCEPT OF MODERN TERRORISM

Terrorism is fundamentally a political event. It is violent and designed to
instill fear in, and influence, its victims, especially potential future victims.
It is a strategy for generating raw political power, in an effort to compel,
coerce, or intimidate its audience into taking actions supportive of the terrorist's demands. Even the threat of terrorism can have a profound effect
by sowing fear among the populace. Terrorism can undermine stability and
create chaos with governments. Moreover, it may harm the economy, the
standard of living, and the quality of life in the target society. Right here
in the United States, the 9/11 attacks caused the stock market to plunge,
depressed the job market, rocked the American airline industry, and made
ghost towns of the hotels and tourist spots in Washington, DC, and New
York City for months after the attack. U.S. airlines posted a net loss of $7
billion in the months following the September 11 attacks. Overall, economic growth fell in 2002, and the loss in national income through the end
of 2003 amounted to at least half a trillion dollars.

Terrorism can be a very powerful political tool, providing an effective and efficient path to actualizing a terrorist's sordid agenda. Whether that objective is changing a government policy, altering the political order, addressing a social grievance, or settling a score, terrorism can help. Terrorism uses violence not only to punish a victim, but to influence those still living. In reality, those killed by terrorist acts are not the real targets of terrorism, the survivors are. The dead can no longer be influenced by terrorism, but the surviving government and general public can.

Terrorism can be especially effective against democratic societies, where political leaders are elected and their policies and records must withstand the continuing scrutiny of voters. A civilian population's discontent with its elected government because of acts of terrorism gives significant leverage to terrorists. Case in point: al-Qaeda's March 2004 train bombings in Spain. Executed just three days before Spain's national parliamentary elections, the slaughter effectively brought down the popular government of Spanish prime minister José Maria Aznar after eight years in office. The attacks were also "rewarded" with the withdrawal of 1,300 Spanish troops from Iraq under the new government of Prime Minister José Luis Rodriguez Zapatero—one of al-Qaeda's preattack demands of Spain. Al-Qaeda's indiscriminate carnage, resulting in 191 deaths, provided the leverage to change the policies of one of Europe's strongest democracies. Iraqi insurgents employed a similar tactic against an Asian democracy. Threatening to behead a kidnapped Philippine national, Manila met the insurgents' demand and withdrew its fifty-member military contingent from Iraq in August 2004. Regrettably, the moves of both of these governments set dangerous precedents that will undoubtedly encourage more acts of terrorism to influence democratic governments.

Terrorism is not only a political event; it is also a form of warfare. War and politics are closely interwoven. Karl von Clausewitz (1780–1831), the Prussian general and author of the famous military treatise "On War," which analyzed the nature of war during the Napoleonic era, posited that war is but an extension of politics by other means. War is a tool for achieving political aims rather than an end in itself—war is, essentially, a continuation of politics with guns instead of words. So is terrorism. Terrorism is politics by other means—in this case, violent means. In fact, sometimes terrorists commit violent acts because they have no other method of expressing themselves politically or challenging the political status quo as is the case in many repressive parts of the world.

Terrorism is psychological warfare. It is also a psychotraumatic event aimed at the survivors of the terrorist act, not the victims. The number of victims physically affected by any one terrorist attack to date is generally limited—9/11 being a significant exception. But the number of people psychologically affected is quite dramatic. Although in some instances only a few people are killed or injured in a terrorist incident, there is a prevalent sentiment in the target population that they could have been the victims themselves. As a result, they may change their habits, views or even voting practices, giving an advantage to the terrorists.

Terrorists use acts of violence to gain recognition and support for their cause. In some simplistic ways, terrorism is a public relations stunt, albeit a risky one. Continued terrorist brutality reminds the target audience that the terrorist group continues to exist and that its demands must be addressed. Moreover, terrorist supporters, sympathizers, and possible recruits are energized by the terrorist group's barbarous successes. Without acts of terror, a terrorist group can become yesterday's bad dream: quickly and easily forgotten.

But violent acts of terror can also galvanize opposition to the terrorist's evil handiwork. For example, some Muslims saw the events of 9/11 as abhorrent while others cheered, looking for ways to join the global jihad (holy war) against the "Western infidels." In fact, Osama bin Laden is revered in some parts of the world as a mythic folk hero who has stood up to both the mighty Soviet Union and the all-powerful United States. But no civilized human being has a positive image of al-Qaeda. Instead of crushing the United States, the 9/11 attacks united America, costing al-Qaeda dearly in losing its terrorist sanctuary in Afghanistan, much of its senior leadership, and a lot of its financial assets. Successful terrorist acts against a perceived enemy can have the added benefit of drawing more financial resources and followers to the cause. Violence is dramatic and, if nothing else, terrorism forces public attention to the terrorist's plight. This has clearly been the case in Iraq, where successful acts of terrorism have drawn more foreign jihadists to the cause of preventing the establishment of a post-Saddam government.

Though other important factors were involved, terrorists can point to a number of perceived political successes just in this century. Terrorism played a role in driving the British from Palestine (1948), Aden (1967), and Cyprus (1960). It ended French colonialism in Algeria (1962). It resulted in America pulling peacekeeping troops out of Lebanon (1984) and Somalia (1994) and it pushed the Israelis from Lebanon (2000) and the Gaza Strip (2005). Terrorism changed a democratically elected government in Spain

(2004). And it forestalled the establishment of a government in Iraq (2003–2005). Some al-Qaeda members have even mentioned the American loss in Vietnam as an example of the effectiveness of terrorism and irregular warfare as a good method for the weak to prevail against the strong. Judging from these events, terrorists have come to believe terrorism works, meaning it will continue to be wielded as a political club by murderous extremists. This means that giving into terrorism creates a "moral hazard"—surrendering to it only encourages more of it.

A QUICK HISTORY OF TERRORISM

Terrorism has been practiced across the centuries by both the political left and right, by nationalist and ethnic groups, by rogue states against their own citizens, and by revolutionaries. In fact, most experts agree that terrorism may have begun as early as the first century in Roman-occupied Judea. Jewish members of the resistance group the Zealots would attack Roman soldiers and Jewish collaborators, attempting to end the occupation. In the eleventh to thirteenth centuries, in modern-day Syria and Iran, the Muslim group known as the Assassins attacked Christian Crusaders and other prominent local Muslim officials. Their daring attacks in the presence of large crowds assured their immediate capture and execution, leading to what is believed to be the first acts of Islamic martyrdom.

Through the eighteenth century, most terrorism originated from religious fervor. Beginning in the nineteenth century, though, terrorist movements acquired a more political and revolutionary orientation. In the late nineteenth and early twentieth centuries, anarchists in Italy, Spain, Russia, and France used terrorism to fight the aristocratic governments and monarchies of the day. Modern-day terrorism is thought to have arisen from the thoughts and writings of nineteenth-century Russian revolutionary Mikhail Bakunin, who wrote the Principles of Revolution in 1869. Bakunin believed that the only way to deal with the autocratic Russian monarchy was to undertake violent acts against it. Influenced by Bakunin, a Russian anarchist group, The People's Will, undertook a series of attacks on the Russian royal family. In fact, the infamous Russian revolutionary Vladimir Lenin was inspired by his older brother Aleksandr's membership in The People's Will. In 1887, Aleksandr was arrested and executed in St. Petersburg, Russia, for his involvement in a conspiracy to assassinate Russian Emperor Alexander II. It left an indelible impression on his younger sibling, sparking a life-long interest in vindicating his brother and removing the Russian monarchy. As we all know, he eventually did so in 1917.

At the dawn of the twentieth century, political assassination became a terrorist art form. Terrorism was responsible for the assassination of Austrian archduke Ferdinand in Sarajevo by a Serbian nationalist in 1914. The assassination ultimately served as one of the seminal events leading to the carnage of World War I. After World War II, terrorism became the political weapon of choice for many nationalist groups seeking independence from colonial rule in the Middle East, North Africa, and Asia. In their struggle to bring an end to British rule in Palestine, radical Jewish groups such as the Stern Gang resorted to terrorism in the late 1940s. The most notorious of these attacks was the bombing of British government offices at the King David Hotel in Jerusalem in 1946, which killed more than a hundred people. These struggles, often involving guerrilla warfare, gave rise to the hotly contested semantic debate about the terrorist versus the freedom fighter. This argument sought to rationalize the use of violence for political liberation purposes as justified, regardless of its civilian victims.[2]

In the latter half of the twentieth century, acts of terror became more common, propelled by fierce nationalism and political ideology, including communism. The 1960s and 1970s saw the evolution of state-sponsored terrorism. Middle Eastern and other terrorist groups received support from the Soviet Union and sent their members to the USSR and communist Eastern Europe for training. The Soviets supported these groups in their efforts to gain influence in the Arab world, undermine Israel and the United States, and support socialist national liberation efforts.

Arab terrorism against Israel increased in the 1960s, especially following Israel's overwhelming victories against Egypt, Jordan, and Syria in the 1967 Six-Day War. Israeli victories led to their occupation of territory populated by Palestinians, such as the Gaza Strip and West Bank. Terrorist groups such as Yasir Arafat's Fatah faction, organized under the Palestine Liberation Organization (PLO), conducted terrorist operations against Israel and Israeli interests abroad. Most notable was the 1972 attack by the Palestinian terrorist splinter group Black September, which took hostage and then killed eleven Israeli athletes at the Olympic Summer Games in Munich, Germany.

In the 1960s and 1970s, leftist terrorist groups outside the Middle East, such as the Japanese Red Army, the Italian Red Brigade, and the German Bader Meinhof Gang, plagued Asia and Europe with terrorist acts, including bombings and kidnappings of prominent officials as well as attacks on

American military bases overseas. Inspired by Marxist and Maoist teachings and supported by the Soviet Union and affluent middle-class leftist sympathizers, these terrorists aimed to bring about the collapse of these nascent democratic governments.

These terrorist groups also started a trend of working together across international borders. For instance, the Bader Meinhof Gang cooperated with Palestinian terrorists in the murder of the Israeli athletes in 1972 and the 1976 hijacking of an Air France flight with 105 Jewish passengers aboard to Uganda. The Air France incident concluded successfully when Israeli commandos raided the plane and freed the hostages after it landed at Entebbe, Uganda. In another incident demonstrating the trend toward internationalizing terror, in 1972, the Japanese Red Army conducted a raid at Ben Gurion airport in Israel. Back at home in Italy, the Italian Red Brigade launched a brutal wave of assaults on politicians, police, journalists, and business executives. The most infamous attack was the 1978 kidnapping and murder of former Italian prime minister Aldo Moro. Intense law enforcement and the waning of interest in the socialist agenda brought a relatively quiet end to these groups.

The late 1970s and the 1980s saw the formation of religiously motivated terrorist groups, such as Hamas and Hezbollah, rising like tempests out of the 1979 Iranian revolution. Many terrorism experts believe the success of the Iranian Islamic revolution against the Western-leaning Iranian monarchy was the watershed event in the development of modern Muslim terrorism. The fact that the Iranian revolution also struck at the United States through the storming and holding of the American embassy in Tehran only made the event more compelling to would-be terrorist groups. Another seminal event was the successful Muslim resistance to the Soviet invasion of Afghanistan in late 1979. The "godless" communist occupation of Muslim Afghanistan resulted in an uproar across the Islamic world, which helped draw foreign jihadists to Pakistan and Afghanistan by the thousands to fight the *infidel* Soviets. This network of Arab resistance fighters in Afghanistan eventually became the core of the terrorist group al-Qaeda in the late 1980s, created by Osama bin Laden himself.

Hostility to the United States' support of Israel and Washington's involvement in the Middle East resulted in numerous acts of terrorism against American interests in the 1980s, including airplane hijackings, hostage taking, and bombings. But perhaps most notable was the 1983 suicide bombing by the Iranian-supported Lebanese Shiite Muslim group Hezbollah on the American embassy and U.S. Marine barracks in Beirut, Lebanon, which killed more than 300 people, including 241 American servicemen. The attack was so successful that the Americans withdrew their peacekeeping forces from Lebanon shortly thereafter. Although the PLO renounced terrorism in 1988, radical Palestinian groups such as Hamas, Palestinian Islamic Jihad, and the Al Aqsa Martyrs Brigade have continued to wage a campaign of terror against Israel. Over one hundred Palestinian suicide bombings have killed over four hundred Israelis in the last few years.

With the fall of the Berlin Wall and collapse of the Soviet Union, the 1990s saw a significant drop in state-sponsored terrorism. Unfortunately, a new form of terrorism soon replaced it. The last decade of the twentieth century saw the formation of terrorist safe havens, such as Afghanistan and Sudan, where terrorists could meet, train, plan, and operate. These places became incubators for the militant Islamic fundamentalism of Osama bin Laden and al-Qaeda. Born in the resistance camps of Pakistan and Afghanistan during the Soviet-Afghan war of the 1980s, al-Qaeda became a global network of loosely affiliated terrorist groups stretching from Europe to the archipelagos of Southeast Asia. This new strain of holy warrior included Muslim terrorists of many nationalities operating in a number of countries around the globe at the same time. Its size and reach was unprecedented in the history of terrorism.

Perhaps the most ominous harbinger of the new age of terrorism was the 1993 bombing of the World Trade Center in New York City by early elements of al-Qaeda. Six people died in the blast, which caused an estimated $600 million in property and other economic damage. This was the beginning of Osama bin Laden's battle with America. Unfortunately, no one in the United States—or elsewhere—seemed to take notice. It was thought to be the sinister act of a rump element of Cold War–era Islamic fanatics. That World Trade Center attack was followed by the ambush of U.S. servicemen in Mogadishu, Somalia, in 1993, which had the backing and support of al-Qaeda operatives. Two years later in 1995, al-Qaeda elements in Saudi Arabia attacked a Saudi National Guard training center, killing two American contractors. In 1996, al-Qaeda and Hezbollah used a truck bomb against the American Khobar Towers housing complex in Dhahran, Saudi Arabia, killing nineteen American servicemen. Osama struck again in 1998, devastating the American embassies in Kenya and Tanzania. And in 2000, al-Qaeda operatives attacked the American destroyer USS *Cole* with a bomb-laden motorboat while it was in port in Aden, Yemen. This attack killed seventeen American sailors and put the destroyer out of service for a couple of years.

Perhaps at the pinnacle of their perfidy, on September 11, 2001, nineteen al-Qaeda hijackers commandeered four U.S. airliners, which took off from Boston, Newark, and Washington, DC. They crashed two of them into New York's World Trade Center; one into the Pentagon; and the final plane into a Pennsylvania field. Almost three thousand people from over 80 countries lost their lives that late summer day and innumerable lives were forever shattered. Al-Qaeda and its terrorist affiliates have conducted a number of significant terrorist acts since 9/11, in places ranging from the idyllic tropical paradise of Bali, Indonesia, to the northwestern African seaport of Casablanca, Morocco to the streets of London. A number of attacks in places like Singapore, Malaysia, the Philippines, Saudi Arabia, Pakistan, and the United States have been prevented, preempted, or disrupted. The Middle East is no less troubled as terrorist suicide bombers continue to take innocent lives in Israel, the new Afghanistan, and post-Saddam Iraq.

Unfortunately, the final chapters of terrorism's dark and destructive history have not yet been written. More death, more carnage, and more chaos are likely to come at the hands of terrorists despite the best efforts of the United States and the international community. One can only hope that there will be less to write about the history of terrorism in the future than there is today.

NOTES

1. U.S. Department of State, *Patterns of Global Terrorism* (Washington, DC: U.S. Government Printing Office, 2002), p. xiii.

2. Harvey G. Kushner, *Encyclopedia of Terrorism* (Thousand Oaks, Calif.: Sage Publications, 2002), p. 361.

BIRTHING MODERN TERROR

Islam is politics or it is nothing.

—Ayatollah Ruhollah Khomenei,
father of the Iranian Islamic Revolution

Known as the godfather of the Muslim suicide bombing, the mysterious Sheik Ahmed Yassin was, in actuality, a sickly, wheelchair-bound quadriplegic. Despite his frail appearance, the sixty-seven year old, nearly deaf and blind Muslim cleric was the driving force behind one of the deadliest terrorist groups in existence: Hamas. Under Yassin's hand Hamas was responsible for a majority of the over 100 Palestinian suicide bombings, killing over 500 mostly civilian Israelis since September 2000. Rejecting outright the existence of Israel, Yassin called for the establishment of an Islamic state in Israel, the Gaza Strip, and the West Bank.

Yassin founded the Islamic terrorist group in 1987 during the first Palestinian uprising as an offshoot of the radical Egyptian Muslim Brotherhood and presided over its meteoric rise to the pinnacles of terrorist power and violence. Hamas quickly gained a reputation for ruthlessness, especially against Palestinians who collaborated with the Israelis. Yassin was jailed by the Israelis in 1989 and sentenced to life in prison for his crimes. He was released in 1997 in exchange for Israeli intelligence agents, who had been arrested in Jordan during a failed operation. Israel came to deeply regret releasing Yassin, who moved to strengthen Hamas and continued his terrorist war against Israel. For Israel, Yassin became a marked man.

By March 2004, Israeli prime minister Ariel Sharon had lost his patience with the Muslim cleric and ordered Israeli forces into action. Leaving his mosque after morning prayers, Yassin and his bodyguards were killed instantly when an Israeli helicopter launched three missiles at his party. In an ironic twist of fate, the man who had fomented so much brutality met an end as violent as some of his victims.

THE ROOTS OF MODERN TERRORISM

Since 9/11, studying the roots of terrorism has become a veritable "cottage industry" for policy-makers, think tanks, and academia. The debate is lively, controversial, complex, often emotionally charged, and rarely conclusive. Some have argued that pursuing a general theory of terrorism, including an overall explanation of its roots, is futile.[1] Despite these obstacles, and considering the stakes at hand, the topic clearly warrants study in spite of the challenges. So why does someone become a terrorist? What propels an individual from the societal mainstream into a life of fanaticism, violence, and crime? There are many reasons for the terrorist phenomenon, including radical religious ideology, poor governance, a lack of economic opportunity, social alienation, demographic pressure, and political isolation, and they are all important to understand in order to determine how to deal with the challenge of terrorism.

RELIGIOUS IDEOLOGY

Though it does not answer all of the questions about the roots of modern terrorism, religious ideology is a significant factor. Religion does not address all of the causes of the current round of terrorism, but to the casual observer, it certainly seems to be the most obvious and prevalent cause lately. When most people think of terrorism today, they see the specter of Osama bin Laden, his fiery religious fervor and his advocacy of a clash of civilizations between the "believing" Islamic and "nonbelieving" Judeo-Christian worlds. Unfortunately, this makes Islam a good place to start the discussion on the roots of modern terrorism.

Islam is one of the world's major religions, founded by the Prophet Muhammad in Arabia in the early seventh century AD. With one billion followers, almost one-fourth of the world's population is Muslim. In fact, due to high birth rates in the Muslim world, Islam is the world's fastest growing religion. But the Muslim world is not monolithic. Muslims can be found in all nationalities, races, and ethnic backgrounds. Most Muslims live outside the Middle East; and only 20 percent of Muslims are ethnic Arabs. Over fifty nations are Muslim-majority states, but its four largest, Indonesia, Pakistan, Bangladesh, and India, are non-Arab.

The word Islam is often translated from Arabic to English as meaning "submission." More specifically, it means "submission to the will of God" (Allah). Islam is a strictly monotheistic religion, and its followers regard Muhammad, who lived in the sixth to seventh centuries AD, as Allah's messenger on earth. Biblical personalities such as Adam, Abraham, Moses, and Jesus are all elements of the Islamic religious tradition. Islam's sacred scripture, the Koran, mentions Moses over 500 times. Despite a history of struggle and strife, three of the world's major religions, Islam, Judaism, and Christianity, actually trace their origins to one man—Abraham. The majority of Islamic scholars and clerics say that Islam is a peaceful, tolerant, even democratic religion.

The Koran contains Allah's revelations to Muhammad. The sayings, deeds, and advice of the Prophet Muhammad, as recounted by his companions and followers, are contained in two books, the Sunna and the Hadith, and are also an important source of belief and practice in Islam. These books are only second to the Koran as a source of Islamic belief. The religious obligations of all Muslims are summed up in the Five Pillars of Islam. These five duties include: the profession of faith in Allah as the one God and in Muhammad as his Prophet; praying five times a day; giving alms to the poor; fasting during the month of the holy season of Ramadan; and making the *hajj* (the pilgrimage) to Mecca, the birthplace of Muhammad and Islam's holiest city, barring any difficulties such as poverty or physical disability.

Sharia, often translated as the "path to the watering place," is a combination of traditional Islamic law and political and social philosophy.[9] It was developed in the eighth to ninth century AD and deals extensively with politics, governance, citizenship, and authority, as based on divine revelation. Muslims adopt *sharia* in their personal lives to a greater or lesser extent as a matter of conscience. Like many religions, Islam draws no distinction between religious and secular life, and it has been formally instituted as law by certain states and enforced by the courts. *Sharia* covers not only religious rituals and the legal code, but many aspects of day-to-day life as well, such as dietary rules, dress, domestic life, and the role of women.

It is implemented to varying degrees in different Muslim countries: from the beheadings in Saudi Arabia for murder to the stonings in Nigeria for adultery to the tolerance of Indonesia. There are four fundamental elements to *sharia*: the books of the Koran and the Sunna; the *ijma* (agreement or consensus of the community); and *qiya* (legal analogies).

Like in Christianity, there are a number of different Islamic sects and movements. The two major sects are the Sunni and Shia. A division between the Sunni and Shia occurred early in Islam's history, brought about by disputes over the succession to the caliphate (an Islamic state ruled by an Islamic leader, a *caliph*). Today, about 90 percent of Muslims belong to the Sunni branch of Islam, which is considered to be the mainstream branch of Muslim faith. (Sunni is derived from the word Sunna.) The Shia (party) broke away in the seventh century over the caliphate succession issue. For example, Iran and Iraq are predominantly Shia, while Saudi Arabia, Egypt, and Pakistan are majority Sunni nations. It is not uncommon for the followers of the different sects to look down on one another, even hate one another.

There are also a number of major movements within Islam, including Sufism, Liberalism, Salafism, and Wahhabism. Sufism is a mystical form of Islam that is generally considered moderate in its outlook. Liberalism is an interpretation-based movement that advocates a reform agenda, which might include such issues as women's rights, political secularism, tolerance, and nonviolent jihad. Of significant note since 9/11 is Salafism. Salafists are traditionalists, who believe the first three Muslim generations (Prophet Muhammad's companions and the two generations after them) are exemplar of how Islam should be lived and practiced. Even more conservative than Salafism, Wahhabism advocates a fundamentalist, puritanical stance in matters of faith and religious practice. Wahhabists see their role as protecting Islam from innovations, deviances, and heresies. Wahhabism is an eponym for the movement's founder, Muhammad ibn al Wahhab, who developed a political brand of Islam in the eighteenth century in the sands of the Arabian Peninsula. It advocates a return to the ways of life of early Islam and espouses a literal interpretation of the Koran. Strict Wahhabists are intolerant of other interpretation of the Koran and view other Muslims who do not practice their form of Islam as heretics and enemies. They are willing to undertake violence to impose their views of Islam on other Muslims. Wahhabism is widely practiced in Saudi Arabia. It is influential in Qatar, Kuwait, and the United Arab Emirates. It has a substantial following in Yemen. Critics say that some extremists such as Osama bin Laden and the Taliban have further distorted and misinterpreted Wahhabism for their own evil purposes.

ISLAMIC FUNDAMENTALISM

Some Muslims, like some in other religions, take a very strict view of their faith. This is often described as religious fundamentalism. Some might even call it religious conservativism. Islamic fundamentalism describes the views of traditional Muslims that restrict themselves to the literal interpretations of Islam's sacred scripts, the Koran and Hadith. Islamic fundamentalists form a part of the broad spectrum of the adherents of the Muslim faith. Some Islamic fundamentalists, also called Islamists, advocate Islam as a political movement, which advocates the replacement of existing secular laws with *sharia*. Fundamentalists may also be very intolerant of the views of other Muslims who do not share their conservative views. They may also see non-Muslims as infidels (nonbelievers). For these people, the world is simply divided into believers and nonbelievers. Fundamentalism comes from many sources and can be generated at the grassroots level or based on years of local tradition. It can also be promoted, or imposed, by a state, as in the case of Saudi Arabia, Iran, or pre-9/11 Afghanistan.

In the eyes of the Islamic fundamentalists, the Muslim world is going in the wrong direction. They want to change its course by returning to a society based on traditional religious values. Fundamentalist Muslims reject Western "decadent" influences, such as modern dress, Hollywood movies, provocative TV, and a liberated role for women, which have permeated their societies. Fundamentalists offer an ideology that promises to deal with the problems that have plagued the Muslim world such as economic stagnation, or even decline. They are in favor of turning back the clock to "simpler times," to the days of Muhammad. For some in the Muslim world, modern society has, unfortunately, not led to a better life, but has instead created a widening socioeconomic gap between rich and poor. In many Muslim societies the rich are getting richer, and the poor are getting poorer. Fundamentalists attribute this negative trend to unwanted, unnecessary changes in Muslim societies. Economic stagnation is a fact in many parts of the Muslim world. Due to a wide variety of reasons, including a population bulge and bad economic policies, even talented, educated young people cannot find work or opportunity or realize their potential. This rejection of modernity and socioeconomic frustration can lead to upheaval as evidenced by the movement that brought the overthrow of the Shah of Iran in 1979 and the assassination of Egyptian president Anwar Sadat in 1981.[3]

In fact, because of the Internet, international travel, and satellite television, many in the Islamic world are more aware of their poverty than they have ever been. They are unhappy and deeply frustrated about it. As a result, they are looking for reform, any type of reform, including the "re-Islamization" of society, if it will change their lives for the better. In the view of the fundamentalist, a more religiously conservative way of life, including fewer freedoms, especially for women, will bring quick and easy solutions to all their problems.

Most Islamic fundamentalist groups insist that *sharia* govern Muslim countries. In actuality, *sharia* does not govern the vast majority of Muslim countries. *Sharia* is currently in place in Iran and Saudi Arabia. Parts of other countries are ruled by *sharia*, including Sudan and Pakistan. Afghanistan, under the Taliban, was ruled by *sharia* as well. Many countries adopt elements of *sharia* for their own penal systems. Islamic fundamentalists also indict Muslim governments that have failed in preserving traditional Muslim ways of life based upon the Koran. They often refer to these governments as "apostate." An apostate is one that abandons one's religious faith or beliefs. Osama bin Laden's al-Qaeda and many of its affiliates aspire to Islamic caliphates ruled by *sharia*. Many Islamic fundamentalists insist that strict Islam is the "answer," but to date they have not offered solutions for what ails the Muslim world, other than religion.

Militant Islam

Some Muslims have taken their strong Islamic beliefs one step further to fanaticism and militancy. Militant Islam, most often springing from fundamentalist religious beliefs, has become the engine of today's terrorism. This new breed of terrorist grew out of the 1979 Iranian Revolution and the 1980–1989 Afghan–Soviet War experience, promoting a culture of jihad and martyrdom. A "holy warrior" is often willing to give his (or, increasingly, her) life to destroy the perceived enemies of Islam in a struggle between "good and evil." With roots in Shiism, the culture of martyrdom was popularized by the 1979 Iranian Revolution, personified in suicide attacks against American and French forces in Lebanon in the early 1980s, and soon spread to Sunni radicals as well.

These violent Muslim radicals blame the West, and particularly the

United States, for the Muslim world's troubled state. Harkening back to the Christian Crusades (eleventh and twelfth centuries), Western colonial rule (nineteenth century), and imperialism (twentieth century), these Islamic militants have convinced themselves that the West is waging a war to destroy Islam. These extremists also believe that Western values such as democracy, separation of church and state (secularism), political and civil liberties, and women's rights are all part of a grand conspiracy by the West to vanquish Islam and subjugate the Muslim world. Al-Qaeda, for instance, has effectively pointed to Iraq, Afghanistan, American bases in Muslim Central Asia, Pakistan's support for the war on terror, and America's support for Israel as proof that Islam is in danger from America and the West. Unfortunately, this "call to arms" has resonated in the Muslim world.

One of the key elements of militant Islam is jihad (struggle). Jihad, arguably, has been more misunderstood and misrepresented than any other single word in Islam. Since Islam has no one single individual, such as the pope, who serves as the ultimate authority on religious concepts, jihad has been used repeatedly by Osama bin Laden and others to justify and legitimize terrorism and violence. As a tenet of the Islamic faith, Muslims are supposed to undertake a jihad to oppose evil, lead a good life, promote and defend the religion against enemies, and contribute to the development of a just Islamic society across the globe.[4] According to the Koran and the Hadith, jihad is a duty that may be fulfilled in four ways: by the heart, the tongue, the hand, or the sword. The first way involves struggling against sinfulness, such evils as vice, passion, and ignorance. The way of the tongue calls for spreading the world of Islam and verbally defending the religion. The hand requires doing "good," avoiding evil, or administering discipline with one's hand. The least central to moderate Islam is the jihad of the sword, or war jihad, involving waging war against Islam's enemies to defend the faith, Muslim territory, or the Muslim people (umma) from attack. This is known as "defensive jihad." A variance of this is "offensive jihad," which advocates taking actions to void the earth of nonbelief, leading to the complete supremacy of Islam. The militants' reinterpretation of jihad calls for the re-creation of an expansive Muslim empire (caliphate). "Believers," who die in combat defending Islam, become martyrs and are guaranteed a place in "paradise." Al-Qaeda and its affiliates are keen to advance the idea that they are involved in a defensive jihad, using a continuing mantra of American and Western oppression of Islam in an effort to justify the more controversial offensive jihad with the Muslim world.

Like any concept, jihad is open to interpretation. In the late twentieth century, extremists misused the concept of jihad as an ideological weapon to justify combat against the United States (e.g., 9/11) and Western influences (e.g., American troops in Saudi Arabia), overthrow apostate Muslim governments (e.g., Egypt), destroy Israel (e.g., terrorism), or establish Islamic societies based on *sharia* in historically Muslim lands (e.g., Southeast Asia). Although these militant radicals may drape themselves in religiosity, their objectives are political and should be viewed as such. The anti-American jihad is focused on getting Washington to withdraw its support from Israel and apostate Muslim states, leaving them vulnerable.

Osama bin Laden and Iraq's infamous Abu Musab al Zarqawi are archetype militant Islamists: self-righteous, intolerant, and violent. Demonstrative of his Wahhabist fundamentalism, bin Laden said on October 7, 2001, referring to the events of 9/11, "These events have divided the world into two camps: the camp of belief, in which there is no hypocrisy, and the camp of unbelief. May Allah protect us and you from the latter. It is necessary for every Muslim to rise up in defense of Islam."[5] Fortunately, these militant Islamic fundamentalists are a minority among Muslims. A vast majority of Muslims have not embraced violence as a means of change as evidenced by voting in Afghanistan, Iraq, and Lebanon.

ECONOMIC AND SOCIAL CONDITIONS

In addition to religious radicalism, two of the most frequently cited reasons for terrorism are the poor economic and social conditions in the Muslim world. Poverty, large populations due to high birth rates, lagging economic growth rates and investment, unemployment, and a lack of educational opportunities abound in Muslim societies today, especially in comparison with the Western world. There is a "youth bubble" in many Muslim countries. In Iraq, 40 percent of the population is below 15; 50 percent in the Gaza Strip; and 38 percent in Saudi Arabia. Unemployment is 30 percent in Saudi Arabia and 50 percent in Gaza.

It was not always this way. In 1000–1200 AD, a period often referred to as the Golden Age of Islam, some Muslim cultures such as Abbasids, centered in Baghdad, were among the most advanced in the world, according to some experts. The culture was highly sophisticated, and responsible for many innovations and inventions in mathematics and science.

The situation in the Middle East is a good example of the simmering economic and social trouble that exists in the Muslim world. Much of the Middle East suffers from high inflation and unemployment, large disparities in income distribution and low wages. This is even true for countries with significant oil wealth. This phenomenon is due to government control of the oil resources and the economy. The energy profits, garnered by the government, do not trickle down through society's economic layers due to the lack of a private commercial sector. It does not help that 70 percent of all Arabs are less than twenty-five years of age.[6] High-energy young people with limited economic and social outlets and opportunity can create an explosive combination in any society.

In some cases, disaffected youth are looking to belong to a cause, even one that espouses violence. In some ways, it is similar to joining a street gang. Many young gang members join to be part of something that gives meaning to their lives. In some cases, they may also admire the group's leader. Belonging to a group—even a terrorist group—gives them stature. In fact, some terrorists are not even bothered by being called "terrorist" and may even proudly embrace it. Ramzi Yousef, mastermind of the 1993 World Trade Center bombing in New York City that killed six people, proclaimed after being sentenced to 240 years in jail, "I am a terrorist, and I am proud of it."[7]

Worse yet, some Muslim religious education is being used to promote violence and terrorism against nonbelieving infidels. Religion can provide an important moral compass and give meaning to our lives, but it can also be used for nefarious purposes such as preaching hatred, prejudice, or violence. For some poor Muslims, the stark choice is either religious schooling or no schooling at all. Perhaps even more important than an education is the fact that the religious schools often offer meals to the students who attend, reducing the burden on parents at home. The real question is whether Muslim religious schools are supplementing secular education or supplanting it, training the next generation of jihadists.

Some Muslim religious schools are purely interested in teaching the peaceful principles of Islam and the 6,666 Koranic verses. Others are teaching intolerance, hatred, and violent jihad. These radical schools are also preparing the next generation of terrorist foot soldiers for a holy war against the infidels and apostate governments. Some schools serve as recruiting stations for adult holy warriors, safe havens for active operatives, supply depots, and clandestine meeting places for planning terrorist operations.[8] For instance, in Pakistan where religious radicalism has been a significant problem, the government estimates that there are twenty-seven thousand or more *madrassas* (private religious Muslim schools).[9] In fact, neither the Pakistani government nor Pakistani religious clerics has any idea how many *madrassas* there are in Pakistan. Conventional wisdom says that the *madrassas* far outnumber Pakistani public schools. Symptomatic of the problem, Pakistan spends only 2 percent of its gross domestic product on education, the lowest in South Asia.

It is estimated that shortly after 9/11, these Pakistani *madrassas* were home to as many as sixteen thousand foreign students from as far away as Southeast Asia. Most of these schools are supported financially by Saudi Arabia and other oil-rich Arab countries intent on spreading the more orthodox forms of Islam such as Wahhabism. It is well known that in the past some of these foreign students have joined al-Qaeda, Southeast Asia's major terrorist group, Jemaah Islamiya, and Afghanistan's Taliban. Many of the *madrassas* have been shuttered since 9/11.

It can only be assumed that at least some of these school's students continue to join radical groups. The world's most populous Muslim nation, Indonesia, where religious schools are called *pesantren*, suffers from a similar challenge, trying to prevent Islamic intolerance, violence, and terrorism in that Southeast Asian nation. Indonesia spends the least on public education in Southeast Asia. An additional problem with schools that focus on Islamic studies, even if they are not preaching radicalism, is that memorizing the Koran poorly prepares students to compete in the modern world.

POLITICAL CONDITIONS

A lack of political freedom—or the "freedom deficit" as some call it—is another cause of terrorism. Regrettably, very few countries in the Muslim world are democracies, with the notable exception of Indonesia, Malaysia, Iraq, and Afghanistan. In contrast, some Middle Eastern, North African, and Central Asian regimes, such as Saudi Arabia, Iran, Syria, Egypt, Libya, Uzbekistan, and Turkmenistan, have historically been among the world's most repressive governments. An absence of political freedom and civil liberties, prospects for significant reform in the Muslim world, and the inability of their citizens to have their voices heard is a source of tremendous tension and frustration. In the Arab world, for instance, seven of twenty-one countries ban political parties. Secretary of State Condoleezza Rice has said that extremism is rooted in the "absence of other channels of political activity."

The historical support of many of these repressive regimes is one of the reasons some Muslims "hate" the United States and the West. This grievance, regrettably, is not without merit as Western governments for many years tolerated repression in the Muslim world for strategic stability reasons, especially during the Cold War when right-wing, repressive governments were considered better than left-wing, communist regimes. The situation in the Arab Muslim world is exacerbated by the lack of free press, inhibiting the free flow of information in many countries. Self-serving, anti-Western propaganda generated by the state-sponsored media outlets on issues such as the Israeli-Palestinian conflict not only is intended to deflect criticism of domestic problems, but also inflames the embers of radicalism in many of these societies—at times unintentionally.

Tragically, Muslim governments and the Muslim world fail to counterbalance their grievances by noticing how the United States came to the aid of the Muslim peoples: Kuwait (Iraqi invasion, 1990), Iraq (Kurd and Shia no-fly zones, 1991–2003), Somalia (civil war, 1993), Bosnia (civil war, 1994), Kosovo (Serb aggression, 1998), and Indonesia (tsunami relief, 2005). In addition, the United States has sponsored several Arab-Israeli peace deals and, most recently, supported a two-state solution in the establishment of a Palestinian state. Repressive Muslim regimes, fraught with widespread corruption and disinformation, often strengthen the rage, hopelessness, and appeal of radical groups to many Muslims.

So who becomes a terrorist? Predicting who becomes a terrorist—and how—is an inexact science. Many defy the stereotype. In the past, one might expect a terrorist to be a young, poor, uneducated, Arab male who was swept up with religious fervor out of frustration with the lack of opportunity in his life. Undoubtedly, there are still some like that, but the profile of terrorist has changed. Many real life examples completely undermine the conventional idea of the likely terrorist. For instance, the 9/11 hijackers, especially the seventeen from Saudi Arabia, were generally middle-aged, traveled, well-educated Arab males from the middle to upper classes of Saudi society. Mohammed Atta, the infamous ringleader of the 9/11 hijackers, completed a degree in engineering in Hamburg, Germany. They were not poor, unemployed, or absent a meaningful future. Osama bin Laden has a university degree and is from one of Saudi Arabia's wealthiest families. His deputy, Ayman al Zawahiri, is an Egyptian pediatrician, who grew up in one of Cairo's poshest neighborhoods. Adding to the complexity of the terrorist mosaic, Pierre Robert, known as the "Blue-eyed Emir of Tangiers," is a blond-haired, blue-eyed Frenchman, who converted to Islam and played a major role in the May 2002 bombings in Casablanca, Morocco, as well as planning other attacks.

As contradictory and confusing as this all sounds, it is important to look at terrorism's root causes because understanding them is the first step in addressing them. Taking action on each cause might reduce any number of potential terrorist foot soldiers from the global jihad. For instance, taking the education of a young man out of the hands of a radical cleric in a Pakistani *madrassa* and placing that same young man in a national school where tolerance is taught could significantly change the trajectory of his life—and others—in a positive way. Though there is no silver bullet for defeating terrorism or ending intolerance and religious radicalism in the Muslim world, tackling its origins will undoubtedly have a salutary effect on the prospects for peace and stability the world over.

NOTES

1. Walter Laqueur, *No End to War: Terrorism in the Twenty-First Century* (New York: Continuum, 2003), p. 22.

2. Bernard Lewis, *The Crisis of Islam: Holy War and Unholy Terror* (New York: Modern Library, 2002), p. 8.

3. Lewis, *The Crisis of Islam*, p. 24.

4. John L. Esposito, *Unholy War: Terror in the Name of Islam* (Oxford: Oxford University Press, 2002), p. 5.

5. National Committee on American Foreign Policy, "Summary of the January 10, 2002, Roundtable on Militant Islamic Fundamentalism in the 21st Century," Security Interests, http://www.ncafp.org/legacy/projects/rd02islam.htm (accessed March 19, 2004).

6. National Committee on American Foreign Policy, "Summary of the January 10, 2002, Roundtable on Militant Islamic Fundamentalism in the 21st Century," Security Interests, http://www.ncafp.org/legacy/projects/rd02islam.htm (accessed March 19, 2004).

7. Rex Hudson, *Who Becomes a Terrorist and Why: The 1999 Government Report on Profiling Terrorists* (Washington, DC: The Lyons Press, 1999), p. 21.

8. Ron Moreau, Sami Yousafzi, and Zahid Hussain, "Holy War 101," *Newsweek*, December 1, 2003, 30.

9. Moreau et al., "Holy War 101," 29.

TRADECRAFT: TARGETS, TACTICS, AND TOOLS

We are terrorists, and terrorism is our friend and companion. Let the West and East know that we are terrorists and that we are terrifying as well. We shall do our best in preparation to terrorize Allah's enemies and our own. Thus terrorism is an obligation of Allah's religion.

—Sheikh Abdullah Azzam, "Father of Global Jihad"[1]

It was just before Christmas 2001. Travelers were rushing to get to loved ones for the holidays or business appointments on the American Airlines Paris-Miami flight. Flight attendants noticed a passenger trying to strike a match in his seat. Smoking is forbidden on just about every flight nowadays, so a passenger lighting a match at his seat seemed particularly odd. It became all the more odd when the passenger, Richard Reid, tried to light the tongue of his sneaker, which strangely had a wire protruding from it.

Since it was only three and a half months after 9/11, several passengers and flight attendants subdued the gangly Briton of Pakistani descent. In the struggle, Reid, a Muslim convert and a self-proclaimed Osama bin Laden disciple, bit a flight attendant. Two French doctors on board injected Reid with sedatives to keep him subdued. The plane landed safely in Boston. Reid had enough plastic explosives in his sneaker to tear a hole in the plane's fuselage. Such a tear in the plane's skin would have caused a rapid decompression of the cabin and likely brought the plane down. Fortunately, this *terrorist "Grinch" was not able to steal this Christmas, but he may not be the last to try.*

THE MEANS AND METHODS OF MODERN TERRORISM

The measure of any terrorist group is its ability to attack its target. The terrorist must lash out violently if the cause is to survive and regenerate itself. Terrorist acts demonstrate capacity, foster unity, and draw attention to the cause. Death and destruction are the sine qua non of the terrorist's game. Finding new ways of wreaking carnage and chaos is a continuing challenge for today's terrorist. They must be ambitious and innovative. But more than that, the modern terrorist is like a virulent, deadly disease that continually mutates itself to ward off the onslaught of new antibiotics. The virus instinctively knows that if it does not change and adapt, it will die. The same is true of terrorism. Like a living organism, terrorism has changed significantly over the last ten years. In fact, the tactics, targets, and tools of the terrorist tradecraft are continuously evolving. Male suicide bombers have become female suicide bombers. Hijacking planes in the United States changes to attempts to hijack planes originating overseas en route to the United States. Terrorist attack scenarios are only limited by the immoral imagination of the modern terrorist. To today's terrorist, everything is fair game.

Naturally, this increase in the sophistication and flexibility of terrorist operations has led to a commensurate increase in the challenges of defending against terrorism. Antiterrorism is a veritable game of cat and mouse, where the stakes are human lives. The modern terrorist has fully embraced today's most advanced technology, including high-speed Internet communications and satellite telephones. This is laughable, since most of today's Islamic terrorists, most notably al-Qaeda, have rejected modernity as incompatible with their fundamentalist religious views. Perhaps, in their own twisted minds, it is all right to use modern weapons to kill infidels, but unacceptable for modern Muslim society. For instance the use of the Internet for terrorist purposes is unprecedented. The Internet is easily accessible, anonymous, fast, inexpensive, and difficult for governments to control. The Web is ideal for terrorist propaganda, fundraising, communicating, information sharing, and data mining. Twenty-first-century terrorism is still evolving as violent extremists look for new ways to overcome the hurdles counterterrorism professionals have put in their way.

TERRORIST TARGETS

The potential terrorist target list is essentially limitless. If the selected target serves the terrorist's need for sowing panic, it is a viable quarry. Ideal targets can be large gatherings of people, packed stadiums, hotels, office buildings, shopping malls. Or bridges, trains, subway systems, airliners, dams, oil refineries, nuclear power plants, sea ports, landmarks, chemical plants, hazardous cargo on trucks and trains—the list goes on and on. Some targets are, of course, more attractive than others. For instance, an empty bus station might be less appealing to a terrorist than a full bus station on a busy holiday weekend. Bringing down a cargo plane may be less inviting than bringing down a large trans-oceanic passenger airliner carrying three hundred or more people. Since the target set is so broad, fortunately, there are some indicators of what the modern terrorist is considering when he looks for a potential target. Based on the rash of attacks in recent years, the modern terrorist is attracted to symbolic, undefended ("soft"), highly populated targets where a large number of casualties are possible, and critical infrastructure targets.

Symbolic Targets

Since an important aspect of terrorism is psychological, symbolism, not surprisingly, is an essential component of a target. The 9/11 attacks are instructive in this regard. The World Trade Center represented the economic might of the United States and symbolized the globalization that Muslim fundamentalists find so objectionable. The Pentagon, as the headquarters of the mighty U.S. military, embodied American power, including its presence in the Middle East. The U.S. military also conducted strikes against al-Qaeda's training camps in Afghanistan in August 1998 in retaliation for the bombings of the American embassies in Kenya and Tanzania. Attacking the Pentagon was not only symbolic, but a matter of revenge for al-Qaeda as well.

The final 9/11 plane, which never reached its intended target, came to rest in a Pennsylvania field after passengers bravely stormed the cockpit. This plane was destined, many believe, for either the White House or the

U.S. Capitol. The symbolism of these buildings is obvious in that they not only house America's political leaders, but also are representative of American freedom, liberty, and democracy—all principles antithetical to al-Qaeda's worldview. Warning: Al-Qaeda has gone back to attack targets it failed to destroy the first time, such as the World Trade Center, which it hit first in 1993. It is likely that al-Qaeda will try to attack the White House and the U.S. Capitol again.

U.S. embassies and consulates—the most powerful symbols of American influence overseas—are prime targets for terrorism, too. The attacks on the American embassies in Kenya and Tanzania in 1998 and the American consulate in Jeddah, Saudi Arabia, in late 2004 demonstrate this fact. Depending on the ability of the local intelligence and security services, American government facilities can be quite vulnerable to attack. Terrorist groups have successfully penetrated Indonesian, Pakistani, Saudi Arabian, and Iraqi security services in the past. The United States closed embassies and consulates in places like Jordan, Indonesia, and Saudi Arabia for short periods, based on intelligence threat information since 9/11. Moreover, there were a number of attacks in the American-occupied "Green Zone" in Baghdad, Iraq. Targets can also be symbolic by singling out ethnic, racial, or religious groups as has been seen in interethnic (e.g., Arab and Kurd) and intersectarian (e.g., Sunni and Shia) violence in Iraq since the beginning of the 2003 occupation.

Soft Targets

Not surprisingly, soft targets—meaning lightly or undefended targets—are also high on the modern terrorist's target list. Nonmilitary targets, such as schools, housing complexes, hospitals, and shopping malls, are vulnerable because they lack the physical security necessary to deter a terrorist. For example, al-Qaeda and its affiliates have successfully attacked a nightclub on the island of Bali, Indonesia (October 2002); hotels in Indonesia (August 2003), Kenya (November 2002), and Morocco (May 2003); synagogues in Tunisia (April 2002) and Turkey (November 2003); housing complexes in Saudi Arabia (May and November 2003); commuter trains in Spain and the UK (March 2004 and July 2005); an elementary school in Russia (September 2004); and theaters in Russia (October 2003) and Qatar (March 2005), not to mention the plethora of attacks in Afghanistan and Iraq against civilians. Iraqis seeking employment in the police or military have been particularly targeted. Another example: The Kuwait militants, arrested in February 2005, had in their possession caches of weapons and diagrams of shopping malls.

Choosing soft targets increases the likelihood of the success of a terrorist act. If a terrorist can avoid having to face concrete barriers, barbed wire, armed security personnel, or well-armed soldiers, his chances of getting close to the target, and the success of the operation, are greatly increased. This is the appeal of soft targets, and al-Qaeda considers it in their operational planning. For instance, based on the debriefings of al-Qaeda operatives, the group decided to attack an undefended synagogue in Istanbul, Turkey, in November 2003 instead of the American airbase at Incirlik, Turkey, because the airbase was too heavily defended, making the likelihood of failure high. Considering that terrorist groups do not have unlimited resources, attacking soft targets gives terrorists the biggest bang for the buck.

Well-Populated Targets

The desirability of targets swarming with potential victims should come as no surprise to even the most casual observer of terrorism. Some modern terrorist groups, such as al-Qaeda, are not only interested in influencing a particular audience—they are bent on killing as many enemies as possible. Al-Qaeda and some affiliated terrorist groups believe that all members of the infidel society are in play. They believe—correctly—that the more women and children killed, the more panic and fear they will create. The World Trade Center, where fifty thousand people worked, and the Pentagon, where twenty-five thousand people were employed, and the school in Beslan, Russia, where over one thousand students and teachers were in attendance, were ideal targets in the modern terrorist's eyes.

Large hotels during vacation or the holiday season or a college football stadium on a fall Saturday afternoon could be filled with tens of thousands of people concentrated in one spot.

No doubt this is why Las Vegas appeared to be on al-Qaeda's hit list for an airplane strike during the 2003 holiday season. Las Vegas is filled with thousands of holiday revelers during the Christmas season, and the city's large hotel complexes, including the casinos, are some of the biggest in the United States. Some of the hotels in Las Vegas have three thousand rooms. Thousands of people could have been killed if a plane was flown into one of these hotel complexes. Moreover, in addition to being highly populated, they are undefended and symbolic of the West's decadent lifestyle—a perfect target in al-Qaeda's eyes.

Critical Infrastructure and Economic Targets

Critical infrastructure is the often-taken-for-granted element of society, both physical and virtual, that keeps our everyday lives humming along. Dams, bridges, power plants, airports, trains, subway systems, the Internet, the banking system, our water and food supply systems, as well as nuclear power plants and industrial complexes, are all considered "critical infrastructure." And it is the "critical" element these systems play in the American way of life that make them desirable targets to terrorists. An attack on a transportation system could kill hundreds in one fell swoop. An assault on a chemical plant or a nuclear plant could release chemicals or radioactive particulate into the air, which could kill or injure many downwind. A cyberterrorism attack on Wall Street computers could grind the world's largest financial markets to a halt, costing billions in lost productivity. The economic element of the targets are also particularly attractive because of the terrorist's belief that some nations' world strength is based not only on their military strength, but their economic might as well. In the mind of the modern terrorist, destroying economic targets, such as Wall Street, the World Trade Center, or airliners, will bring target societies to their knees. They can only be encouraged by the "success" of al-Qaeda's 2001 World Trade Center attack.

TERRORIST TACTICS

Terrorist tactics include hijackings, kidnappings, and bombings. Al-Qaeda and its affiliates use both small- and large-scale attacks to accomplish their goals. Attacks range from simple car bombings—as we have seen in Iraq, Saudi Arabia, and elsewhere—to the unspeakable attacks of 9/11 against the World Trade Center and the Pentagon. As antiterrorism forces step up their counterterrorism efforts, terrorist groups look for new and innovative ways get at their targets. The face of terrorism we see today will be different tomorrow.

Bombings

The most prevalent and effective tactic of the modern terrorist is the bombing. In fact, with the exception of the 9/11 hijackings, bombings have accounted for more deaths than any other terrorist tactic. Bombs are flexible in their application, relatively inexpensive to produce, and are simple to build. Because of the element of surprise and destructive powers of a bomb, terrorist bombings have not only physical impact, but a psychological one as well. As we have seen during the Iraqi insurgency and elsewhere, bombs are an ideal terror weapon.

A bombing can be accomplished in several ways. There is the human suicide bomber that we're so familiar with today. Bombs can be parked nearby or driven into a target in a vehicle. A bomb can be carried on a motorcycle or a bicycle or be placed at, or near, a target in such things as a backpack, a suitcase, or a trashcan. For example, backpacks were used in the March 2004 train bombings in Madrid, Spain. A bomb can be detonated manually, by a cell phone, a laser, or a timer. Sometimes suicide bombers detonate the explosives themselves and sometimes others explode the human bomb package. This prevents a failed operation in case the suicide bomber is shot or incapacitated while trying to get near his or her target. The possibilities are almost endless. Obviously, the lethality of the bombing is determined by the proximity of the bomb to its target and the size of the bomb itself. Instructions for making bombs can be found on the Internet, and terrorist groups have produced CD-ROMs on the subject for worldwide distribution to other terrorist groups and cells. A typical al Qaeda bombing might include multiple, near simultaneous, bomb attacks in close proximity to one another, against soft or symbolic targets, causing mass casualties as in London in 2005.

Suicide Attacks

One of the most disturbing aspects of this new age of terror is the increasing use of suicide attacks.[2] This tactic distinguishes the modern Islamic brand of terrorism from the more politically motivated terrorism of decades past, especially in Europe and South America, where the survival of the terrorist attacker was a high priority. However, suicide attacks are not new. Islamic culture has a long suicide attack tradition, dating back to the Assassins, a Shiite sect, of the eleventh to thirteenth centuries in modern-day Syria and Iran. The Assassins were infamous for attacking Christian Crusaders and prominent local Muslim officials in large public places, assuring the attackers' immediate capture, execution, and martyrdom. Many believe that this ancient practice set the precedent for today's Muslim terrorist suicide bombings.

The suicide attack serves the main purpose of assaulting an enemy, but it has other purposes as well. For Islamic terrorists, perishing in a jihad brings martyrdom, entrance into heaven, and eternal salvation. For many Muslims, heaven is a place of milk and wine rivers and honey lakes. The martyr will see Allah's face, be joined by seventy chosen relatives, and enjoy the services of seventy-two virgins. Female martyrs are promised to dwell forever alongside the husband or fiancé they left behind. The weight of earthly rules, including *sharia*, and responsibilities will no longer hang upon them like millstones in the afterlife. In fact, suicide bombers have been known to smile widely and joyfully just before blowing themselves up. It can also result in bringing personal and familial notoriety, new recruits to the cause, or revenge, or it can even give significant meaning to one's mortal life.

Many experts consider the 1983 bombing of the U.S. Marine barracks in Beirut, Lebanon, by Hezbollah to be the beginning of the modern suicide bombing campaign. A truck laden with explosives killed 241 American servicemen and injured 80 others when it drove into the barracks late at night. At the same moment, across town, another truck bomb struck the French peacekeeping compound, killing fifty-eight and wounding fifteen. The subsequent American withdrawal of its peacekeeping forces has been cited by terrorists, including al-Qaeda, as an example of the effectiveness of suicide attacks and of the lack of stomach Americans have for casualties.

Most suicide bombers are carefully selected and trained by their terrorist organization sponsors. The attackers understand what they are doing and the consequences to themselves and others. Although suicide for reasons of personal distress is forbidden in Islam, like in most religions, to give one's life in the name of God is considered a divine act. But suicide bombing is not unique to religious-oriented terrorist groups. Other nationalist terrorist groups, such as the Tamil Tigers of Sri Lanka (LTTE), have used suicide bombings to great effect. In fact, the LTTE killed a number of political luminaries with suicide attacks, including Indian prime minister Rajiv Gandhi (1991) and Sri Lankan president Ranasinghe Premadasa (1993).

Although the Muslim faith has long opposed martyrdom for women, they have begun serving as suicide bombers. For instance, Chechen women are active in suicide bombings, especially those who have been widowed or lost a loved one in a conflict. The Palestinian terrorist groups Hamas and Al Aqsa Martyrs Brigade have both used female bombers in Israel and the Palestinian territories. Uzbek women served as suicide bombers in attacks in Uzbekistan in April 2004. In general, women are considered less violent and do not arouse suspicion with security personnel that a man might. Previously, the suicide bomber could be easily stereotyped: a young, unemployed, uneducated, fervently religious male. This is no longer the case, and as a result, coming up with a suitable working profile of who might be a suicide bomber is much more difficult.

Suicide attacks provide several advantages to terrorist operations. First, suicide attacks generally result in higher casualties than other types of attacks. The pedestrian suicide bomber is a "precision-guided munition" and the ultimate "smart weapon," usually able to get closer to its target than a car bomb. Professor Robert Pape of the University of Chicago has estimated that between 1980 and 2001, thirteen people died on average in every suicide attack, as compared with just one killed using other forms of terrorist attacks (excluding 9/11).[3] The efficiency and effectiveness of mass suicide bombing campaigns may assist the terrorist's cause by raising the threat so significantly that it pressures the target audience into succumbing to the terrorist's demands.

Second, suicide attacks generate more media attention than other types of terrorist attacks. The combination of the emotion involved in a suicide and the carnage of a bombing is too much for any media outlet to resist. This publicity gives volume and texture to the terrorist's message, which could further his or her cause. Suicide attacks create a tremendous amount of fear in the target audience because of the perception that the suicide attackers may not be able to be identified and, therefore, cannot be deterred or stopped.[4]

Third, a suicide attack may draw more attention to the cause and subsequently bring more prestige, recruits, and funding to the terrorist effort. The suicide bombing demonstrates to both friends and foes alike that the cause is a serious one. It can move supporters, who then decide to join the cause or provide a financial contribution. Families of Palestinian suicide bombers, for example, often received a death benefit of $25,000 (a significant sum to most Palestinians) from sympathizers, including some Arab governments such Libya and Saddam Hussein's former regime.

Lastly, suicide attacks are simple and low tech. No escape routes are required. And little to no intelligence can be gained from the dead bomber. (Although some suicide truck bombers have been blown from their truck cabs in Iraq and survived.) Most personal suicide belts are laced with nails, screws, or ball bearings to ensure that the largest number of people are killed or injured by the shrapnel. More victims will die from the shrapnel than the bomb blast. Even those who survive the blast may have to live with the legacy of the incident through the shrapnel left in their bodies. Since the invasion of Iraq in 2003, there have been over 150 suicide attacks.

The knowledge to carry out these types of attacks is available, not surprisingly, on the Internet through al-Qaeda's one-volume "Manual of Jihad" and their thirteen-volume "Encyclopedia of Jihad."[5] Jihad message boards also provide information such as how to make an explosive suicide vest or a bomb. Since 9/11, there has not yet been an additional incident of a human suicide bomber here in the United States. Many experts believe that it is only a matter of time, however, before a terrorist suicide bombing takes place here, and at some large gathering such as an airport, school, sporting event, or shopping mall.

Hijackings

There have been over one hundred hijackings of airliners by terrorists and others since the late 1960s when "skyjacking" became popular.[6] (The first U.S. hijacking took place in 1961 when a National Airlines flight was taken to Cuba.) In most cases, a hijacking used to mean the forced diversion of a plane from its intended flight route, several days of holding the passengers hostage, and, perhaps, some limited killings of passengers or crew before their release. The events of 9/11 changed all that. Undoubtedly, for at least some period of time, the passengers of those four hijacked planes believed they were going to be flown somewhere and held hostage while the hijackers made a number of demands of the U.S government before being flown to Cuba or somewhere else. Unfortunately, that wasn't the case and a hijacking will never be looked at again in the same way.

There is also a tremendous concern about the hijacking of cargo aircraft. The Department of Homeland Security (DHS) has warned that al-Qaeda may be plotting to fly cargo planes from overseas into targets in the United States such as nuclear plants, bridges, dams, tunnels, or other critical infrastructure. The American intelligence community still believes that al-Qaeda wants to commit additional hijackings. DHS is also concerned that al-Qaeda may have recruited insiders, such as pilots, flight attendants, and cargo crews to facilitate the commandeering of an aircraft. Airplanes have become weapons. They have become the terrorist's intercontinental ballistic missile, capable of striking a large array of targets from afar. With almost ten million domestic and over seven million international flights per year in the United States, the challenge of preventing attacks on airlines is immense. With over ten billion dollars spent on commercial airline security measures since 9/11, officials worry that terrorists will shift to noncommercial aircraft such as helicopters and private planes.

Kidnappings

Kidnappings and hostage taking had fallen off in popularity as a terrorist tactic until the American occupation of Iraq in 2003. Beginning in late 2003 and continuing through the present, Iraqi insurgents, foreign fighters, and al-Qaeda cohorts, bent on disrupting the burgeoning democracy in the newly Saddam-free Iraq, have kidnapped and murdered civilians of all nationalities who were working in Iraq. By some estimates, there were as many as five kidnappings a week in Iraq in 2004. Perhaps the most infamous hostage taking in recent years was the kidnapping and murder of American civilian Nicholas Berg by al-Qaeda's Abu Musab al Zarqawi in May 2004. The brutal beheading of Berg, a twenty-six-year-old Pennsylvanian who had gone to Iraq to help set up communications systems, was recorded on videotape by Zarqawi, then broadcast worldwide on the internet in an effort to dampen enthusiasm for democracy in Iraq. Zarqawi, like most modern terrorists, was not interested in negotiating a ransom for Berg's release—a symbolic execution of an infidel was always the goal.

Other Tactics

International terrorists continue to look for new ways to spread death and destruction. The modern terrorist is not satisfied with hijacking planes or even suicide car bombings, especially as we erect defenses against these terrorist tactics. Like an animal on the prowl, he continues to look for new prey—and for new ways to kill that prey. Today's terrorist is looking for seams of vulnerability in our defenses, especially where he can affect not only our well-being, but also our economy. Lesser known types of terrorism, including cyberterrorism, maritime terrorism, and agricultural terrorism, can be as devastating as those with which the world is already familiar.

Think of it: A terrorist hacker enters the computer system of a local dam, opening the floodgates and deluging a local town with a wall of water in the middle of the night without warning. How about cyberterrorists entering the country's financial system to grind Wall Street, commerce, and the banking system to a halt? Perhaps even worse yet: Terrorists hack into the nation's air traffic control system, causing chaos in the skies over major cities like Chicago or Atlanta. This is not fantasy—it could happen if terrorists use "weapons of mass disruption."

Another potential terrorist target is global shipping, both passenger and merchant. Any number of the world's 120,000 cargo ships, tankers, or passenger liners could be used in a 9/11-style attack against a large port facility in a highly populated area. A large ship, or ships, could be scuttled to close a key waterway, such as the Strait of Hormuz in the Persian Gulf, disrupting international commerce. A cruise liner, such as the new $1.3 billion Queen Mary 2, could be attacked by a small boat laden with explosives, like the USS *Cole* was attacked by al-Qaeda in Yemen in October 2000. Al-Qaeda attacked the French supertanker *Limburg* in a similar manner off the coast of Yemen in October 2002. Alternatively, terrorists could take cruise line passengers hostage as happened with the Italian cruise liner *Achille Lauro* in 1985 at the hands of Abu Abbas' Palestinian Liberation Front. There have also been threats about flying aircraft into passenger liners.

The water and food that nourishes us can also be used as a vehicle for terrorism. Without question, the world's food and water supply are vulnerable to terrorist attack. Although it does not receive the media attention that other types of terrorism do, agricultural terrorism, or agroterrorism, can be just as deadly. Poisoning the civilian food and water supply with chemical, biological, or radioactive agents can cause illness, death, economic loss, and panic. A large, successful attack can easily overburden public health resources.

TOOLS

Ultimately, terrorists will use whatever tools are necessary to achieve their objectives. Of greatest concern is the continuing use of explosives, employment of surface-to-air missiles against civilian passenger aircraft, and use of weapons of mass destruction, including chemical, biological, radiological, and nuclear weapons. In early 2005, the FBI raised concerns about a string of incidents involving lasers being used from the ground to blind airline pilots. No direct terrorist links have yet been found, but the Patriot Act, signed into law in 2004, imposed harsh penalties for directing lasers at aircraft.

Explosives

Explosives are the weapons of choice for the modern terrorist. They are readily available, versatile, inexpensive, concealable, and deadly. They can be high tech, such as in military high explosives, including plastic explosives, or relatively low tech in the form of chemical fertilizers and/or gasoline. They can be concealed on a suicide bomber's body or placed in the trunk of a car. Explosives can be manually detonated in the case of a suicide bomber or a hand grenade, or set off by remote control, timer, or cell phone, allowing the terrorist to escape unharmed. Some explosives, such as plastic explosives, are currently undetectable by airport metal detectors. This technical shortcoming allowed the infamous Shoe Bomber, Richard Reid, to board a flight from Paris to Miami in December 2001 with plastic explosives hidden in his sneakers, completely undetected by security personnel. Another British Muslim was also recruited to mimic Reid's attack via Amsterdam, but withdrew just before the operation.

Surface-to-Air Missiles

One of the most troubling aspects of the terrorist threat is the global availability of surface-to-air missiles (SAM). These weapons have been used, and will likely be used again, against civilian airliners or cargo planes. The man-portable air defense systems (MANPADS) are ubiquitous, cheap, and capable of downing a large aircraft if employed accurately by a trained individual, especially when the aircraft is most vulnerable, during take-off or landing. It is widely believed that as many as 1 million MANPADS were produced; 500,000 are in existence around the world, including 150,000 in circulation. The remaining 350,000 are believed to be in military stockpiles. These missiles can be purchased, on the black market, for as little as $1,500–$5,000 each. The most common missile is the SA-7 GRAIL, produced by the former Soviet Union and sold widely during the Cold War. There are also probably some American-made STINGER and British BLOWPIPE systems around from the Soviet-Afghan war in the 1980s.

Al-Qaeda operatives used SA-7 MANPADS in an unsuccessful attempt to bring down an Israeli El Al airliner taking off from Mombasa airport in Kenya in November 2002. That same month, Hong Kong arrested three al-Qaeda operatives trying to buy SAMs. In 2003, in a joint operation with the Russians, the FBI arrested an international arms merchant at Kennedy airport in New York City after he had smuggled into the United States an advanced Russian SA-18 surface-to-air missile. Missiles are small and lightweight (20–25 lbs.) and are therefore easy to transport and conceal. Nicaragua, for example, acknowledged possessing as many as 1,000 MANPADS from Soviet purchases under the Sandinista government in the 1980s, but informed sources believe that 200 SA-7s missiles are in private hands and a similar number of SA-16s and SA-18s are outside of the Nicaraguan military's control. Some experts feel that the SAM is ideal for shipping in a seaborne container and could easily be smuggled into the United States, since DHS estimates that only about 3 percent of the nine million containers arriving in the United States every year undergo a thorough inspection. A MANPAD could also be smuggled across an American land border as well. In its annual testimony to the Senate Select Committee on Intelligence in February 2005, the U.S. State Department reported, "the danger that groups or individuals antithetical to the United States will obtain MANPADs or advanced explosives is both high and immediate."

Weapons of Mass Destruction

Whether a terrorist group would use a weapon of mass destruction (WMD), such as a nuclear, chemical, biological, or radiological weapon, is controversial and under significant debate among scholars, policy-makers, and counterterrorism practitioners.[7] The problem is that the technology, materials, and knowledge required to build one of these weapons are more readily available than at any time in the past. Clearly, using a WMD would fulfill the modern terrorist's objective of causing a high number of casualties and immense psychological impact, but it would not necessarily be a suitable weapon for all terrorist groups. For instance, for Hamas to use a WMD against Israel would probably be counterproductive, since the effects of the weapon would likely be harmful not only to the Israelis but also to the Palestinian people who live in close proximity. Depending on the weapon, it might also leave large areas of land uninhabitable, undermining Hamas's desire to reclaim Israel for the Palestinians.

Nevertheless, some American policy-makers feel strongly about al-Qaeda's use of WMD. Former undersecretary of state John Bolton said, "There can be no doubt that, if given the opportunity, terrorist groups such as al-Qaeda would not hesitate to use disease as a weapon against the unprotected; to spread chemical agents to inflict pain and death on the innocent; or to send suicide-bound adherents armed with radiological explosives on missions of murder."[8] Of course, al-Qaeda would not be bound by the same sort of moral dilemma that limits Hamas' freedom of action if it decided to use WMD against a non-Muslim country, such as the United States. Because of the complexities of transporting, producing or purchasing, and storing WMD, it is much more likely that in the near term al-Qaeda and its affiliates would use radiological weapons, also known as "dirty bombs," against intended targets.

There is no doubt that al-Qaeda and other terrorist groups will innovate and vary their targets, tactics, and weaponry in an effort to keep their opponents off balance. For if these groups fail to perpetrate new acts of terror, in the face of ever-increasing vigilance on the part of their opponents, their cause will falter and die. The challenge for the civilized world is to do whatever it can to prevent, preempt, and disrupt modern terrorists from achieving their evil ends.

NOTES

1. Walter Laqueur, *No End to War: Terrorism in the Twenty-First Century* (New York: Continuum, 2003), p. 236.

2. Some prefer to call these "homicide attacks," choosing to emphasize the plight of the victims as opposed to the bomber. This is understandable, but for the purposes of this book, the term "suicide bomber" will be used since it is the most common way to describe this act currently.

3. "Special Report: Suicide Bombers," *The Economist*, January 10, 2004, p. 21.

4. Audrey Kurth Cronin, "Terrorist and Suicide Attacks," CRS Report for Congress, August 28, 2003, pp. 9–11.

5. "RAND Center for Middle East Public Policy and Geneva Center for Security Policy 3rd Annual Conference," found in Bruce Hoffman, "Al Qaeda, Trends in Terrorism and Future Potentialities: An Assessment," held in Santa Monica, Calif., May 5, 2003, pp. 16–17.

6. Harvey G. Kushner, *Encyclopedia of Terrorism* (Thousand Oaks, Calif.: Sage Publications, 2002), p. 361.

7. A radiological weapon is not considered a WMD.

8. "The Second Global Conference on Nuclear, Biological, and Chemical Terrorism," remarks by Undersecretary of State John Bolton, found in the 2003 Gilmore Commission Report, held at The Hudson Institute, Washington, DC, November 1, 2002.

COLLECTING CASH AND RECRUITS

Money is the lifeblood of terrorist operations today. We're asking the world to stop payment.

—President George W. Bush, September 23, 2001

If Osama bin Laden is the face of al-Qaeda, Ayman al Zawhiri is the "brains." Long abandoning the basic medical rule: "Primum non nocere" (first, do no harm), the Egyptian pediatrician gave up a medical career to pursue a life of religious fanaticism, becoming the second most wanted man in the world. As Osama's deputy, al Zawhiri is the driving force behind al-Qaeda's searing radicalism and the mastermind of the September 11 attacks. While Osama serves as the poster child for militant Islamic fundamentalism, al Zawhiri brought cunning, ruthlessness, and experience from the leading terrorist Egyptian Islamic Jihad movement to the #2 spot in al-Qaeda. Often seen beside Osama in videotapes, the bespectacled al Zawhiri continues to spread his message, including tapes that taunt President George W. Bush and promise more attacks on the United States. In one tape, al Zawhiri challenged Bush's claim that nearly two-thirds of al-Qaeda's known leaders had been captured or killed since 9/11: "We remind Bush that he didn't destroy two-thirds of al-Qaeda. On the contrary, thanks be to Allah, al-Qaeda is still in the holy war battleground raising the banner of Islam in the face of the Zionist-Crusader campaign against the Islamic community." Not surprisingly, some consider the capture of al Zawhiri to be more important than nabbing Osama bin Laden.

TERRORIST FINANCING AND RECRUITING

The abundance of terrorist blood money and the recruiting of new terrorist "foot soldiers" are two of the biggest problems facing the international community today on the terrorism front. A terrorist group, like any organization, needs cash and people to support its mission. Although terrorist attacks can be relatively inexpensive, terrorist organizations require a continuous influx of funding for recruiting new members, training operatives, and planning and conducting operations at home or abroad. New recruits are needed to replace those arrested or killed in conventional or suicide attacks. Without money and new recruits, any committed terrorist organization like al-Qaeda, Jemaah Islamiya, Hezbollah, or Hamas will wither on the vine.

TERRORIST FINANCING

In the world of terrorism, there are always new and evolving challenges. In this vein, terrorist groups are using a variety of mechanisms to raise and move money. Unfortunately, cutting off the flow of money to terrorist organizations is no simple task. Arguably, it is the most vexing challenge for counterterrorism officials today. Terrorist groups are always looking for weak links in the barriers that are put in their way. Although there has been progress in stemming the flow of terrorist money since 9/11, terrorists still have too much cash. On the positive side of the balance sheet, according to the U.S. government, al-Qaeda's cash flow has been reduced by two-thirds, and over $140 million, belonging to 435 individuals or groups linked to al-Qaeda, has been frozen since September 11. In addition, over 170 countries have issued orders to freeze terrorist assets; more than 100 nations have passed new laws; and more than 80 countries have established terrorist finance intelligence units, making it more difficult for terrorists to transfer money and receive assistance. Furthermore, the UN passed a number of resolutions requiring all 191-member states to freeze the assets of 320 individuals and 115 groups associated with al-Qaeda.

Unfortunately, terrorists continue to operate, as evidenced by the attacks across the globe. Money is still available despite well-intentioned international efforts to stem it. Pakistan, Afghanistan, Indonesia, the Persian Gulf states, and even some European countries remain problems in fighting terrorist financing due to a lack of political will and stringent enforcement. A failure to dry up terrorist funding streams will undoubtedly prolong the war on terror and lead to more death, destruction, and despair at the hands of cold, calculating terrorists.

Fundraising is critical to terrorist operations. A terrorist operation can be cheap, but it is not free. Money is required to buy weapons, fund travel, rent safe houses, pay hush money, buy off officials, obtain forged passports and documents, cover members' living expenses, recruit and train new operatives, and distribute propaganda, to name a few (see Box 4.1, The Costs of Terrorism).

Depending on the size and types of activities of the terrorist organization, it can take millions of dollars annually to finance a group. It can also take much less. For example, American intelligence officials believe that al-Qaeda's global operations require an annual budget in the tens of millions of dollars, perhaps as much as $50 million.[1] This figure may, or may not, be accurate as knowledge of al-Qaeda's finances remains limited, especially since the organization is now decentralized across the globe. It is likely that no one has complete knowledge of al-Qaeda's finances, including those inside the organization. As a reasonable estimate, the $50 million figure does provide a benchmark for determining al-Qaeda's operational capacity and capability, judging the quality of our intelligence, and evaluating the effectiveness of programs designed to clamp down on terrorist financing. Some believe that maintaining the global Islamist terror network, including non-al-Qaeda groups such as Hamas and Hezbollah, actually costs billions of dollars per year.[2] This might be reasonable considering the sustained level of attacks in Iraq. But it may actually be much less than that, depending on the level of activity.

Box 4.1. The Costs of Terrorism

- September 11 attacks: $300,000–$500,000
- Synagogues, British consulate, and bank bombings in Istanbul, Turkey: $150,000
- Disco bombing in Bali, Indonesia: $50,000
- USS *Cole* attack in Aden, Yemen: $50,000
- Synagogue bombing in Djerba, Tunisia: $35,000
- Madrid, Spain train bombing: $7,500

Sources of Income

As President Bush said: Money is the lifeblood of terrorism. From where do terrorist organizations get their money? Terrorist funding comes from a number of different sources, including sympathetic, private "deep-pocket" donors, state sponsors, criminal activities, legitimate businesses, charities, and even drug running. Each terrorist group operates differently. Some rely heavily on donations, while others are intimately involved with criminal syndicates. Perhaps the most famous terror financier of all is Osama bin Laden, who provided the seed money for al-Qaeda in the late 1980s from his own vast $300 million family fortune. Bin Laden used his business acumen to fund al-Qaeda operations for some time, but lost a significant portion of that when Sudan expelled him and froze his assets. It has been rumored that he may be worth as little as $30 million today. According to the 9/11 Commission, al-Qaeda receives $30 million in donations annually. Beyond al-Qaeda, according to some sources, private Saudi citizens have continued to provide 50–60 percent of Hamas' annual budget.[3]

Muslim Charities

Perhaps the most troubling and morally reprehensible source of terrorist funding is the Muslim charity. These charities, like other organizations identified as "charitable," are obviously meant for good works, such as religious, humanitarian, educational, and social undertakings. The Islamic faith has a tithing practice (zakat), and faithful Muslims are expected to give 2 percent of their annual income to the poor every year, according to the Koran. Unfortunately, in some parts of the world, wealthy Muslim charities are being abused to fund, launder, and disburse money to terrorist organizations unbeknownst to the donor. The CIA believes al-Qaeda and other terrorist groups have unwittingly penetrated one-fifth of all Islamic nongovernmental organizations (NGO), including major charities.[4] Experts have called Saudi Arabia the epicenter of Muslim charity terrorist funding, but money is coming from other areas as well, including Europe and North America.

Using charities to fund terrorism has advantages and disadvantages for the terrorists. First, the charities' support for terrorism can often be done clandestinely, away from the prying eyes of contributors and the government. On the other hand, the funding stream from these charities to terrorists can be unpredictable. Good government oversight can lead to closure of wayward charities, ending their terrorist involvement. But competent oversight is not always available due to the varying capability of a country's financial or security services. More pointedly, a host government may not have the political will to act against a charity. Some governments have been reluctant to crack down on errant charities because these charities are at least partially involved in legitimate good works in needy communities. In some cases, it would be very controversial for the government to close them—especially if it is perceived that is being done at the behest of the West, especially the United States.

This is particularly true in the Third World. Even when charities are designated as supporting terrorism by such benign organizations as the United Nations, they are difficult to shutter and many continue to operate. This is because in many of these poor countries, the charities mix good works, such as building schools and clinics and aiding the poor, with clandestinely funding radicalism and terrorism. These governments are often willing to live with charities funding terrorism to ensure that the charity continues to do social and humanitarian works. This often changes when terrorism strikes at home, as is the case with Saudi Arabia, which began a significant crackdown on terrorist financing after the 2003 terrorist attacks in the kingdom.

Since its inception, al-Qaeda and other Islamic terrorist groups have relied on Islamic charities to fund their operations. One of the largest Islamic charities, the International Islamic Relief Organization (IIRO), is based in Saudi Arabia and has been implicated in funding al-Qaeda, Hamas, and, perhaps, even Hezbollah. The IIRO, an arm of the Muslim World League (an organization that bills itself as a global NGO whose mission is the propagation of the Islamic faith), has offices across the globe, including Africa, Asia, Europe, and Latin America. It also supported al-Qaeda training camps in Afghanistan prior to 9/11.[5] Osama bin Laden's brother-in-law Muhammad Jamal Khalifa ran the IIRO office in the southern Philippines during the early 1990s, where it supported Islamic separatism and the Abu Sayyaf Group, according to a UN report.[6] Although the Saudis have cracked down on IIRO, experts are still concerned about its activities. IIRO is currently active in tsunami-ravaged Indonesia, and analysts are concerned that the organization is spreading a radical religious message that could spur extremism or lead to aid for Jemaah Islamiya.

Another charity accused of funding terrorism, including al-Qaeda, is the al Haramain Islamic Foundation. Also a Saudi Arabia–based charity, it reportedly raises $30 million annually and was active in over forty countries. There are branches in terrorist hotspots like Indonesia, Kenya, Tanzania,

Somalia, Bosnia, and Pakistan. The Somali branch of al Haramain is believed to have funneled money to Al Ittihad al Islami (AIAI), an African Muslim terrorist group located in Somalia and active in eastern Africa. AIAI has been implicated in the attack on American soldiers in Mogadishu, Somalia, in 1993. Al Haramain's African operations have also been implicated in funding the bombing of the American embassies in Kenya and Tanzania in 1998.

The Indonesian branch of al Haramain has been supporting the Southeast Asian al-Qaeda affiliate Jemaah Islamiya. Al Haramain funded the November 2002 Bali, Indonesia, disco bombing that killed over 200 people.[7] In Europe, the Russian government has complained about al Haramain funding the Chechen rebels fighting in the protracted struggle in the Caucasus. A number of Muslim charities have been closed in the United States as well because of al-Qaeda ties, including the Global Relief Foundation, Benevolence International Foundation, and the Holy Land Foundation for Relief and Development. In 2004, an American branch of al Haramain, located in Oregon, was closed. It was accused of having links to al-Qaeda and al-Qaeda-affiliated Chechen terrorists. Also in 2004, the Saudi Arabian government said it was dissolving al Haramain and other Saudi charities and folding them into the Saudi National Commission for Relief and Charity Work to provide greater oversight of private donations from Saudi Arabia. The United States has identified thirty-five international charities as being involved in terrorist financing.

Business Sponsors

Businesses are another problem in the terrorist financing world. Some firms, known as "front companies," that pose as legitimate businesses, provide a covert funding stream and launder money for terrorist organizations. These companies can be as small as a "mom and pop" shop or as large as a multinational corporation. Take for instance the al Taqwa financial empire, which was highlighted in a 2003 United Nations report.[8] Al Taqwa was a large multinational corporation involved in financial transactions, import-export, and real estate ventures based in Italy, operating in the Middle East, Europe, and the Caribbean. It has reportedly funneled tens of millions of dollars to al-Qaeda, Hamas, and other terrorist groups through Muslim charities and informal, unregulated remittance networks known as *hawalas*. Once under suspicion of wrongdoing, these businesses are often quickly liquidated by their owners and reappear under new names—sometimes in different countries—to continue their legitimate—and illegitimate—business, including funding terrorism.

For example, Osama bin Laden ran a number of businesses in the Sudan, including a large complex of construction companies doing contractual work for the Sudanese government during the early 1990s. The companies employed al-Qaeda operatives and funded the nascent terrorist organization before Osama was evicted from Sudan under pressure from the Saudi and American governments and fled to Afghanistan. On the smaller end of the business scale, in a Spanish al-Qaeda cell, which indirectly supported the 9/11 attacks, one al-Qaeda operative ran a photocopy shop in a Madrid suburb where he also produced propaganda advocating holy war. Another member directed real estate companies. Other Middle Eastern or North African–born members of the Spanish al-Qaeda cell ran such companies as a carpentry shop, a ceramics factory, and an audio equipment store, according to Spanish court documents.

Terrorist groups also use criminal activities to fund their operations, including extortion, smuggling, drug trafficking, kidnapping for ransom, credit card fraud, software and music piracy, and petty theft. Smugglers with ties to terrorist groups are acquiring millions of dollars from illegal cigarette sales and funneling the cash to organizations such as al-Qaeda and Hezbollah right here in the United States. The traffickers purchase a large volume of cigarettes in states where the cigarette tax is low, such as Virginia and North Carolina, ship them up to Michigan, Maryland, New York, Pennsylvania, and New Jersey, selling them at local prices and pocketing the profit. For example, in 2000–2001, Hezbollah operatives were arrested for running discounted cigarettes from Charlotte, North Carolina, to Detroit, Michigan, where they were sold at a significant markup. When the ring was busted, it was estimated that they had sent several million dollars in profits to Hezbollah in Lebanon. According to government officials, illegal cigarette trafficking or "cigarette diversion" is now rivaling drug trafficking as a funding choice for terrorist groups. In 2005, two Yemeni operatives were convicted in U.S. courts for using their Brooklyn shop to funnel money to Hamas and to al-Qaeda operatives in Afghanistan and Bosnia.

Terrorists have also turned to trafficking narcotics to generate revenue. It had long been speculated that al-Qaeda was involved in the drug trade, but there was little evidence of it until late 2003. Al-Qaeda—and the Taliban—appear to be capitalizing on the burgeoning opium trade in Afghanistan, using the drug trade as a principal funding source. Afghanistan is the world's leading source of heroin and opium, responsible for nearly 90 percent of the world's opium production, according to the United Nations. The UN estimates that Afghanistan's opium crop is currently worth $2.3 billion annually, generating about $30 billion a year in turnover as it snakes its way from Afghanistan to its main destination Europe.[9] It is not clear how much income al-Qaeda is reaping from this harvest, but some have suggested that al-Qaeda may be earning in excess of $28 million annually from the Afghan poppy crop.[10]

For example, from mid-December 2003 to early January 2004, the U.S. Navy intercepted four small boats with al-Qaeda ties in the Persian Gulf and North Arabian Sea carrying hashish, heroin, and methamphetamines. On December 15, 2003, the U.S. Navy destroyer USS *Decatur* seized a boat in the Strait of Hormuz in the Persian Gulf that was carrying two tons of hashish worth $8–10 million. Another shipment of drugs seized on New Year's Day, 2004, had a street value of $11 million.[11] Since most opium leaving Afghanistan goes north through Central Asia into Russia and then to Europe, it appears that al-Qaeda may be looking for new routes, destinations, and clients, perhaps including the United States. Although most Muslims object to narcotics use, in al-Qaeda's eyes selling drugs to infidels to fund a holy war is fine. Regrettably, the Afghan poppy harvest rose over 60 percent in 2004.

State Sponsorship

During the Cold War, many terrorist groups received support from the Soviet Union, Eastern European Bloc states, or other Soviet client states, including some Arab nations. But with the fall of the Berlin Wall, state sponsorship has dwindled to just a few rogue states. Iran, Syria, Pakistan, and Saudi Arabia have been implicated to greater or lesser extents in financing terrorist groups. For instance, Lebanon's Hezbollah reportedly receives financial support from Iran to the tune of $100 million per year.[12] Some reporting indicates it may be as high as $200 million. For years, both Iraq (under Saddam Hussein) and pre-2004 Libya provided the families of Palestinian suicide bombers with $25,000 each for the acts of terrorism committed against Israel by their kin. Pakistan's intelligence service, the ISI, supported terrorist acts against India by Pakistani terrorist groups in India over border disputes in Kashmir.

Distribution

Once a terrorist group solicits and collects its donations, it has to get the money to its operatives for their use in the field. This is especially true for al-Qaeda, whose network is truly global. Operating a global terrorist organization is more difficult, especially since 9/11. A perfect, albeit tragic, example of this is the 9/11 hijackers, who piloted the planes that struck the World Trade Center and the Pentagon. Some of the pilot hijackers received their basic and advanced flight training in the United States. Since they were essentially unemployed, they needed money for living expenses as well as flight lessons. Al-Qaeda had to get money to them in the United States somehow without raising the suspicion of government banking authorities. Money can be moved in a number of ways across international borders, including couriers, the international banking system, *hawalas*, charities, or NGOs, or through money laundering.

Couriers, in some instances, reduce the risk of detection because there are fewer people involved in the transfer process, leaving the international financial surveillance system unaware of large deposits, withdrawals, or transfers. According to the U.S. Treasury Department, al-Qaeda and other terrorist groups are increasingly using couriers to smuggle bulk cash across international borders. For example, in mid-December 2003, six Arabs with suspected al-Qaeda links were arrested in Syria carrying $23 million in cash, according to administration officials.[13] If true, this is believed to be the largest netting of terrorist cash since September 11.

International Banking System

Prior to 9/11, the preferred way of moving terrorist money was through the international banking system. It was quick, easy, safe, and effective. That changed after 9/11, when the international community began to freeze terrorist-associated assets and implement surveillance and interdiction methods. But despite the risk, the banking system is still used. For instance, in Southeast Asia, Jemaah Islamiya reportedly uses automatic teller machines (ATMs) to get money to operatives. All an operative needs is an ATM card and a personal identification number (PIN) to withdraw cash from just about anywhere in the world without raising suspicion. Small deposits and withdrawals, especially, will go completely unnoticed by banking authorities. Fortunately, because of global efforts, it is now harder for terrorists to use the traditional banking system to move tainted money.

Money Laundering

Money laundering is not just for common criminals and drug runners any longer; it is integral to terrorist financial operations. Under U.S. law, money laundering means the "movement of illicit cash or cash equivalent proceeds into, out of, or through United States financial institutions." It means trying to make money from illegal transactions, such as drug sales, look like money from legal transactions such as a weekly salary from a legitimate place of employment. Money laundering is big business. The International Monetary Fund has pegged the global volume of money laundering at 2 to 5 percent of the world's gross domestic product (GDP), meaning $600 billion to $1.8 trillion.[14] It is not clear what portion of this is related to terrorism, but it demonstrates how pervasive criminal money laundering is, and how easy it is for terrorists to launder money.

To reduce the risk to their financial transactions, terrorists have moved their financial operations to areas where antiterrorism enforcement is not as stringent or effective, including Africa, the Middle East, and Southeast Asia.[15] In these parts of the world, there is limited capacity and or political will to regulate these financial activities. Terrorists are also using "shell companies" and offshore trusts to conceal terrorist financing and protect the people and entities involved in terrorist funding. Because the global financial system's surveillance and interdiction efforts have intensified, al-Qaeda, in particular, has moved its financial transactions outside the traditional banking system, relying more on commodity trading in gold, gems (including West African conflict diamonds), weapons, and now drugs, to move money. Deposed Liberian president Charles Taylor reportedly laundered al-Qaeda cash with conflict diamonds from neighboring Sierra Leone, benefiting both Taylor and the terrorist group.

The *Hawala*

The *hawala* is a unique, unregulated, unofficial banking and financial system used primarily in the Muslim world to send money domestically or overseas through trusted agents. It performs the function of a bank, and they are quite common in rural areas where legitimate banks are not common. In many cases, *hawaladars* (money dealers) operate in open-air markets and provide the most reliable, safe, convenient, and inexpensive means for moving money, such as the remittance of immigrant wages back home. *Hawalas* operate in over 50 countries in the Middle East, South Asia, Southeast Asia, Africa, and, even the United States. Because they are unregulated, based on trust between two *hawaladars*, and leave no paper trail, they are ideal for transferring terrorism funds outside of official banking channels. For example, a drug dealer approaches a *hawaladar* in Dubai,

United Arab Emirates, with $10,000 for the purchase of opium from a Kabul, Afghanistan–based drug dealer. For payment of $10,000, plus a 1 percent fee, the Dubai *hawaladar* will call or wire instructions to a Kabul *hawaladar* for him to pay $10,000 to the Kabul drug dealer. The *hawaladars* will eventually settle their accounts among themselves, sometimes through an official banking system. Fortunately, some countries such as Pakistan and the United Arab Emirates are instituting *hawala* regulations.

TERRORIST RECRUITING

The United States claims that 15 of the top 37 of al-Qaeda's 9/11 leadership have been arrested or killed since the September 11 attacks. It adds that over 3,000 al-Qaeda suspects in over 100 countries have been arrested since then as well. These are impressive numbers, but the question is how many al-Qaeda militants are there in total? And are the ranks of those who have been detained or killed being refilled with new recruits? These are important questions; the answers are not clear. An understanding of al-Qaeda's operational structure remains incomplete. Recruiting new members remains critical to a terrorist organization's viability, especially as the effort to contain and destroy terrorist groups today is at a fever pitch in many parts of the world.

Many of al-Qaeda's initial recruits came from the Arab resistance fighters, who fought against the Soviet occupation of Afghanistan from 1979 to 1989. After the war, many returned to their homelands and took up a normal life. Others returned home to the Middle East, Europe, North Africa, South Asia, and Southeast Asia and assumed the lives of radicals, going to mosques, recruiting members, or establishing operational terrorist cells. Some new recruits are seduced by the strident sermons of radical clerics or succumb to high-pressure recruiters who come to their mosque with a message of jihad. Because police in many countries, such as Germany, were not permitted to enter mosques, these houses of worship became havens for terrorist recruiting, planning, and fundraising. Now that authorities are aware of the presence of recruiting activities in the mosques, the houses of worship are monitored, meaning the radicals have now moved to teashops, Islamic bookstores, and *souks* (markets), away from the prying eyes and ears of the local security services. Surviving veterans of the jihad in Iraq are sure to return home ready to recruit and train new members.

Other recruits are enticed by Osama bin Laden's messages of holy war as seen on al-Qaeda and other radical websites. His call to action is also distributed on audiotapes or CDs, or broadcast on Arabic television such as Qatar's al Jazeera and the United Arab Emirates's al Arabiya. Still others are recruited through the radical curricula of religious schools. Recruiters also trawl universities, looking for young, educated radicals whose intellect makes them top-notch terrorist recruits. Though the strength of al-Qaeda is not exactly known, it is widely speculated that al-Qaeda trained as many as 120,000 new recruits in their Afghan training camps from 1996 to 2001. Islamist websites are particularly troubling. These websites, which can be viewed worldwide, include Koranic calls to jihad, photographs, videos, encouragement to terrorists, and terrorist application forms. There are even Web-based magazines, including one started recently by al-Qaeda in Iraq.

The New Breed

Al-Qaeda looks outside the Arab and Muslim world for new recruits as well. New adherents are being sought in Italy, France, Germany, Britain, Spain, Norway, Sweden, Canada, and the United States, to name a few. Citizens, legal residents, or people with legal passports who can move freely across international borders and blend into a local society are particularly attractive. Arab males living abroad outside the Muslim world are one natural recruitment target, but some others are more surprising: young Islamic converts, including Caucasians, Latinos, Blacks, and women. These new recruits raise less suspicion among security personnel because they defy the young, Arab, male terrorist stereotype. In fact, an al-Qaeda training manual lists potential recruits as persons disenchanted with their country's policies: convicted criminals, especially smugglers; adventurers; workers at coffee shops, restaurants, and hotels; security personnel at borders, airports, and seaports; and people in need.[16]

In the United States, al-Qaeda cells have been broken up in Buffalo, Detroit, Portland, and Seattle. Some of these cell members trained in al-Qaeda camps in Afghanistan. According to law enforcement officials, there are an unknown number of al-Qaeda sleeper cells in the United States, which probably entered the country prior to 9/11 before the crackdown on immigration and visitation was implemented. There is concern that Islamic radicalism is being brought to American prisons by religious clerics, ministering to disenchanted inmates who feel victimized by the American system and are not opposed to violence as a means of expression. Some radical

Islamic literature from Pakistan and Saudi Arabia has also made its way into the American prison system, where 10–20 percent of the prison population is Muslim.[17] Some of these people could become terrorist operatives, but it is more likely that they would become sympathizers, donors, informants, or part of a support network for future al-Qaeda operations in the United States. Jose Padilla, a Latino gang member originally from New York, who converted to Islam, went beyond the sympathizer stage. He was arrested in May 2002 in Chicago for plotting to detonate a "dirty bomb" in the United States. He converted to Islam in a Florida jail, was reportedly recruited by Osama bin Laden's top lieutenant, Abu Zubaydah, and was controlled operationally by al-Qaeda's now-arrested operations boss, Khalid Sheikh Mohammed.

In too many cases, European Muslims feel alienated and isolated in European society. Some Muslim communities have unemployment as high as 60 percent, making Europe a prime recruiting territory. Since 2003, European law enforcement has arrested al-Qaeda-affiliated Ansar al Islam operatives in six countries, including Denmark, Norway, Sweden, Germany, Italy, and Spain. The Kurdish Ansar al Islam is suspected of as many as 50 suicide bombings in Iraq. The network had recruited at least 100, and, perhaps, as many as 3,000, Islamic militants for Iraq duty, 70 of them from Italy. Italian authorities say an Arab male suicide bomber from Italy helped conduct the attack on the UN's Baghdad headquarters in August 2003 that killed twenty-two, resulting in the death of the UN envoy Sergio de Mello and the withdrawal of UN teams from Iraq. Another recruit from Italy attacked Baghdad's al Rasheed hotel in October 2003 where then U.S. deputy secretary of defense Paul Wolfowitz was staying during a visit to Iraq. Islamic extremists are clearly exploiting the Iraq war to recruit new jihadists.

France's community of Muslim converts is also a rising concern, according to French law enforcement officials. Frenchman Pierre Robert, known as the "Blue-eyed Emir of Tangiers," was sentenced in late 2003 to life in prison in Morocco for recruiting and training Moroccan extremists after the May 2003 suicide bombing in Casablanca that killed forty-five people. The French government estimates the number of converts at about 100,000 in a population of eight million Muslims living in France. In the United States, there are two million Muslims; approximately 17 percent are converts.

Britons of Pakistani descent were involved in the 2005 London bombings. In Germany, home to three million Muslims and the way station of three of the nineteen 9/11 hijackers, there are concerns as well. Christian Ganczarski, a Caucasian German and Muslim convert with ties to former al-Qaeda operations chief Khalid Sheikh Mohammed, was arrested by the French in June 2003 as a suspected conspirator in the bombing of a Tunisian synagogue on the island of Djerba, which killed twenty-one people in April 2002. Officials believe that Khalid Sheikh Mohammed used a number of non-Arab Europeans, including Swiss and Spaniards, to confuse Tunisian authorities and divert attention from the actual suicide bomber, Nizar Nawar.

European law enforcement authorities note that many converts are ferociously ideological and anxious to show their zeal and worthiness to their new faith by doing such things as joining a jihad. Osama bin Laden reportedly views converts as an especially valuable and a unique talent pool for his cause. Perhaps the most surprising trend is the increase in female terrorists. Islamist groups have long opposed female suicide bombers, noting that females are not worthy of martyrdom. Nevertheless, women are increasingly undertaking violent terrorist acts, including suicide operations in Chechnya, Israel, and Uzbekistan. Because women are typecast as being less prone to perpetrating violence, they usually raise less concern among security personnel, making them ideal recruits—and operatives—for al-Qaeda and other terrorist groups.

All of this is not to say that everyone is suspect. But terrorists are continually seeking new ways to try to outsmart the infidels. Terrorism is evolving and so must the defense against it, whether it's stopping the flow of dirty money or reducing new recruits to the terrorist cause. We must continue to adapt to the efforts of terrorist financiers and recruiters. Thinking outside the box is a continuing requirement, not a luxury, for those fighting terrorism.

NOTES

1. Gregory Vistica and Douglas Farah, "Syria Seizes Arab Couriers $23 Million," *Washington Post*, December 20, 2003, p. A16, col. 1.

2. Rachel Ehrenfeld and R. James Woolsey, *Funding Evil* (Santa Monica, Calif.: Bonus Books, August 2003), p. 2.

3. *Strategic Comments*, "Financing Islamic Terrorism: Closing the Net," vol. 9, no. 10 (December 2003), p. 2, www.iiss.org/stratcom (accessed March 19, 2003).

4. Rohnan Gunaratna, *Inside al Qaeda: Global Network of Terror* (New York: Berkley Publishing Group, 2003), p. 8.

5. UN Security Council, letter dated December 1, 2003, from the Chairman of the Security Council Committee established pursuant to resolution 1267 (1999) concerning Al-Qaida and the Taliban and associated individuals and entities addressed to the president of the Security Council, UN S/2003/1070, p. 15.

6. UN Security Council, S/2003/1070, p. 16.

7. UN Security Council, S/2003/1070, p. 16.

8. UN Security Council, S/2003/1070, p. 21.

9. United Nations Office on Drugs and Crime, *Afghanistan: Opium Survey 2003*, October 2003, http://www.unodc.org/pdf/afg/afghanistan_opium_survey_ 2003_exec_ summary.pdf, p. 1 (accessed April 14, 2004).

10. Mark Steven Kirk, quoted in Guy Taylor, "Heroin Money Fuels Terrorists; Three Groups Linked to Afghanistan Trafficking," *Washington Times*, February 13, 2004, p. A03.

11. Associated Press, "Navy Seizes Boat Suspected of al Qaeda Drug Smuggling," *Washington Times*, December 20, 2003, p. A1, col. 1; Associated Press, "Navy Nets Another Boatload of Drugs Linked to al Qaeda," *Washington Times*, January 3, 2004, p. A4.

12. Daniel Byman, "Should Hezbollah Be Next?" *Foreign Affairs* (November/ December 2003), p. 61.

13. Gregory Vistica and Douglas Farah, "Syria Seizes Arab Couriers $23 Million," *Washington Post*, December 20, 2003, p. A16, col. 1.

14. UN Security Council, S/2003/1070.

15. UN Security Council, second report of the monitoring group established pursuant to resolution 1363 (2001) and extended by resolutions 1390 (2002) and 1455 (2003), on sanctions against al-Qaida, the Taliban, and individuals and entities associated with them, UN S/2003/1070 December 2, 2003, p. 4.

16. Jerry Seper, "Terrorists Recruited from U.S. Seen as Rising Threat," *Washington Times*, June 18, 2002, p. A3.

17. Laura Sullivan, "New Twist on Jail Conversion al Qaeda May Seek Followers in Prisons, U.S Fears," *Chicago Tribune*, November 30, 2002, p. 8.

5

AL-QAEDA: TERROR CENTRAL

Even the Western world realizes that Western civilization is unable to
present any healthy values for the guidance of mankind. It knows that
it does not possess anything which will satisfy its own conscience and
justify its existence . . . Islam is the only system which possesses these
values and this way of life.

—Sayyid Qutb, founder of modern militant jihad

*Fellow prison inmates remember Abu Musab al Zarqawi as the cell block
"tough," a guy known for giving out orders, which others obeyed out of
pure, raw fear. Zarqawi grew up in rough-and-tumble circumstances in his
native Jordan, and mostly showed an affinity for drinking, fighting, and
attempting to overthrow the government in his youth, ultimately landing
him in jail. He later came to adopt Islam with the same intensity as he pursued his former vices. Generally viewed as a dull-witted "hothead," few of
Zarqawi's acquaintances can see him as the successful leader of the bloody
al-Qaeda insurgency in Iraq, responsible for guerrilla attacks, suicide
bombings, kidnappings, and, even, videotaped beheadings of infidels. Zarqawi has come a long way since his Jordanian cellblock days to being
Osama bin Laden's lieutenant, al-Qaeda's "Prince in Iraq," and the world's
second most well-known terrorist.*

OSAMA BIN LADEN

No one would expect a man of privilege and erudition to become such a
ruthless killer. Perhaps that is why self-anointed Muslim cleric and al-

Qaeda kingpin Osama bin Laden is the most infamous person alive today. For having stood up to two of the most powerful nations in the history of mankind, the Soviets in the 1980s and the Americans for more than a decade, this shy, quiet Saudi "holy warrior" has become a figure of mythic proportions in the Muslim world—and one of the world's most wanted terrorists.

The enigmatic, but charismatic, leader of al-Qaeda was born in Saudi Arabia in 1957, the seventeenth son of Mohammed bin Laden, a wealthy Saudi business owner of Yemeni descent. No child of the slums, Osama's father ultimately rose to become the wealthiest contractor in all of Saudi Arabia as the head of the Saudi Binladen Group. When he died in a 1967 plane crash, Mohammed bin Laden was worth a reported $10 billion. Osama, ten years old at the time of his father's death, inherited $300 million. His worldview reportedly began to develop while he was a teen, as his family's construction business worked under contract to the Saudi government on two of the Muslim world's holiest sites—the mosques at Medina and Mecca. Being awarded such a contract bestowed great honor on the bin Laden family, and the work had an immense spiritual impact on Osama. He rapidly developed the belief that the Muslim world needed to be protected—by any means necessary—from the encroaching modern world of infidels. He began to associate with Islamic fundamentalist groups in Saudi Arabia that discussed worldwide Islamic domination and violent jihad.

But it was a militant Jordanian professor, Abdullah Azzam, a radical fundamentalist Wahhabist, who probably did the most to bring about Osama's religious fanaticism. Teacher by day, radical by night, Azzam was an underground member of the Islamic extremist militant organization the Muslim Brotherhood and is thought to be a founding member of the Palestinian terrorist group Hamas. Azzam's students at King Abdul Aziz University in the Red Sea coastal town of Jeddah, Saudi Arabia, including Osama, a student of management and economics, were fed a steady diet of Muslim militancy based on the teachings of the Egyptian radical Sayyid Qutb. Qutb, who was executed by Egypt in 1966 for plotting to overthrow the government, is considered to be the founder of modern militant jihad theology. Qutb's teachings promoted the idea that non-Islamic (i.e., nonfundamentalist) Muslim governments were illegitimate (i.e., apostate) and that faithful Muslims had a duty to overthrow them and establish Islamic rule.

Azzam expanded on Qutb's theology of overthrowing apostate Muslim governments and preached his own vision of global jihad to his students.

Abdullah Azzam said before his suspicious assassination in Afghanistan in 1989, "This duty will not end in Afghanistan: jihad will remain an individual obligation until all other lands that were Muslim are returned to us so that Islam will reign again: before us lie Palestine, Bokhara [modern-day Uzbekistan], Lebanon, Chad, Eritrea, Somalia, the Philippines, Burma, Southern Yemen, Tashkent, and Andalusia [southern Spain]."[1] Osama bin Laden internalized these ideas and made them his own—and, eventually, al-Qaeda's.

There is no greater enemy than the United States, bin Laden noted in a November 2002 "Letter to America," published in a British newspaper. America is to blame for the Palestinian conflict with Israel, the Chechen conflict with Russia, the Kashmiri Muslims' struggle with India, and the Abu Sayyaf Group's conflict with the Philippine government. The only remedy in bin Laden's eyes is for the United States to abandon the Middle East, convert to Islam, and end the immorality of its culture. Or Americans can die.

Osama's fervor for Islam and militant jihad exploded with the Soviet invasion of Afghanistan in December 1979. He immediately went to South Asia to organize, fund, and fight with the *mujahideen* (holy warrior) resistance. Initially, he coordinated the flow of Arab holy warriors into Afghan resistance training camps in Pakistan. By most accounts, Osama entered Afghanistan himself in 1982, engaging in combat against the Soviets in at least one battle and earning a warrior reputation among the other fighters. By the time the Soviets pulled out of Afghanistan in February 1989, Osama led a military contingent of 20,000 fighters, which he used to his vast wealth to care for. He later returned to Saudi Arabia to recruit and train other Arab volunteers to fight in Afghanistan. And Saudi Arabia was only too glad to let bin Laden take some of the radicals out of the kingdom.

The Afghan resistance's victory against the Soviets gave Osama the sense that militant jihad could be successfully waged against the mightiest of powers—Azzam and Qutb were right. The Muslim world could overcome its humiliation at the hands of the West and Israel. America was corrupt and the American people must be held accountable for the policies of their government.

In 1989, shortly after Azzam's death, the messianic bin Laden forged an alliance with Qutb's followers in Egypt and formally launched al-Qaeda (the Base) to destroy the infidels and remold societies to his strict Wahhabist views of Islam.

BROTHERS IN ARMS

There was another soldier on the field in Afghanistan in the 1980s who, with encouragement and assistance from bin Laden, would come to be as reviled by the peace-loving world as Osama himself. Abu Musab al Zarqawi, for his role in organizing a ruthless string of attacks by insurgent groups in a newly free Iraq, in 2004 caught up with bin Laden on the most-wanted list, earning a price on his head of $25 million—the same reward offered for bin Laden.

A Jordanian terrorist with militant sympathies for the Palestinian movement, Zarqawi acted as an independent contractor for most of his career. From his early days as a petty criminal to attempted bombings and kidnappings in Amman and Israel to his better-known work leading insurgent efforts in Iraq after the United States ousted Saddam Hussein, Zarqawi has never missed an opportunity to attack innocent populations—both Muslim and non-Muslim—who don't share his extreme interpretation of Islam.

While their goals are similar, it would be a mistake to attribute the same motivations to Osama and Zarqawi. Like many in the Muslim Middle East, both were humiliated by Israeli's defeat of the Arabs in the 1967 Six-Day War—it was not only an ignominious military loss, but a disgraceful defeat for their pride as well. As a result of the war, many Palestinians living in the West Bank and Gaza Strip were brought under Israeli control. Osama blamed the plight of the Palestinian people squarely on the United States, considering Israel a mere puppet of American money and influence. Zarqawi, who has been described as nothing more than a "barely literate gangster" by some of his former associates, could not see that far across the Atlantic. To him, Americans, Jews, and nonfundamentalist Muslims were all equal parts of the same, "nonbelieving" global evil. Zarqawi was content to continue his efforts against the infidels closer to home in the Middle East.

Zarqawi's past shines some light on his motivations. Unlike the wealthy bin Laden, Zarqawi—born Ahmedal-Khalayleh—grew up in a small mining town north of Amman, in extreme poverty. Both of his parents died early and he spent most of his youth perfecting his street-crime skills, and for that spent some time in a Jordanian jail. Sometime after being charged with sexual assault in the 1980s, he started hanging around mosques and educating himself, to the best of his limited abilities, on the Koran. He married a cousin at twenty-two, but left Jordan for Pakistan six months after his nuptials.

Rallying to bin Laden's call for Muslim fighters to repel the Soviet invasion in Afghanistan, Zarqawi slipped out of Pakistan to join the battle. He made it right about the time the Soviets were leaving, so he returned to Jordan, passing five years in a Jordanian prison for illegal arms possession and by some accounts, plotting to kill Jewish and America tourists. He was released under a general amnesty in 1999 and fled Jordan. He began roaming Afghanistan, Pakistan, and northern Iraq, rallying his own band of extremist fighters.

Zarqawi became a "man without a country." Having been run out of Jordan and Afghanistan, he finally got comfortable in the mountains of Kurdish northern Iraq. From there, he could carry out various terrorist activities against infidels in both Jordan and other surrounding areas. Israel was still his main enemy—until, that is, the American military disrupted his plans by bringing a wave of democracy into his backyard.

COMMON THEMES

Osama returned to Saudi Arabia a hero for his victorious actions in Afghanistan. Filled with religious zeal and an overwhelming sense of power, he soon parted ways with the Saudi royal family when he began to openly criticize them for allowing Americans to station troops in the kingdom following Iraq's invasion of Kuwait in August 1990. The Saudi government feared Iraq's mighty Republican Guard would press through Kuwait into the oil fields of the Saudi kingdom. Osama gallantly offered himself and his battle-hardened—and loyal Muslim—Afghan resistance fighters to the Saudi royal family to defend the kingdom from Saddam Hussein's marauding armies. The House of Saud rejected Osama's proposal outright and went with the American deployment of 500,000 troops. A deeply humiliated Osama saw this as nothing more than the occupation of Islam's holiest land with foreign infidels. This rejection by his homeland, more than anything else, launched Osama's terrorist destiny and drive for world Islamic domination.

A continuing source of annoyance to the Saudi royal family for his outspokenness, in 1991 Osama moved across the Red Sea to Sudan with some of his al-Qaeda followers and opened a construction firm. He hired many of his former Afghan resistance fighters and began contracting with the Sudanese government. This is where Osama's real life of terror began. Osama, with the apparent knowledge of the Sudanese government, in 1992 opened his first terrorist training camps in Sudan, while also funding camps in and near Afghanistan. He also built an extremist network in the Philippines, Egypt, and Saudi Arabia. Because of his radicalism and continuing outspokenness against the Saudi royal family, Riyadh finally withdrew his citizenship and froze his assets in 1994 and pushed the Sudanese to deport him. In 1996, under pressure from the United States and Saudi Arabia, Sudan expelled him. Osama fled with his followers to Afghanistan where he set up dozens of terrorist camps to train thousands of militants in the terrorist "black arts." It was in these camps that Zarqawi later developed his expertise in poisons and explosives.

In Afghanistan, with no one to stop him, bin Laden stepped up the recruiting and training of al-Qaeda fighters. He struck a deal with the ruling, fundamentalist Taliban. They would allow Osama to establish al-Qaeda training camps, ensuring easy entry and departure to Afghanistan for his operatives and new recruits. In exchange, Osama provided money and fighters for the ethnically Pashtun Taliban's protracted civil war with the opposition Tajik-Uzbek Northern Alliance that held the northeastern part of Afghanistan. Osama's support of the Taliban was a significant boost to their success in the civil war. The Taliban, under Mullah Omar, was grateful. Despite the international community's repeated calls to expel or extradite Osama for his terrorist acts, the Taliban refused, acknowledging that they needed Osama for their war with the Northern Alliance.

But while it was the Taliban that gave Osama asylum, the key to his successful encampment there was actually Pakistan. Nominally headed at the time by Prime Minister Benazir Bhutto, Pakistan's military intelligence (Inter-Service Intelligence, or ISI) held the real power. ISI had watched thousands of unwelcome Afghan war refugees pour over the border into Pakistan, creating instability. If Osama could help the Taliban establish order in Afghanistan, Pakistan could send the refugees home and have a potentially cooperative ally next door. ISI's acceptance of the Taliban and bin Laden came back to haunt the nation later, as President Pervez Musharraf dodged assassination attempts after 9/11 for helping the United States track down displaced Taliban and al-Qaeda members and struggled to rid his country of the reputation for tolerating terrorists and extremists.

Osama remained in Afghanistan until he was forced to flee in fall 2001, when American forces moved in and overthrew the Taliban. Osama escaped through the Tora Bora Mountains with the likely assistance of local tribesmen, willing to take a hefty bribe. Today, he, like Zarqawi, is a terrorist without a country, on the run, and with a price tag of $25 million on his head. Bin Laden has been rumored to have health problems related to his kidneys, requiring dialysis, which could explain why Ayman al Zawahiri, a physician and head of the Egyptian Islamic Jihad before it merged with al-Qaeda, is such an important adviser to bin Laden.

AL-QAEDA

Al-Qaeda, with its loosely affiliated network of terrorist co-conspirators, is the world's first truly global terrorist network. Its quest for world Islamic domination and its terrorist operations—from North America to Europe to the Middle East and into Southeast Asia—are unprecedented. Most terrorist organizations restrict their ambitions to a specific geographic area or a target country. For instance, the Basque terrorist-separatist group Euskadi ta Askatasuna (ETA) operates in Spain and is only interested in an independent homeland in northern Spain. It does not seek to place a Basque flag in capitals around the globe as al-Qaeda wishes to do with a green Islamic flag. Al-Qaeda follows the lead of Sayyid Qutb and Osama bin Laden in its belief that the West represents a threat to Islam, and no Muslim can rest until all other religions and ways of life are vanquished in favor of Islam.

In fact, al-Qaeda, originally a terrorist group, has now become al-Qaeda the terrorist movement. This evolution—from group to ideology—makes al-Qaeda arguably more dangerous now than ever before. From a small core of dedicated extremists motivated by the Afghan conflict with the Soviet Union, al-Qaeda has grown into a global campaign to change the world's current political order. Al-Qaeda—like a "multinational corporation"—has subsidiaries, sometimes consisting of groups, small terrorist cells, or even "Lone Wolf" operatives, in many countries around the world that draw inspiration from Osama bin Laden's message of global jihad. Estimates suggest that al-Qaeda has a presence in more than one hundred countries, including the United States. This means that al-Qaeda has members in over half of the world's 191 nations, a terrorist presence unparalleled in the history of terrorism. Because of al-Qaeda's proven ability to integrate unnoticed into a society until called to action, it is very likely that they are operating in a number of countries of which we are not yet aware.

Without question, al-Qaeda is the world's deadliest, largest, and wealthiest terrorist organization. Bin Laden believes that violence is the only power the infidels understand. It has been behind some of the world's most spectacular terrorist acts, most notably 9/11. But al-Qaeda's terrorist activity goes back well before 2001. Al-Qaeda and its network are believed to be behind a number of major terrorist attacks, including the bombing of the World Trade Center (1993: 6 Americans killed); attacks on U.S. servicemen in Mogadishu, Somalia (1993: 18 Americans killed); the strike on the Saudi National Guard Training Center in Riyadh, Saudi Arabia (1995: 5 Americans killed); the assault on the American military housing complex at Khobar Towers, Dhahran, Saudi Arabia (1996: 19 Americans killed); the bombing of the American embassies in Tanzania and Kenya (1998: 257 killed, including 12 Americans); the assault on the American naval warship USS *Cole* in Aden, Yemen (2000: 17 American sailors killed); the attacks on the World Trade Center, the Pentagon, and a United Airlines flight (2001: 2,995 killed from 80 nations).

Since 9/11, al-Qaeda has been implicated in the nightclub suicide bombing in Bali, Indonesia (2002: 202 killed, including 7 Americans); the car bombings of the housing complex bombing in Riyadh, Saudi Arabia (2 attacks in 2003: 8 Americans in first attack; 4 in second attack); the strikes on the Casablanca, Morocco, hotel and restaurant (2003: 45 killed); the bombing of the Jordanian embassy in Baghdad, Iraq (2003: 10 killed); the blasts at the UN headquarters in Baghdad, Iraq (2003: 22 killed, including 3 Americans); the strikes on the British consulate and bank and synagogues in Istanbul, Turkey (2003: 24 killed); the train bombings in Madrid, Spain (2004: 191 killed); suicide attacks in Tashkent, Uzbekistan (2004: 45 killed); American consulate in Jeddah, Saudi Arabia (2004: 5 killed); Hilla, Iraq (2005: 125 killed); London subway (2005: 50 killed); and a number of lesser terrorist events, including a number of bombings, assassinations, and beheadings in Iraq since 2003 under Zarqawi's evil hand. Zarqawi is believed to have personally beheaded at least two hostages. Al-Qaeda's thirst for the blood of nonbelievers is unprecedented.

Despite its record of death and destruction, al-Qaeda is not invincible or even infallible. A 1994 plot to blow up eleven airliners over the Pacific out of the Philippines and a plot to assassinate the late pope John Paul II were foiled. Al-Qaeda operatives were arrested in Jordan, the United States, Canada, England, Spain, Germany, Italy, and Syria in connection with attempts to conduct attacks during the Millennium activities in 1999–2000. Planned hijackings of Air France and British Airways flights in late 2003 and early 2004 appear to have been thwarted by American, French, and British intelligence and law enforcement authorities, as were attacks planned around the American presidential election in 2004. The U.S. government reports that it has thwarted well over one hundred different known terrorist attacks since 9/11 both at home and abroad.

AL-QAEDA'S OBJECTIVES

Al-Qaeda's objective is to establish a global, pan-Islamic, theocratic caliph-ate (kingdom) that stretches from the historically Muslim lands of Spain in the West to Indonesia and the islands of the Philippines in the East. Osama, naturally, considers Israel to be a historically Muslim state as well. By work-ing with other fundamentalist Muslim allies, al-Qaeda intends to overthrow non-Islamic regimes and expel Westerners and infidels from Muslim coun-tries. The Kingdom of Saudi Arabia is particularly important to Osama because it is the birthplace of Islam. Al-Qaeda sees the United States as the premier enemy of Islam, the most significant impediment to the establish-ment of a worldwide Islamic caliphate, under *sharia*, and the most ardent supporter of Israel in its struggle with the Palestinians. Osama also despises the United States because he believes that America took undue credit for the demise of the Soviet Union. In Osama's twisted mind, the Soviet's defeat in Afghanistan at the hands of the Afghan and Arab *mujahideen* changed the course of history, bringing the Soviet Union to its knees and ending the Cold War. The end of the Cold War was not due to the untiring efforts of the United States and the West.

Naturally, Israel is al-Qaeda's second sworn enemy. But surprisingly, al-Qaeda has never successfully attacked an Israeli target,[2] which is part of the reason that Abu Musab al Zarqawi declined for many years to pledge his allegiance to al-Qaeda. Like bin Laden's mentor Azzam, Zarqawi thought Israel was the next logical target after the Soviet-Afghan conflict, while bin Laden had his sights set on the United States. However, by 2003, the two "uberterrorists" looked past their differing strategies and worked together to rid Iraq of infidels.

Al-Qaeda plans to bring other apostate Middle Eastern states under its rule, cripple Israel's most ardent supporter, the United States, before crushing the Jewish state itself. After vanquishing Israel, Israeli lands will be returned to the Palestinian people and Islamic rule. Its other target countries are Morocco, Jordan, Saudi Arabia, Yemen, and Pakistan, which bin Laden has labeled oppressive, unjust, and apostates. He vowed that the people of these nations would be "liberated."

DECLARING WAR

Although most people are not aware of it, al-Qaeda actually declared war on the United States. So, indeed, the moniker "war on terror" is appropriate. In 1991, Osama bin Laden issued a *fatwa*, called the "Jihad on the Americans Occupying the Country of the Two Sacred Places." This religious edict refers to the American troop presence in Saudi Arabia, beginning before the first Gulf War in 1991. After the war, American forces began a semipermanent presence in Saudi Arabia, which lasted until 2003. Controversy exists among Muslims over Osama issuing *fatwas*. Generally, a *fatwa* can be issued only by a religious cleric. Osama is not a religious cleric, but he fancies himself one.

In 1998, al-Qaeda issued two new *fatwas*: "The Islamic World Front for Jihad against the Jews and Crusaders" and "The International Islamic Front for Jihad against America and Israel." Not content with declaring war just on the United States, al-Qaeda expanded its 1996 *fatwa* to include Israel and the "Crusaders." By referencing the Crusades, a series of wars by Western European Christians to recapture the Holy Land from the Muslims in the eleventh to the thirteenth centuries, al-Qaeda in effect declared war on the West. The *fatwas* concluded that America, despite its power, could be defeated and it was the duty of all Muslims to kill U.S. citizens (both civilian and military) and their allies everywhere.

AL-QAEDA IN IRAQ

While bin Laden initially supported the overthrow of Saddam Hussein to make way for an Islamist, rather than secular, ruler in Iraq, he later came to see Hussein as a potential ally against a common enemy: the United States. In 1994, Hassan al Turabi, head of the Sudanese branch of the Muslim Brotherhood, brokered a meeting between bin Laden and a senior Iraqi intelligence officer in Khartoum. Bin Laden is believed to have asked for help in procuring weapons and requested land in Iraq for training camps. That request, and bin Laden's additional overture to Hussein in 1997, were reportedly ignored. It was bin Laden's 1998 *fatwa* against the United States that finally got Saddam's attention and several meetings between Saddam's deputies, the Taliban, and bin Laden followed, mostly arranged by bin Laden's top deputy and personal physician, Ayman al Zawahiri. The meetings resulted in an invitation for bin Laden to relocate to Iraq in 1999, which bin

Laden declined, preferring his surroundings in Afghanistan. But it became obvious to bin Laden just a few years later that he needed "representation" in Iraq. He had communicated with Zarqawi over the years and while bin Laden deemed Zarqawi to be too violent and extreme in his interpretation of Islam at one point, it became clear by 2004 that al-Qaeda needed Zarqawi, who had been in northern Iraq since 2002, to address the American occupation in Iraq.

Zarqawi's special talent for sneak attacks manifested itself into suicide bombings and kidnappings as Iraq's fledging democracy tried to get off the ground. He gained notoriety in the terrorist world for the brutal, 2004 videotaped beheading of American Nicholas Berg in Iraq, as well as other grotesque terrorist acts there. Not surprisingly, bin Laden—perhaps eager to take credit for Zarqawi's successes—extended repeated "invitations" for Zarqawi to pledge his allegiance to al-Qaeda and bin Laden. Zarqawi declined across the board, and then for reasons that aren't clear, he accepted the invitation offered by one of bin Laden's associates in late 2004.

In late 2004, bin Laden anointed Zarqawi: "prince of al-Qaeda in Iraq." By 2005, Zarqawi had personally taken credit for twenty-five attacks in Iraq, most of which killed far more Muslims than Americans. In early 2005, bin Laden exhorted Zarqawi to take the fight to the United States, "We have to expand our attacks on the enemy outside Iraq." Today, Zarqawi, arguably, is the world's single-most dangerous terrorist.

TARGETS

Muslims, especially nonbelievers, have never been off limits as al-Qaeda targets, even though bin Laden has sought alliances with Shia Muslims for some operations (much to Zarqawi's dismay). As Iraq has shown, al-Qaeda's "kill circle" has become more indiscriminate. Al-Qaeda now strikes soft, undefended civilian targets frequented by Muslims and infidels alike such as businesses, hotels, restaurants, and housing areas. Al-Qaeda has killed thousands of Iraqis in an effort to foment civil war in Iraq among the Shia, Sunni, and Kurds. It has even attacked mosques in both Iraq and Pakistan. These rash acts have eroded al-Qaeda's support base among some groups, which object to the wanton violence against other Muslims. Once tolerant of al-Qaeda, countries like Saudi Arabia and Pakistan clearly have the terrorist group in their sights.

THE ORGANIZATION

The exact number of al-Qaeda operatives is unknown and the groups' size probably ebbs and flows, depending on recruitment, retention, detentions, and world events such as the rallying cry of Iraq. But it is widely estimated that al-Qaeda trained as many as 120,000 militant Muslim radicals in their camps in Sudan and Afghanistan from the early 1990s through 2001. Surely, today, only a fraction of those trained militants are active. Today's al-Qaeda probably numbers in the thousands, not tens of thousands. But some experts believe that al-Qaeda is actually growing in number as it transforms itself from a terrorist group to a terrorist movement. Many of its members, who were displaced by Operation Enduring Freedom in Afghanistan in fall 2001 have dispersed to South Asia, the Horn of Africa, Southeast Asia, Europe, and the Middle East, to places where they are among sympathizers and supporters. Among their haunts are Morocco, Tunisia, Algeria, Kenya, Somalia, Ethiopia, Sudan, Saudi Arabia, Iraq, Yemen, Qatar, Kuwait, Syria, Egypt, Iran, Afghanistan, Pakistan, India, Indonesia, Malaysia, the Philippines, Cambodia, Russia, Spain, Germany, France, Britain, Bosnia, Switzerland, Italy, Canada, and the United States, to name a few.

Looking at the transformation of al-Qaeda after it lost its training camps and operations base in Afghanistan, former CIA case officer Marc Sageman noted that al-Qaeda had become more of a social movement than a terrorist organization. Rather than controlling the jihadist movement, al-Qaeda is now more like "a collection of local people with local grievances who share the same ideology. They follow the methodologies and precepts of al-Qaeda, but without direct links to the group." In some ways, al-Qaeda has become a terrorist political party, which provides ideology, direction, and visible leadership, to local groups that advance the cause at the grassroots level. Many attacks will be in the name of al-Qaeda, even if they are not actually organized and perpetrated by al-Qaeda itself.

As such, al-Qaeda and its affiliates operate in small, clandestine cells. Not all members may be active at any one time. Some covert operatives may be "sleepers"—members who infiltrate local communities posing as a neighbor, local merchant, or student, remaining dormant until they are activated by a signal or a predetermined time and date to undertake support functions or conduct terrorist operations. Because sleepers live such low-profile lives, they may be able to conduct reconnaissance and preparations for a terrorist act without any suspicion until it is too late. A sleeper may remain dormant and undetected for years. Authorities in the United States have long expressed concern that al-Qaeda's public statements broadcast on television or Internet websites are embedded with coded messages that could contain an activation cue for a terrorist operation by local agents.

Al-Qaeda, for all its gripes with modernity, has hypocritically embraced modern technology. Unquestionably, it is one of the most technologically sophisticated terrorist groups ever. This, of course, is a requirement for al-Qaeda's global operations. Al-Qaeda relies on satellite and cell phones, computers, e-mail, websites, chat rooms, and encrypted communications for getting its terrorist business done. It simply could not operate around the world as it does without advanced technology. This is also one of the reasons that al-Qaeda has sought to recruit educated operatives, such as engineers, who can effectively and efficiently work in the digital age.

THE FUTURE

Today's al-Qaeda is clearly different from what it was on 9/11. It has lost its sanctuary in Afghanistan and much of its senior leadership. It is damaged, but it is not dead as evidenced by the number of al-Qaeda-associated attacks around the world since September 2001. Instead of admitting defeat and surrendering after the American invasion of Afghanistan in 2001, al-Qaeda has undergone an "extreme makeover." Al-Qaeda, with Osama bin Laden as its spiritual head, has become the vanguard of a decentralized, international Islamist ideological movement, stretching from North America to Europe to East Asia.

This transformation from terrorist group to violent, international political crusade arguably makes al-Qaeda more dangerous than it was before. This is evidenced by al-Qaeda's reign of terror in Iraq as well as attacks in new places such as Qatar and the continuing arrests of al-Qaeda operatives in Spain and the UK, for example. Al-Qaeda will continue to operate in a disaggregated fashion unless another terrorist sanctuary is found. But then again, congregating in one place makes al-Qaeda vulnerable like it was in Afghanistan, so such a situation is rather unlikely. In a sense, it is a "virtual" terrorist group. Al-Qaeda will more likely continue to evolve into local grassroots organizations that will rely on al-Qaeda's ideology for direction and local operatives, trained by returning jihad veterans, for execution. The number of attacks may decline, while their lethality increases. Al-Qaeda may shift its emphasis to economic and infrastructure targets in places like Saudi Arabia in an effort to destabilize the government. It will undoubtedly continue to look for new ways to exploit unpopular American policies in the Muslim world. A new phenomenal attack in the United States on the scale of 9/11 would likely rejuvenate al-Qaeda, allowing it to continue internationalizing its distorted view of global jihad.

Al-Qaeda is likely to remain a threat to peace and stability on many fronts even if senior al-Qaeda members such as Osama bin Laden and Ayman al Zawahiri are captured or killed. There is no single point of failure for the organization. The extremist ideology of al-Qaeda will not die with bin Laden or Zawahiri. Bin Laden created an ideology that will outlive his death. As Osama said: "I am not afraid of death. Rather, martyrdom is my passion because martyrdom would lead to the birth of thousands of Osama." Nor will bin Laden's theology die with al-Qaeda's defeat in Iraq. There is no political compromise. Al-Qaeda will die when the ideology of al-Qaeda is defeated. That may take some time.

In the interim, violence will continue to be the key to al-Qaeda's relevance as an international force. Al-Qaeda's epic battle may not have yet been waged; its strategic horizon is far in the future. Al-Qaeda will continue to capitalize on the notion that the West is an unappeasable threat to Islam; violent jihad is the only way to defend the Muslim world; and with patience and constancy of purpose, victory is possible.

NOTES

1. Peter Bergen, *Holy War, Inc.: Inside the Secret World of Osama bin Laden* (New York: Free Press, 2002), p. 53.

2. Harvey G. Kushner, *Encyclopedia of Terrorism* (Thousand Oaks, Calif.: Sage Publications, 2002), p. 20.

6

TERROR HOT SPOTS

If you have $30 million, go to the black market in Central Asia, contact any disgruntled Soviet scientist, and a lot of . . . smart briefcase bombs are available. . . . They have contacted us, we sent our people to Moscow, to Tashkent, to other central Asian states and they negotiated, and we purchased some suitcase bombs.

—Ayman al Zawahiri, Al-Qaeda deputy commander, March 2004[1]

As sixteen-year-old Hussam Adbo approached the Hawara Checkpoint on Israel's West Bank, he changed his mind. The Palestinian boy with a new crew cut and big brown eyes decided he couldn't press the switch of his eighteen-pound suicide vest concealed under his oversized red jersey, blowing himself, Israeli soldiers, and other Palestinian bystanders to pieces. Although considered gullible and easily manipulated by friends and family, he decided he did not want to die that March 2004 day. It is not clear who sent the boy to a certain death, but he said he wanted to reach paradise, which he was taught in school was the reward for suicide bombers. The afterlife would be sweet with rivers of honey and wine and the company of seventy-two virgins. His mother, unaware of her son's death wish or who had sent him on this mission, was grateful that her son had second thoughts that day and would have to wait for another day to reach paradise.[2]

THE MIDDLE EAST

There are plenty of terror hot spots across the globe today. From the UK to Iraq to the Philippines, terrorists are on the move—recruiting, planning,

training, and operating. And it is not only al-Qaeda. Foreign terrorist organizations such as Hamas, Hezbollah, and Palestinian Islamic Jihad are
important not only because of their violent means of trying to resolve political disputes, but because of their long-standing opposition to a comprehensive Middle East peace between the Israelis and Palestinians—some of
these groups have been part of the region's political landscape for over
twenty years. An equitable settlement to the Israeli-Palestinian conflict is
of tremendous interest to the United States—and others. For this reason,
America should pay close attention to these terrorist groups at all times.
They have struck—and have the continuing potential to strike—American
interests at a time of their choosing in the Middle East and beyond.

One of the most dangerous terrorist groups in the Middle East is Hezbollah. This radical Shia Muslim group takes its inspiration from the 1979
Iranian Revolution and the radical teachings of its then leader, the late ayatollah Ruhollah Khomeini. This organization, which literally means the
"Party of God," was formed in 1982 in the midst of the Lebanese civil war.
Its original goal was the establishment of an Islamic state in Lebanon similar to that formed in Iran. Hezbollah's mission was later expanded to militarily oppose the 1982 Israeli invasion of southern Lebanon. The terrorist
group is also dedicated to liberating the city of Jerusalem, which it considers an Islamic holy city, and destroying Israel. The strength of Hezbollah is
probably a few hundred hard-core operatives and several thousand supporters. Hezbollah operates in the Lebanese capital, Beirut, in the infamous Bekaa Valley to the east of Beirut, and in southern Lebanon along
the Israeli border. In addition, it is suspected of having terror cells worldwide within the Lebanese Shiite diaspora, including in the United States.
It draws much of its support from Lebanon's over one million Shiites, the
country's largest religious group.

The group does not reserve its hatred only for Israel. The United States
is also in its gun sights: Hassan Nasrallah, Hezbollah's secretary-general,
has said, "Death to America was, is, and will stay our slogan."[3] Like Iran, its
ideological mentor, Hezbollah sees the United States as the "Great Satan."
Hezbollah has provided training and support to other Middle Eastern terrorist groups as well, including Palestinian Islamic Jihad, Hamas, and other
anti-Israel rejectionist groups, which have helped tatter the Israeli-Palestinian peace process. It is likely that Hezbollah also has a keen interest in Iraq
due to the Shiite majority population in the southern part of the country,
which borders Iran. Hezbollah could easily decide to cause trouble in Iraq
for the new government should its Shia brethren be slighted in some man-

ner. Many believe that it has meddled there already. Hezbollah undoubtedly has a small number of operatives in Iraq that could be called into service at any time.

Hezbollah is unique among terrorist groups in that it also has a strong political movement, holding 14 seats in the 128-seat Lebanese parliament. Hezbollah does social work, funding hospitals, dental clinics, schools, and cultural societies, which makes the group popular with the Lebanese Shia community. It even builds roads and houses. The terrorist group also owns a newspaper, and a satellite television and radio station. The satellite television station, al Manar, was recently banned across most of Europe and in the United States for inciting violence. For example, according to the U.S. government, al Manar broadcast a video with lyrics calling the United States the "mother of terrorism" and urging attacks with "rifles and suicide bombers" against what it termed the "invaders" in Iraq. Al Manar glorifies suicide bombings, calls for attacks on Israel, and recruits for the Hezbollah cause. France also banned al Manar, saying its programs are militant and anti-Semitic. One program made the charge that Zionists are attempting to transmit dangerous diseases like AIDS through exports to Arab countries.

Both Syria and Iran have significant influence with Hezbollah. It is believed that Hezbollah takes its operational direction from Iran and has allied with Syria to advance its political agenda in Lebanon. The relationship with Syria is a marriage of necessity, not choice. Secular Syria wants to keep Israel in check and regain the Golan Heights, which it lost to Israel in the 1967 Six-Day War. For its part, fundamentalist Hezbollah finds sanctuary and logistics support in Syria. The Bekaa Valley, halfway between Beirut and Damascus, serves as the conduit for Hezbollah's outside support, especially from Iran. The valley is infamous for serving as a training ground for Hezbollah militia fighters and terrorists. Although the Bekaa Valley is in Lebanese territory, it is controlled by Syria, which maintained fifteen thousand troops in Lebanon until recently. Hezbollah also receives support from Iran, including training and weapons, not to mention political, diplomatic, financial, and organizational aid. It is estimated that Iran provides upward of $100 million annually to Hezbollah.

Syria and Iran, using Hezbollah as a proxy terrorist guerrilla force, can attack Israel with relative impunity and plausible deniability. In 1982, Israel invaded southern Lebanon to expel Palestinian guerrillas, which had been conducting cross-border strikes from Lebanon into Israel since the 1967 Arab-Israeli war. Syria and Iran used Hezbollah to oppose the Israeli intervention of southern Lebanon, ultimately leading to Israel's withdrawal in

2000. Some terrorists point to the Israeli withdrawal from Lebanon as proof that terrorism is an effective political tool. Hezbollah continues cross-border attacks into Israel from Lebanon, vowing to continue the "resistance" attacks until Israel evacuates Shebaa Farms, an area captured from Syria in the 1967 war, but claimed by Lebanon. Possessing thousands of short-range Katyusha and Fajr rockets, Hezbollah can strike Israeli targets far south of the Lebanese-Israeli border.

Before September 11, 2001, Hezbollah killed more Americans than any other terrorist group. The suicide bombing attack on the Marine Barracks in Beirut, Lebanon, in 1983, which killed 241 American sailors and marines, was the biggest single terrorist attack suffered by the United States in its history until 9/11. Hezbollah struck the U.S. embassy in Beirut in 1983 and the American embassy annex the following year. After the Marine barracks bombing and the attacks on the U.S. embassy in Beirut, the United States in 1984 decided to withdraw its peacekeepers from Lebanon. Hezbollah sees this as victory for terrorism. Hezbollah terrorists are responsible for the death of a U.S. Navy sailor executed during the TWA 847 hijacking in Athens, Greece, in 1985. Hezbollah also kidnapped and killed a number of Westerners in Lebanon during the 1980s, including the Beirut CIA station chief William Buckley. It has attacked American interests outside of Lebanon as well. In 1996, Hezbollah was implicated in the bombing of the U.S. military barracks at Khobar Towers in Saudi Arabia, killing 19 American servicemen and injuring 515 Americans and Saudis. Moreover, it has shown global reach by attacking the Israeli embassy in 1992, killing twenty-nine people, and a Jewish community center in 1994, in Buenos Aires, Argentina, killing ninety-five.

Noting the strength and reach of Hezbollah, former deputy secretary of state Richard Armitage said, "Hezbollah may be the A-team of terrorists," while "al-Qaeda is actually the B-team."[4] Not disagreeing, former CIA director George Tenet testified before Congress in 2003, "Hezbollah, as an organization with capability and worldwide presence, is [al-Qaeda's] equal, if not a more capable organization. I actually think they are a notch above in many respects."[5] Considering al-Qaeda's successful terrorist record, that is no small tribute. Hezbollah has achieved great standing in the Muslim world because of its successful resistance to the Israeli occupation of southern Lebanon and its attacks on American forces in Beirut, leading to their withdrawal. Many Arab governments see Hezbollah members as "freedom fighters" and do not feel threatened by them despite their close association with fundamentalist Iran and advocacy of Islamic rule. These states believe that Hezbollah's enmity is aimed at Israel and they are content to stay within Lebanon. Hezbollah is the only group, or nation for that matter, that has been able to force Israel to cede territory, first retreating to a security zone in southern Lebanon and then leaving Lebanon completely in 2000. Some will see the Israeli withdrawal from the Gaza Strip in the same way. The fact that Hezbollah took on both the United States and Israel in Lebanon and won—in the eyes of many—may encourage al-Qaeda and others to try to do the same elsewhere. It is not clear how Syria's withdrawal from Lebanon will affect Hezbollah. It could push the group into greater militancy in a power struggle with other Christian and Muslim groups or force it further into the legitimate political process.

Hamas (an acronym for a word similar to "zeal" in Arabic) is the main Palestinian Islamic terrorist group in the Middle East. Hamas, also known as the Islamic Resistance Movement, was formed in 1987 during the early stages of the Palestinian *intifada* (uprising) as an outgrowth of the Palestinian Muslim Brotherhood. This Sunni Muslim group is focused on opposing the Middle East peace process and establishing an Islamic state in Palestine by destroying Israel. The group, best known for its suicide bombings inside Israel, has both political and terrorist agendas. The Hamas political platform allegedly says, "There is no solution for the Palestine problem except through jihad."

The organization's terrorist element operates clandestinely, while the political wing works openly through mosques and social service organizations to recruit new members, raise money, organize political activities, and distribute propaganda. Like Hezbollah in Lebanon, Hamas has run candidates in local elections, including electing members to the Gaza Strip municipal councils in January 2005. It will likely continue to participate in future Palestinian elections. It is unclear what effect this will have on its militant views. Like the Lebanese Hezbollah, it also built schools, clinics, and hospitals. In less charity-minded efforts, Hamas has also ruthlessly killed Palestinians who have collaborated with the Israelis, and members of rival Palestinian groups. Hamas' strength is concentrated in the West Bank and Gaza Strip in Israeli territory, which Israel won from Jordan and Egypt during the 1967 Six-Day War. The number of Hamas operatives is unknown, but it is believed that supporters and sympathizers run in the tens of thousands. Unlike Hezbollah that has operated abroad, Hamas currently restricts its terrorist activities to the West Bank, Gaza Strip, and Israel. The group's leadership is located primarily in the West Bank and

Gaza Strip, but may also reside in Syria, Lebanon, and the other Persian Gulf States.

Hamas' financial support comes primarily from legitimate Hamas-run businesses, Palestinian expatriates, and wealthy benefactors throughout the Muslim world. Some speculate that Hamas may receive up to 10 percent of its funding from Iran.[6] It is also believed that some fundraising takes place in Western Europe and North America. Hamas has not targeted U.S. interests directly to date; however, American citizens have been killed due to their proximity to Hamas terrorist operations in the West Bank, the Gaza Strip, and Israel.

Palestinian Islamic Jihad (PIJ) is another militant Sunni terrorist group, allied with Hamas. PIJ was founded in Egypt, but found a home in the Gaza Strip in the 1970s, following the 1967 Arab-Israeli war when the Israelis took control of that small strip of land from Cairo. The exact strength of PIJ is unknown, but despite its ferocious reputation, it is considered small, numbering perhaps a few hundred members. PIJ's leadership is suspected of residing in Syria and Syrian-dominated Lebanon at Damascus' invitation. It is committed to establishing an Islamic Palestinian state and the destruction of Israel through violent jihad. PIJ also opposes moderate Arab states that they believe have been corrupted by the West. It rejects the Palestinian Authority and sees its willingness to negotiate with Israel as a betrayal of the Palestinian people. Although a Sunni Arab group, it reportedly was inspired, like Lebanon's Hezbollah, by the 1979 Shiite revolution in Iran. PIJ receives some financial backing and support from Iran, including payments to the families of suicide bombers, who attack Israeli targets. PIJ has conducted attacks against Israeli military and civilian targets in the West Bank and Gaza Strip. It has not yet targeted the U.S. interests, but considers America an enemy because of its support for Israel. PIJ activities directly affect U.S. interests because their terrorist deeds have undermined the Palestinian-Israeli Middle East peace process.

BEYOND THE MIDDLE EAST

Terrorist activity, as demonstrated by al-Qaeda's criminal reach, has become a global phenomenon. It is certainly not limited to a small patch of earth in the Middle East, centered around Israel, where terrorism was— until the invasion of Iraq in 2003—arguably, the most active worldwide. In the last few years, global terrorism has touched Indonesia, the Philippines,

Pakistan, India, Afghanistan, Uzbekistan, and China in Asia; Morocco, Tunisia, and Kenya in Africa; Turkey, Spain, and Russia in Europe; and Iraq, Israel, Egypt, Kuwait, Qatar, and Saudi Arabia in the Middle East, just to name a few.

Russia and the Caucasus

Russia continues to suffer at the hands of terrorists. Most terrorism in Russia revolves around the question of Chechen Muslim separatism in the southern Caucasus region of the vast nation. Foreign fighters, predominantly Arab jihadists, who have ties to international terrorist organizations, such as al-Qaeda, support the local Chechens in their effort to form an independent Muslim state. The Chechen fighters have conducted terrorist acts in Chechnya as well as Russia, including the Russian capital, Moscow. A number of the Chechen groups have been designated as foreign terrorist organizations by the U.S. government.

Russia has been the scene of some of the most dramatic terrorist acts in recent history. In September 2004, Chechen separatists seized a grade school in Beslan, Russia, taking hostage over 1,000 students and teachers. This is believed to be the largest incident of hostage taking in terrorism history. The ensuing standoff ended in explosions and a blaze of gunfire, leaving 330 dead and over 700 injured. Prior to Beslan, in October 2002, a Moscow theater with eight hundred attendees was seized. Over 120 hostages died in the ensuing Russian SWAT team raid due to the use of an unusual narcotic gas by the Russian assault forces. The Chechen terrorists often make use of female suicide bombers, known as "Black Widows." These women have usually lost a loved one at the hands of the Russian forces and are exacting their revenge by acting as suicide bombers against Russian civilians. A number of these female suicide attacks have taken place in Moscow. Farther to the South, Georgia is also an area of concern, especially Georgia's Pankisi Gorge, where al-Qaeda-affiliated terrorists and Chechen fighters have taken up residency.

Central Asia

Long dubbed the "Stans" by Central Asia watchers, the five former Soviet Muslim republics of Kazakhstan, Turkmenistan, Kyrgyzstan, Tajikistan, and Uzbekistan in Central Asia are hot spots for radical Islamic fundamentalism and terrorism. The region is rife with poverty, political repression, corruption, cronyism, and arms and drug trafficking. The majority of people in these countries live below the poverty line. In fact, the region is much poorer than it was under Soviet rule, which ended in 1991, making it a potential breeding ground for Islamic militancy.

Central Asia, once home to Marco Polo's great Silk Road trading route, is now the stomping grounds of the Islamic Movement of Uzbekistan (IMU). Allied with the Taliban and al-Qaeda, the IMU desires a caliphate (Islamic state) in Central Asia, based in the Fergana Valley. The IMU is believed to number in the range of two to five thousand fighters, operating in Kyrgyzstan, Tajikistan, Uzbekistan, Kazakhstan, Afghanistan, and even Pakistan. Prior to 9/11, the IMU operated freely in Afghanistan, protected and supported by the Taliban. During Operation Enduring Freedom in Afghanistan, coalition forces killed many IMU fighters. Relatively quiet since the fighting in Afghanistan in 2001, IMU fighters, including IMU leader Tahir Yuldash, showed up in clashes with Pakistani forces along the Afghan-Pakistani border in March 2004. An IMU splinter group conducted a spate of suicide attacks in March 2004 in Uzbekistan.

The Central Asian region is also home to the radical fundamentalist group the Islamic Liberation Party or Hizb ut-Tahrir (HT). Like the IMU, HT also wants to establish a caliphate in Central Asia. To date, HT has not been implicated in any violent acts in pursuing a Muslim state, yet it is reasonable to conclude that it is supportive of other like-minded Islamic fundamentalist groups and their tactics. It is perhaps the most feared group in Central Asia because of its size: twenty thousand members. Hizb ut-Tahrir has been known to be anti–United States, anti-Israel, and anti-Western, and supportive of suicide operations as well. HT claimed that the United States and Britain are at war with Islam and has exhorted all Muslims to engage in a jihad against these countries. It is reportedly active in Kazakhstan, Kyrgyzstan, Tajikistan, and Uzbekistan and as many as thirty other countries worldwide, including in Europe. Many experts believe there are, at least, informal connections between al-Qaeda, IMU, and HT.

Southeast Asia

Despite the attention rightfully given to al-Qaeda and the Middle East, Southeast Asia is a major battleground in the war on terror. Some have posited that there are more al-Qaeda operatives in Southeast Asia than in the rest of the world combined. Indonesia's Jemaah Islamiya is the most feared terrorist group in Southeast Asia. Its goal is the creation of a pan-

Islamic state, incorporating the Muslim areas of Indonesia, Malaysia, Singapore, the southern Philippines, and southern Thailand. Jemaah Islamiya was almost completely unheard of until the months after 9/11, when a plan to attack American, Australian, British, and Israeli embassies and diplomatic buildings, as well as American ships and sailors in Singapore, was uncovered by local authorities in December 2001.

The connection between Jemaah Islamiya and al-Qaeda was confirmed by a videotape discovered in an al-Qaeda camp in Afghanistan during Operation Enduring Freedom in fall 2001, which showed Jemaah Islamiya's surveillance footage of intended targets in Singapore. Many of Jemaah Islamiya's members fought in Afghanistan or received al-Qaeda training there in the late 1990s. The group's strength is often estimated to be in the range of three to five thousand members. Jemaah Islamiya has perpetrated several significant terrorist acts, including the October 2002 nightclub bombing in Bali, Indonesia, and the J. W. Marriott hotel bombing in August 2003 in the Indonesian capital, Jakarta. Coincidentally, the Bali nightclub bombing occurred on the second anniversary of the USS *Cole* bombing (October 12, 2000). The terrorist group is also suspected of dozens of other smaller terrorist incidents in the Philippines and Indonesia in 2004, and a spate of bombings in 2004–2005 in southern Thailand.

After Jemaah Islamiya, the Abu Sayyaf Group (ASG) is arguably the most active terrorist group in Southeast Asia. The ASG, which has kidnapped several hundred Philippine nationals and foreigners in the last several years, operates in the Muslim-dominated southern Philippines. Some of the ASG's leaders fought against the Soviets in Afghanistan, trained in al-Qaeda camps in the 1990s, and have radical Islamic tendencies. They have also been involved in bombings and assassinations in the Philippines, including operations against U.S. troops. Although the group has primarily operated in the southern Philippines, it has operated in Malaysia as well. ASG violence continued into 2005, particularly bombings in the Philippines capital, Manila, and the southern island of Mindanao. In early 2005, the U.S. State Department warned that JI, MILF, and the ASG were planning multiple attacks in the Philippines.

Latin America

Narcoterrorism is what most people think of when it comes to Latin America and the subject of terrorism. In South America, the Revolutionary Armed Forces of Colombia (FARC) is the most dangerous terrorist organization. Since the early 1990s, the FARC has been battling Colombian government forces for control of the countryside. But more is going on in Latin America on the terror front than meets the eye. Other international terrorists are present in Latin America as well, including Hezbollah and Hamas. The U.S. government believes that al-Qaeda is also present in the southern hemisphere. Though there have been no recent terrorist attacks by al-Qaeda or Middle Eastern groups in South America, Hamas and Hezbollah are believed to be involved in fundraising in the triborder area of Paraguay, Brazil, and Argentina through drug running, arms trafficking, money laundering, and smuggling. It is likely that al-Qaeda is also raising funds in this region for its global operations.

Africa

One may not first think of Africa when thinking of international terrorism. It has not been a terrorist hot spot for long, and sub-Saharan Africa has been particularly free of terrorist activity. However, from Morocco to Tunisia to Kenya to Tanzania, Africa is no longer a stranger to the carnage of international terrorism. In Eastern Africa in 1998, al-Qaeda bombed the America embassies in Nairobi, Kenya, and Dar es Salaam, Tanzania, killing 257 and wounding over 5,000 (mostly Africans). In November 2002, twelve Kenyans and three Israeli tourists were killed in a bombing of an Israeli-owned hotel in the coastal town of Mombasa. On that same day, a surface-to-air missile was fired at an Israeli El Al civilian airliner as it took off from Mombasa airport. Fortunately, the missile failed to reach its target. Across the continent in North Africa, in April 2002, a gas truck exploded at a historic Tunisian synagogue on the island of Djerba, killing twenty-one, mostly German, tourists. In May 2003, al-Qaeda bombings killed twenty-eight and wounded more than one hundred in Casablanca, Morocco. More than half of the suspects arrested for the 3/11 Madrid bombing were Moroccan.

Due to ongoing conflicts, porous borders, extreme poverty, and insufficient law enforcement, terrorism analysts worry that failing states in Africa, especially the Horn of Africa, could become the new sanctuary for international terrorists, especially states with large Muslim populations. This would not be unprecedented. Sudan, which appears on the mend after years of civil strife, served as al-Qaeda's home from 1991 to 1996. The Horn of Africa, especially Somalia, a Muslim nation of eight million, is one of the most troubling spots in Africa and has been designated a front in the war on terror by the Bush administration. Many experts are troubled that the

Sunni Muslim country could replace Afghanistan as an al-Qaeda sanctuary. Despite more than a dozen attempts at national reconciliation since 1991, there is no functioning central government in Somalia, and Washington has no official diplomatic relations with Mogadishu. Islamic radicals, with al-Qaeda ties, have threatened holy war if peacekeepers are introduced into Somalia to install a new government. A combination of continuing instability, warlordism, open borders, a long coastline on the Arabian Sea, and proximity to terrorist-troubled Yemen and the Arabian Peninsula makes it an ideal terrorist sanctuary. In fact, it is believed that the al-Qaeda terrorist operations in Kenya in 1998 and 2002 originated in Somalia. The country, home to al-Qaeda affiliate Al Ittihad al Islami, is also suspected to be rife with weapons, such as MANPADS (man-portable air defense systems), antitank weapons, and explosives smuggled in from the Arabian Peninsula. Africa's combination of corruption, porous borders, large Muslim populations, Islamic radicalism, and weak and failing states makes it fertile soil for the growth of international terrorism.

South Asia

South Asia is another major front in the war on terror. In Afghanistan, rump Taliban fighters and al-Qaeda fighters have continued their resistance, especially in southern and southeastern Afghanistan along the Pakistani border area. Pakistan has killed or captured over three hundred al-Qaeda operatives since 9/11. There have been attacks against coalition forces, international aid workers, Afghan security forces, and civilians, resulting in hundreds of deaths since the end of 2001. There are also reports of foreign fighters from Chechnya, Uzbekistan, and other Arab states in Afghanistan, too.

Pakistan, itself, has been the source—and victim—of radical Islamic elements. Pakistan's border with Afghanistan is a stronghold for the Taliban and al-Qaeda, and may be the hiding place of Osama bin Laden, his deputy Ayman al Zawahiri, and Taliban leader Mullah Omar. Foreign fighters, including Uzbeks and Chechens, clashed with the Pakistani army in spring 2004. Al-Qaeda-associated terrorists have tried to assassinate Pakistani president Pervez Musharraf more than once, dating back to December 2003, because of his cooperation with the United States, the secular nature of Pakistan's government, and peace overtures toward India. American journalist Daniel Pearl was kidnapped and killed by al-Qaeda operatives in Pakistan in early 2002, and the U.S. consulate in Karachi, Pakistan, was attacked in June 2002. In 2005, a Shiite festival in Quetta was attacked, resulting in the death of thirty. Pakistan has a history of sectarian violence between the majority Sunni and minority Shia extremist groups. A number of senior al-Qaeda operatives, including operations chief Khalid Sheikh Mohammed, were arrested in large Pakistani cities such as Karachi and Rawalpindi. Osama bin Laden and Ayman al Zawahiri may be there as well.

Indian-controlled, Muslim-majority Kashmir has been the site of significant terrorist activity since 1947 when India and Pakistan became independent nations. Pakistani extremist elements, some supported by Pakistani intelligence, have pushed India and Pakistan to the brink of conventional—and nuclear—war more than once over the last few years. Terrorist groups, such as Lashkar-e-Tayyiba, have attacked the Indian parliament, army bases, and local government buildings, killing scores. Although there has been a recent hiatus of terrorism between India and Pakistan, the peace remains fragile.

Europe

After the March 2004 train massacre in Madrid, Spain, Europe no longer comes as a surprise terrorist hot spot. The continent has long been awash in al-Qaeda and has served as a planning and staging area for some of the world's most dangerous terrorists in recent years. In fact, a number of 9/11 hijackers spent time in Hamburg, Germany. Lead hijacker pilot Mohammed Atta, who flew the first plane into the World Trade Center, was in Madrid, Spain, two months before September 11. Since 2001, al-Qaeda cells and operatives have been broken up in Spain, Italy, Germany, France, Belgium, Britain, the Netherlands, and Switzerland. The Spanish alone have foiled four additional bomb plots since the March 2004 attacks. Turkey was the site of a terrorist attack in November 2003 when al-Qaeda attacked two synagogues, the British consulate, and a British bank in Istanbul. The British have broken up a number of terrorist cells there, but still suffered a major attack in July 2005. The recruiting of Muslim immigrants and native European Muslim converts are a particular concern to law enforcement authorities. There has also been a significant recruiting effort in Europe for jihadists for Iraqi duty, especially in Italy. Some al-Qaeda members, who fought in Bosnia during the 1992–1995 war, still reside there. In November 2004, Islamic terrorists in the Netherlands assassinated Theo Van Gogh because of the Dutch filmmaker's documentary on Muslim women.

Sometimes, the foiled terrorist plots are just as frightening. In recent years, the French disrupted attacks directed at the American (suicide bombers) and Russian (chemical attack) embassies in Paris by young Muslims trained in Afghanistan and Chechnya. Regrettably, almost no part of the world can claim that the scourge of international terrorism has not affected it in some manner. Terrorists will continue to look for places to recruit, train, and plan terrorist operations in their effort to overthrow governments worldwide and advance their agendas. We must be prepared.

NOTES

1. Associated Press, "Al-Qaeda Claims to Have Nukes," March 22, 2004, www.foxnews.com/story/0,2933,114806,00.html (accessed March 22, 2004).

2. Editorial, "A Virginal Innocence: The Hussam Tragedy" *The Montreal Gazette*, March 26, 2004.

3. Daniel Byman, "Should Hezbollah Be Next?" *Foreign Affairs* (November/December 2003), p. 54.

4. Byman, "Should Hezbollah Be Next?" p. 55.

5. Byman, "Should Hezbollah Be Next?" p. 57.

6. Kenneth Katzman, "Terrorism: Near Eastern Groups and State Sponsors, 2002," CRS Report for Congress, February 13, 2002, p. 7.

GLOBAL TERROR, INC.

We strongly and fully support Osama bin Laden's jihad against the heretic America and as well we support our brothers in Afghanistan, the Philippines and Chechnya.

—Public statement of the Algerian GSPC terrorist group, 2003

You would not think that one of the world's deadliest terrorists would be short and pudgy. But Khalid Sheikh Mohammed, a Kuwaiti, who turned Osama bin Laden's desire to kill Americans and others into a nightmarish reality, is just that. The bespectacled (now former) al-Qaeda operations chief and mastermind of the September 11 attacks was also active in the terrorist group's attempts to acquire chemical and biological weapons. Crisscrossing the globe with a Pakistani passport and seven aliases, Khalid has been implicated in attacks against a Tunisian synagogue, the kidnap and murder of Wall Street Journal writer Daniel Pearl in Pakistan, and the Bali bombing in Indonesia.

He has also been charged in plots to blow up eleven American airliners flying over the Pacific (Operation Bojinka) in 1995, and to assassinate the late Pope John Paul II during the Pontiff's visit to the Philippines that same year. Khalid also directed al-Qaeda operatives to target bridges, gas stations, and power plants in a number of locations in the United States, including New York City. Smart, but not smarter than the law, he was captured by Pakistani security officials working with the CIA in March 2003 while sleeping soundly in an al-Qaeda safehouse in Rawalpindi, Pakistan.

AN INTERNATIONAL NETWORK

Already enough of a problem to handle separately, international terrorist groups are becoming more interlinked and networked than ever before. They have become a "network of networks." There is an increasing, disturbing trend among Islamic terrorist organizations to cooperate, coordinate, and consult with one another for their own local purposes as well as the purpose of advancing global jihad and Islamism. Among the Muslim terrorist groups this has led to what might be called a "jihad division of labor." Each Muslim terrorist group pursuing its own local or regional goals supports the global fundamentalist Islamic terrorist objective of changing the current global political order and creating a worldwide pan-Islamic "superstate." Al-Qaeda's ideology has become a powerful, dangerous inspiration to the world's disparate Muslim fundamentalist terrorist groups. Al-Qaeda is now both a terrorist group and a terrorist "theology." Under significant pressure from law enforcement and military operations since 9/11, al-Qaeda has morphed from an operational terrorist group itself into a loose network of thirty to forty terrorist groups globally.[1]

A terrorist network is useful in that it can facilitate operations by providing sanctuary and support to traveling operatives, collecting and training recruits, sharing intelligence, raising and distributing funds, and spreading propaganda, not to mention advancing the cause widely through terrorist acts. As a result, today's terrorists are more decentralized, unpredictable, and harder to combat than ever. The phenomena of terrorist groups working together is not unprecedented, but al-Qaeda's willingness to train, equip, fund, and motivate affiliated terrorist organizations, which agree to strike Western targets, takes previous terrorist cooperation to a new level. This terrorist multiplier effect makes al-Qaeda's ideals and operations even more potent. Al-Qaeda's more devolved network allows it to move its objectives forward in a global offensive without the burden and danger of undertaking the operations itself. These decentralized attacks require less time to plan, less logistical support, and less supervision, and therefore, can be done more frequently. This new strategy makes the al-Qaeda movement an increasingly more challenging problem. Instead of fighting one terrorist army (i.e., al-Qaeda) on one front, the international community must fight several terrorist armies (i.e., the al-Qaeda network) on a number of fronts.

Take, for instance, the obstacles facing al-Qaeda in pulling off the 9/11 attacks. Al-Qaeda first needed to get operatives into the United States through the use of passports and visas. Next, they needed to assimilate the operatives into American society by getting them, among other things, driver's licenses and bank accounts. In fact, some of the potential hijackers did not get into the United States because they had been denied visas overseas at American embassies and consulates or, in at least one instance, turned around at American immigration here in the United States. All of this took multiple years of planning and effort, going back to 1993, before the 9/11 operation could be undertaken. Clearly, it would have been much easier to conduct a 9/11-like terrorist operation if the operatives were already in the country, members of the local community, spoke the language, and knew the customs. Now, with a locally based, global network in place, if al-Qaeda wants to conduct an attack in a certain country, for example Turkey, all it has to do is communicate with the local Turkish al-Qaeda cell and, perhaps, transfer some funding. This cell has its own network of supporters and operatives, who blend into the local community and know how to get things done in Turkish society. They are, therefore, best equipped to pull off a terrorist attack like the one in Istanbul in November 2003, which was done by a local al-Qaeda cell. This is undoubtedly how recent attacks in Qatar (theater), Saudi Arabia (American consulate Jeddah), and Pakistan (Shia mosque) were undertaken and how future attacks will be done as well.

An operational terrorist cell may include hardened Afghanistan, Chechnya, or Iraq war veterans as well as raw, local, radicalized recruits. Al-Qaeda trained as many as 120,000 radicals from as many as fifty nations in their Afghan training camps from 1996 to 2001. They also trained an unspecified number of recruits in Sudan prior to 1996. Many of the trainees returned to their homeland to form their own cells after leaving the al-Qaeda camps in Afghanistan and Sudan. Al-Qaeda's philosophy of "training the trainer" in their Afghanistan camps would allow al-Qaeda's militants to competently develop new recruits into radical jihadists by training them in handling weapons or bomb making in the area of a future attack. Large training camps and sanctuaries, such as the Sudan or Afghanistan, though extremely useful, are no longer needed.

According to the 2003 Gilmore Commission report, the cooperation among the Southeast Asian terrorist groups, Jemaah Islamiya, the Moro Islamic Liberation Front (MILF), and the Abu Sayyaf Group (ASG), is instructive.[2] The MILF runs terrorist training camps in the southern Philippines that are used by the ASG, MILF, Jemaah Islamiya, and, perhaps, other terrorist operatives, such as from Malaysia's Kumpulan Mujahadin Malaysia (KMM). In these camps, supported at least in part by al-Qaeda funding, operatives collaborate and train for operations across Southeast

Asia. Moreover, the report adds that even groups that have different religious orientations, such as al-Qaeda (i.e., Sunni), Hamas (i.e., Sunni), Palestinian Islamic Jihad (i.e., Sunni), and Hezbollah (i.e., Shia), train and work together, to a greater or lesser extent, because of their common enemies and objectives.[3]

With each new terrorist attack, there are a number of new previously unheard of terrorist groups or cells identified. For instance, the previously unknown Salafia Jihadia, an offshoot of the terrorist Moroccan Islamic Combatant Group, may be responsible for the attacks in Morocco in 2003. After a year of investigation, Spanish police and their European colleagues are still unraveling the conspiracy surrounding the 2004 Madrid bombings. Moroccans, Syrians, Algerians, Palestinians, and Egyptians have been arrested. The 2005 car bomb attack at a theater in Qatar may have been done by a local al-Qaeda cell under the operational control of a group called al-Qaeda in Arabia. New terrorist groups and cells continue to appear in Iraq. The proliferation of terrorist groups, like international franchises, is evidence of the power, inspiration, and success of the al-Qaeda movement. This trend will undoubtedly increase the law enforcement and intelligence challenges associated with the terrorist problem, making terrorist groups more difficult to discover, track, or eliminate.

AL-QAEDA'S GLOBAL TERRORIST WEB

Describing the links between terrorist groups today is an imprecise exercise. Ties are often clandestine, and murky at best. Sometimes they are formal; other times informal. The links can be permanent or temporary. With terrorist cells operating all over the world, it is sometimes difficult to determine which cell belongs to which organization, and whether members of that cell represent one or more terrorist groups. In other words, it is often impossible to determine where one terrorist group ends and another begins. Some terrorists belong to multiple groups. For instance, Riduan Isamuddin (also know by the *nom de guerre* "Hambali"), the former head of operations for Southeast Asia's Jemaah Islamiya, was also a member of al-Qaeda before he was arrested in August 2003 in Thailand. He served in Afghanistan during the Soviet resistance and trained in al-Qaeda camps there following the war. He was a close associate of former al-Qaeda operations chief Khalid Sheikh Mohammed, as well. Hambali was both al-Qaeda and Jemaah Islamiya. An Indonesia Jemaah Islamiya operative was arrested in the Philippines in early 2005 for his involvement in an Abu Sayyaf Group bombing in Manila.

Al-Qaeda will work with other terrorist groups, even criminal organizations, to advance its goal of global jihad. The breadth of al-Qaeda's global terrorist network is unprecedented. Reasonable estimates indicate that al-Qaeda has links with as many as forty groups, if not more, terrorist groups in places like Egypt, Yemen, Somalia, Libya, Morocco, Tunisia, Algeria, Israel/Palestinian territories, Lebanon, Iraq, Qatar, Kuwait, Afghanistan, Pakistan, Uzbekistan, China, the Philippines, Indonesia, Malaysia, Spain, and Russia, to name some of them. It also has an incalculable number of terrorist cells in countries around the world, including in the United States.[4]

The Middle East

Al-Qaeda is deeply involved with Middle Eastern terrorist groups. Its relationship with Hezbollah and Hamas may be of the greatest concern because of the raw capabilities and reach of each group. Although their individual political objectives do not completely coincide, their willingness to work together could lead to a deadly terrorist alliance like the world has never known. It is believed that Hezbollah is training Hamas members in Lebanon's Bekaa Valley, where some al-Qaeda members were also likely trained. Hezbollah probably taught al-Qaeda the simultaneous suicide attack bombing technique, which has now become an al-Qaeda trademark, and trained some al-Qaeda operatives in security and intelligence operations as well. Hezbollah first used this simultaneous bombing technique in 1983 when it attacked the U.S. Marine barracks in Beirut and attacked the French military headquarters nearby.[5] The Sunni-Shia differences between al-Qaeda and Hezbollah are not necessarily an obstacle to cooperation. A suspected Hamas member was also convicted in Israel in 2003 of ties to al-Qaeda, having learned bomb making in an al-Qaeda training camp in 1998.[6] Al-Qaeda also maintains a relationship with Asbat al Ansar (League of Followers), a Lebanon-based, Sunni radical group that has used violence since the early 1990s to destabilize the Lebanese government and rollback Western influences.

Al-Qaeda has taken the fight to Iraq as well, intending to expel the infidels and prevent the establishment of a democratic secular state. Iraq's most wanted man, al-Qaeda terrorist Abu Musab al Zarqawi, is leading the effort. Zarqawi pledged fealty to Osama and, in turn, the al-Qaeda leader has called him his "lieutenant." Zarqawi and his followers, going by several different names, including "Tawhid and Jihad" and "Al-Qaeda in the Land of the Two Rivers," are undoubtedly responsible for many of the over 150 suicide attacks, assassinations, and beheadings in Iraq since the spring 2003 invasion of Iraq. Zarqawi's group is believed to be doing some operational coordination and cooperation with Saddam Hussein's Baathist loyalists, foreign jihadists who have infiltrated Iraq, and common criminals as well. The Pentagon believes these groups total 12,000–20,000 hard-core members. Zarqawi's group itself may only number 2,000, but is responsible for some of the most spectacular attacks in Iraq, including the attack on the UN headquarters, the Najaf mosque, and the Hilla health clinic.

Ansar al Islam (Supporters of Islam) is a group of Iraqi Kurds and Arabs that formed in September 2001, intent on establishing an independent Islamic state in northern Iraq, opposing both the Kurds and former Iraqi Saddam Hussein. The group trained in al-Qaeda camps in Afghanistan, received funding and equipment from al-Qaeda, and provided protection to al-Qaeda members. It has been implicated in a number of attacks in Iraq since the overthrow of Saddam Hussein in April 2003 and has become infamous for recruiting suicide bombers in Europe, especially in Italy and Germany. In an almost certain Ansar al Islam attack, in February 2004, it attacked the headquarters of the two main Kurdish political parties in Irbil, Iraq, killing nearly one hundred people in a dual suicide bombing, reminiscent of al-Qaeda tactics.

Many believe that al-Qaeda and Egypt's main terrorist group Al Gamaa al Islamiya (The Islamic Group) have strong links. The group, comprised of as many as several thousand members and sympathizers, supported Osama bin Laden's 1998 *fatwa* calling for attacks against the United States. Like many radical Muslim terrorist groups, it has called for the overthrow of the Egyptian government in favor of an Islamic state. Its most infamous terrorist attack came in 1997 at Luxor, Egypt, killing fifty-eight tourists. Al Gamaa has never specifically attacked a U.S. facility but has made threats to do so. The group probably has a presence in Europe, Afghanistan, and Yemen and receives funding from al-Qaeda.

Al Jihad is an Egyptian Islamic extremist group bent on overthrowing the Egyptian government and attacking U.S. and Israeli interests. The group carried out attacks against Egyptian officials and facilities, including assassinating former Egyptian president Anwar Sadat in 1981, attempting in 1993 to assassinate the Egyptian interior and prime ministers, and the bombing of the Egyptian embassy in Islamabad, Pakistan, in 1995. An attempt to attack the U.S. embassy in Tirana, Albania, in 1998 was thwarted. Al Jihad has operatives outside Egypt, focusing on Yemen, Afghanistan, Pakistan, Lebanon, and the United Kingdom. It obtains funding from al-Qaeda and other terrorist groups.[7]

Africa

From Morocco in the west to Tanzania in the south, Africa continues to be a major concern for terrorist activity. More traditional terrorist groups are being joined by new upstart organizations bent on stirring the over 400 million African Muslims for their radical benefit. The Algerian Armed Islamic Group (GIA), perhaps the most infamous terrorist group in Africa, is seeking an Islamic state in the secular country of Algeria. The GIA has mostly targeted foreigners in Algeria, killing more than one hundred men and women since 1993, using assassinations and bombings. It is renowned for slitting the throats of its kidnap victims. The GIA has also been accused of bombings in France, Algeria's former colonial ruler. The organization was formed in the early 1990s by returning veterans of the Soviet-Afghan war. It is believed to have al-Qaeda connections.

The Salafist Group for Call and Combat (GSPC) has replaced the GIA as the most active terrorist group in Algeria. As the most powerful terrorist organization inside the northern African country today, it maintains contact with other extremist groups, including al-Qaeda. The GSPC's focus has been the Algerian government, including military targets. It probably has operatives in Europe, too. In addition, the GSPC is believed to be spreading its radical ideology to the bordering countries of Niger and Mali, which both have large Muslim populations.[8] It is most famous for the kidnapping of a group of German tourists in August 2003, which brought a ransom of $1 million. In the spring 2005, the GSPC was suspected of killing fourteen at a fake roadblock.

The Libyan Islamic Fighting Group (LIFG) is an anti-Libyan government group. It promotes the overthrow of Libyan secular strongman Moammar Qaddafi. The LIFG tried to assassinate Qaddafi in 1996, but failed. Many of the group fought in Afghanistan and as a result have ties to al-Qaeda. According to the U.S. State Department, LIFG is one of the groups believed to be involved in planning the Casablanca suicide bombings of May 2003. They likely receive support from Osama bin Laden and participate in other international jihadist networks.

The Moroccan Islamic Combatant Group (GICM) plans to establish an

Islamic state in Morocco and supports al-Qaeda's international efforts against the United States and its allies. Many of its members received training in al-Qaeda's Afghan camps and associate with other North African extremists, especially in Europe. It is estimated that between 200 and 300 Moroccans trained in al-Qaeda camps in Afghanistan and Pakistan. GICM is also believed to be one of the groups involved in planning the Casablanca suicide bombings of May 2003. GICM is the forerunner of the newest Moroccan terrorist group, Salafia Jihadia, which is accused of perpetrating the five nearly simultaneous suicide bomb attacks in Casablanca, Morocco, in May 2003 that killed thirty-three people, plus the dozen suicide bombers. Most of the Casablanca targets were Jewish, but one suicide bombing took place at a Spanish restaurant, very close to the Spanish consulate. A few of the suspects in the March 2004 bombings in Madrid were Moroccan and there is the possibility that Salafia Jihadia or GICM were involved in the train bombings that killed 191. Ties to al-Qaeda are believed to be strong.

The Tunisian Combatant Group (TCG), like many of its terrorist brethren, supports an Islamic state for Tunisia and targets Western interests. The group is believed to have ties to al-Qaeda as well as to North African terrorist groups, such as the Algerian Salafist Group for Preaching and Combat, as well as the broader international jihadist movement. Al Ittihad Al Islami (Islamic Union), Somalia's largest militant Islamic terrorist group, likely has ties to al-Qaeda.[9] AIAI's original intention was to establish an Islamic state in Somalia. Like some Palestinian and Lebanese terrorist groups, such as Hamas and Hezbollah, AIAI does social work in the community, garnering respect among the populace. Some believe that AIAI, with al-Qaeda backing, was responsible for the attacks on U.S. Army Rangers in Mogadishu, Somalia, in 1993, leaving eighteen dead and over eighty wounded during Operation Restore Hope.

Islamic Army of Aden (IAA) became noteworthy in 1998 when it openly declared its support for Osama bin Laden, called for the overthrow of the Yemeni government, and advocated attacks on Western interests in Yemen. Its terrorist record shows a number of kidnappings and bombings prior to 2001, but had been relatively quiet until 2003 when it attacked a medical convoy. There are a number of Yemenis in al-Qaeda, and some of them returned to Yemen after the fall of Afghanistan in 2001. Top al-Qaeda member Mohammed Hamdi al Ahdal, accused of masterminding the attacks on the USS *Cole* in October 2000 and the French oil tanker *Limburg* in October 2002 off the coast of Yemen, was arrested in November

2003 in Yemen. Yemeni and other non-Arab al-Qaeda members may try to reconstitute themselves under the umbrella of IAA.

Asia

There are more Muslims in Asia than in the whole of the Middle East, making Asia particularly vulnerable to Islamic radicalism. Add to that some relatively weak governments, and it spells trouble for counterterrorist efforts in that part of the world. Jemaah Islamiya (JI) is East Asia's largest and most deadly terrorist group. Based in Indonesia, with al-Qaeda ties, it is at the center of the Southeast Asian terrorism problem. Responsible for the October 2002 Bali, Indonesia, disco bombing, the August 2003 Jakarta, Indonesia, Marriott hotel attack, and the September 2004 Australian embassy attack, JI has cells in the Philippines, Malaysia, Singapore, Thailand, Cambodia, and Australia. Many believe Jemaah Islamiya is gaining strength and now may have an Indonesian hard-line splinter group called Mujahedeen Kompak.[10] In June 2003, Thai authorities disrupted a JI plan to attack several Western embassies and tourist sites there. The capture of JI operations head Hambali, in August 2003 in Thailand after he fled Indonesia, hurt the organization. Hambali was in Thailand to plan an attack on the Asia Pacific Economic Cooperation (APEC) conference to be held in Bangkok in October. Twenty-one world leaders were scheduled to attend, including President George W. Bush. It is assessed that JI is still able to target Western interests and recruit new members.

In East Asia, in addition to close ties with Indonesia's Jemmah Islamiya, al-Qaeda has ties with the Abu Sayyaf Group (ASG). The ASG is a southern Philippines-based terrorist organization that has Afghanistan alumni among its cadre and is believed to have received funding from al-Qaeda. In some operations, Osama bin Laden's brother-in-law Mohammed Jamal Khalifa served as the money middleman. It has been involved in a number of bombings, assassinations, hostage takings, and beheadings in recent years, including three bombings in Manila and two other cities that killed eight in February 2005. The southern Philippine Moro Islamic Liberation Front (MILF) is not currently listed as a foreign terrorist organization by the U.S. government, but it appears to have strong ties to the ASG, Jemaah Islamiya, and al-Qaeda. The MILF is struggling for an independent Islamic state on the southern Philippine island of Mindanao. Recent reporting indicates that the MILF may be hosting terrorist training camps in its semiautonomous territory for the ASG and JI operatives, who are learning bomb making. They may also be providing refuge for terrorists in flight from such operations as the Bali bombing. In March 2005, the U.S. State Department issued a travel warning, stating: "Terrorist groups, including Jemaah Islamiya and the Abu Sayyaf Group, and radical elements of the Moro Islamic Liberation Front are planning multiple attacks throughout the Philippines."

Malaysia's Kumpulan Mujahadin Malaysia (KMM), like Indonesia's Jemaah Islamiya, hopes to unite the Muslim parts of Indonesia, the Philippines, and Malaysia into a pan-Islamic state. The group has close ties with Jemaah Islamiya and may have ties with Philippine groups, such as the Abu Sayyaf Group and the Moro Islamic Liberation Front. KMM operatives have ties to al-Qaeda through militant training in Afghanistan. Many KMM members were arrested in December 2001 in Malaysia along with JI members for plotting terrorist acts against Western targets, including U.S. Navy ships.

In China's far western Muslim province of Xinjiang, the Eastern Turkestan Islamic Movement (ETIM) is suspected of having continuing al-Qaeda terrorist ties. ETIM is a Muslim separatist group comprised of native Uighurs, which may have received training and financial assistance from al-Qaeda, and supports the formation of an Islamic "Eastern Turkestan" consisting of Turkey, Kazakhstan, Kyrgyzstan, Pakistan, Afghanistan, and China's western Xinjiang province. A number of Uighurs were captured among the al-Qaeda and Taliban fighters in Afghanistan in late 2001 during American military operations there. Another was captured in Pakistan in March 2004 during military operations against al-Qaeda members in the Pakistani tribal areas. Besides being suspected of a number of bombings in China, ETIM attempted to bomb the U.S. embassy in Kyrgyzstan in 2002.[11]

Central Asia

Concerns about the rise of Muslim extremism dates back to the Soviet era, when these states were part of the Soviet Union. Rising poverty and repression create an explosive mixture right in the new Afghanistan's backyard. The Islamic Movement of Uzbekistan (IMU) is the largest terrorist group in Central Asia. Some have suggested that Osama bin Laden founded the IMU with the intent of establishing an Islamic state in Uzbekistan, beginning with the overthrow of the Uzbek government, the region's most powerful state. The IMU conducted attacks in the Fergana Valley where the Uzbek, Kyrgyz, and Tajik borders converge. It fought with the Taliban and al-Qaeda in Afghanistan against coalition forces in late

2001. The IMU also committed a series of car bombings and kidnappings, including kidnapping four American mountaineers in August 2000. Because of a crackdown by the Uzbek government, the group had been most active recently in Kyrgyzstan, Tajikistan, and along the Pakistan-Afghanistan border, including a 2003 plot against the U.S. embassy in Kyrgyzstan, until a spate of suicide bombings in Uzbekistan in April 2004.

South Asia

Large Muslim populations, nationalist rivalries, and the presence of weapons of mass destruction are reasons for concern in this part of the world. Failure to counter terrorism in South Asia could have dire consequences for peace and stability in this regional crucible. Pakistan has a number of active terrorist groups, including Harakat ul Mujahidin (HUM). This Pakistani militant radical group operates primarily in the disputed, Indian-controlled, Muslim-dominated province of Kashmir in western India. Of note, HUM signed Osama's 1998 *fatwa* calling for attacks on the United States and Western interests and had training camps in Afghanistan until late 2001. In 2003, HUM began using the name Jamiat ul Ansar (JUA), which was quickly banned by Pakistani authorities.

Lashkar e Tayyiba (LT) is one of the largest Pakistani terrorist groups fighting against India in Kashmir. Some believe LT was formed by the Pakistani Inter-Service Intelligence agency to oppose Indian rule in Kashmir. It has been implicated in a number of bombings in India, especially in the city of Srinagar. LT has also cooperated with Pakistan's Jaish-e-Mohammed in the December 2001 attack on the Indian parliament, which killed nine and injured eighteen. Prior to the end of 2001, it trained in Afghanistan and had contact with al-Qaeda. Senior al-Qaeda lieutenant Abu Zabaydah was arrested in an LT safehouse in Pakistan in March 2002. LT also maintains ties with other radical Islamic groups around the world and may be sending fighters to Indonesia.[12]

Lashkar I Jhangvi (LJ) is another Sunni militant group located in Pakistan with ties to Afghanistan. LJ is noted for its sectarian violence against Shiites and Christians, but may have been involved in a number of other politically motivated bombings, including an attack on the U.S. consulate in Karachi in June 2002. Pakistani authorities believe LJ was responsible for the bombing in July 2003 of a Shiite mosque in Quetta, Pakistan. LJ's ties to al-Qaeda are murky, but LJ members fled to Afghanistan when the group was outlawed in Pakistan in 2001 for its involvement in sectarian violence.

It is assumed that it made connections with the Taliban and al-Qaeda there. Another group with ties to al-Qaeda in Pakistan is Jaish e Mohammed (Army of Mohammed) or JEM. Like HUM, JEM is focused on the issue of Indian control of Kashmir. It has conducted a number of high visibility raids on the Indian side of the Kashmiri line of control, including the most infamous one, an attack on the Indian parliament in December 2001. JEM has received support from the militant groups Harakat ul Jihad al Islami and the Harakat ul Mujahedin. JEM also had training camps in Afghanistan, and is believed to have received money from Osama bin Laden.[13] The group has been implicated in the death of *Wall Street Journal* writer Daniel Pearl in early 2002 in Pakistan. In December 2003, JEM may have been behind two assassination attempts against Pakistani president Pervez Musharraf. The group has splintered into factions recently.

Europe

Europe has long been a crossroads for international terrorism. The existence of al-Qaeda-affiliated terrorist cells as witnessed by the travels of the 9/11 hijackers in Europe, the Madrid attacks in March 2004, the recruitment of jihadists across Europe for duty in Iraq, and the large number of foiled terrorist plots demonstrate that Europe could go up in terrorist flames at any time. Al-Qaeda-affiliated terrorist cells almost assuredly still exist in France, the UK, Germany, Italy, Switzerland, Belgium, the Netherlands, Norway, Russia, and Turkey. Many of these cells in Western Europe are comprised of immigrants or illegal travelers from North Africa and South Asia, especially Morocco, Tunisia, Turkey, Algeria, and Pakistan. Russia seems to be the terrorist front with the most activity.

Three Chechen terrorist-separatist groups participated in the Dubrovka Theater seizure in October of 2002, wherein 800 hostages were taken in an attempt to force Russia to withdraw from Chechnya.[14] The first, the Islamic International Brigade (IIB), is comprised of native Chechens, Arabs, and other foreign fighters. The IIB may receive support from Georgian, Azerbaijani, and Turkish al-Qaeda and other Sunni international terrorist groups. The second group, the Riyadus-Salikhin Reconnaissance and Sabotage Battalion of Chechen Martyrs (RAS), is speculated to be quite small, with perhaps only fifty fighters. The RAS allegedly receives support from foreign sources, including al-Qaeda. The third major Chechen terrorist group is the Special Purpose Islamic Regiment (SPIR). The SPIR has also executed Chechens, who have collaborated with the Russian forces in

Chechnya. Like other Chechen groups, it may receive support from abroad, including al-Qaeda. Chechen fighters have been discovered in al-Qaeda and Taliban enclaves along the Pakistan-Afghanistan border. There have been allegations that Chechen militants have undergone chemical weapons training in Georgia's Pankisi Gorge. Elements of these same groups were likely involved in 2004 attacks on the Moscow subway; the assassination of Chechen president Akhmad Kadyrov; raids on Russian Interior buildings in Ingushetia and Russian military bases; and the seizure of the grade school in Beslan.

The world of terrorism is evolving—and not necessarily in a favorable direction for those who oppose it. Networked terrorism is turning out to be the wave of the future. Smaller local groups, inspired by al-Qaeda's vision of global jihad, are taking up the former mantle of larger terrorist groups, such as al-Qaeda, by perpetrating terrorist acts against common targets around the world. Combining new faces and new places with hardened, ideological veterans, is proving to be a force multiplier for the global terrorist movement led by al-Qaeda. The global, interconnected nature of today's terrorism is proving to be more unpredictable and harder to track than ever. Terrorist successes may encourage others to join the global movement in the belief that they can, in fact, advance their agenda through violence. This new brand of terrorism will prove to be even more challenging in the years to come and, ultimately, harder to defeat.

NOTES

1. Reuters, "Al-Qaeda Seen Shifting to 'Terror Consultant' Role," November 24, 2003.

2. "Advisory Panel to Assess Domestic Response Capabilities for Terrorism Involving Weapons of Mass Destruction," 2003 Gilmore Commission Report. (Arlington, Va.: RAND, December 15, 2003), p. 11.

3. "Advisory Panel to Assess Domestic Response Capabilities," p. 12.

4. J. T. Caruso, acting assistant director, Counter Terrorism Division, Federal Bureau of Investigation, "Al-Qaeda International," before the Subcommittee on International Operations and Terrorism Committee on Foreign Relations, United States Senate, Washington, DC, http://www.fbi.gov/congress/congress01/caruso 121801.htm (accessed January 7, 2004).

5. Faye Bowers, "Attacks in Kenya Signal al-Qaeda's Expanding War," *Christian Science Monitor*, December 2, 2002, http://www.csmonitor.com/2002/ 1202/p04s01-usgn.html (accessed January 7, 2004).

6. Foreign Desk, "Palestinian Sentenced to 27 Years: An Israeli Military Court Convicts Man of Training with Al-Qaeda. He Denies the Charge," *Los Angeles Times*, February 4, 2003, p. A4, WL 2382919.

7. "Patterns of Global Terrorism 2002," U.S. Department of State, Washington, DC, http://www.state.gov/s/ct/rls/pgtrpt/2002/pdf/ (accessed January 5, 2004).

8. Raymond Bonner, and Don Van Atta, "Regional Terrorist Groups Pose Growing Threat, Experts Warn," *New York Times*, February 8, 2004, p.1.

9. Robert S. Mueller, director, Federal Bureau of Investigation, "The War on Terrorism," before the Select Committee on Intelligence of the United States Senate, Washington DC, February 11, 2003, http://www.fbi.gov/congress/congress03/mueller021103.htm (accessed January 7, 2004).

10. Raymond Bonner, "Report Cites Emergence of New Islamic Militia in Indonesia," *New York Times*, February 4, 2004, p. 1.

11. "Patterns of Global Terrorism 2002."

12. Bonner and Van Atta, "Regional Terrorist Groups Pose Growing Threat," p. 1.

13. "Patterns of Global Terrorism 2002."

14. "Patterns of Global Terrorism 2002."

TACKLING TERRORISM

No one pretends that democracy is perfect or all-wise. Indeed, it has been said that democracy is the worst form of government except all those other forms that have been tried from time to time.

—Winston Churchill to the British House
of Commons, November 11, 1947

A *lot of the passengers had left the luxury cruise liner that day for tours ashore, but about 100 stayed behind as the ship anchored offshore in Egyptian waters. Many of them had probably wished they had decided to take the tour because they were taken hostage by four heavily armed Palestinian Liberation Front terrorists, who demanded the release of fifty Palestinians in Israeli jails. It was October 1985 and the Italian cruise ship* Achille Lauro *became the scene of two days of intense drama for its 400 passengers and crew.*

The terrorists, led by Abu Abbas, agreed to release the ship in exchange for a pledge of safe passage from Egyptian president Hosni Mubarak, but not before killing a wheel-chair bound American tourist, sixty-nine-year-old Leon Klinghoffer, and throwing his body overboard. But when an Egyptian Air plane tried to fly the hijackers to freedom in Tunisia, U.S. Navy F-14 Tomcat fighters intercepted the airliner and forced it to land at a U.S. base in Sigonella, Sicily. The terrorists were taken into custody by Italian authorities. The United States and Italy fought for jurisdiction over the terrorists, but the Italians refused to extradite any of the men. Most of

the terrorists were tried and sentenced, but, inexplicably, Abbas was
allowed to go free to Yugoslavia. He later settled in Baghdad, where U.S.
forces captured him as they swept into Iraq's capital in April 2003. Abbas
died in American custody of natural causes in March 2003, where he should
have been since 1985.

THE TERRORISM CHALLENGE

There is no silver bullet for ending international terrorism, especially this
violent wave of Islamic terrorism. Considering terrorism's long, dark history, if there were a magical cure, someone surely would have invented it
by now. This war on terror will be fought on many fronts, and in many
different ways. It will not be won on a battlefield in a single day of glory.
The courage of American generals and the might of the U.S. military cannot
defeat the scourge of terrorism by itself. The long arm of the law and the
FBI's law enforcement powers alone cannot trump international terrorism.
The best tradecraft of the CIA's best spies cannot. Defeating the current
Islamic terrorist plague is going to require a multifaceted, multinational,
multiyear effort.

It is clear that the United States—and others—have made tremendous
progress in the war on terror. Without question, we are safer today than we
were that fateful September 11. But as President George W. Bush has said
many times: "We're safer, but we're not safe." He is right. Despite the
many successes of the antiterror campaign, terrorism remains a potent
threat to American interests and international security. The U.S. State
Department has a list of over 100,000 names worldwide of suspected terrorists or people with terrorist ties.[1] No one knows how many more names
should be on that list. Before their camps in Afghanistan were shut down,
al-Qaeda trained as many as 120,000 potential jihadists.[2] How many more
have joined the al-Qaeda movement since then is anyone's guess. Despite
progress, there is still more to be done to defeat the specter of international
Islamic terrorism.

WIN THE PEACE IN IRAQ AND AFGHANISTAN

In 1944, an FDR presidential campaign button said: "We are going to win
this war and win the peace that follows." FDR understood the failures of

the Versailles Treaty that ended World War I, but precipitated the horrors of World War II. He knew that winning the military campaign was only half the battle. The peace after the conflict ends must also be won. The same is true today. It is critical that the postconflict peace be won in Iraq and Afghanistan. The United States and the international community must transition both of these countries to free, open, stable democratic societies and away from their dark, repressive pasts. This needs to be done not only because that is what we set out to do, but also because the rest of the Middle East—and the Muslim world for that matter—have their eyes on this Herculean effort.

If the international community fails, these countries could become new sanctuaries for terrorists, or even despots, supporting the foolish notion that democracy and Islam are incompatible. Moreover, failure will create political power vacuums that might be filled by opportunistic powers such as Iran or Syria. If we succeed, we will give hope to all those in the Muslim world oppressed by heavy-handed governments, but especially in key places like Egypt, Libya, and Saudi Arabia.

A glance at the map shows that Iraq is arguably the center of gravity in the Middle East. It borders Iran, Syria, Saudi Arabia, Jordan, Kuwait, and Turkey. Successfully transforming Baghdad from dictatorship to democracy is a key to altering the face of the Middle East for the better—once and for all. A secular Iraq could help contain the spread of Iranian fundamentalist influence, causing Tehran's ayatollahs to rethink their quest for political and military hegemony in the Persian Gulf. A strong Iraq could undermine Syria's support for terrorist groups such as Hezbollah, Hamas, and Palestinian Islamic Jihad, bringing hope to the Israeli-Palestinian peace process and bolstering political sovereignty to Lebanon.

A democratic Iraq would give hope to those who toil under the yoke of repressive regimes, which breed radicalism and hatred of America. With the January 2005 Iraqi elections already an inspiration to hundreds of thousands, if not millions in the Middle East, an Iraqi democratic government would promote freedom across the Muslim world. A secure Iraq in which insurgents and foreign terrorists are vanquished would dishearten terrorists and would-be terrorists worldwide.

The same is true for Afghanistan. Afghanistan has long served as a bridge between the Muslim worlds of the Middle East, South Asia, and Central Asia. One of the reasons so many have tried to conquer it over the years, most notably the Mongol Ghengis Khan, the Turkic conqueror Tamerlane, the Indians, Iranians, British, and Russians, is because of its strategic location in that part of the world. Placing a free, stable nation in the midst of repressive, neighboring regimes in Iran, Pakistan, China, Turkmenistan, Uzbekistan, and Tajikistan can have only a positive effect on that turbulent part of the globe.

Democratizing and stabilizing Iraq and Afghanistan is a necessary down payment in winning the war on terror and improving the prospects of global peace and security. President Bush is right: "The establishment of a free Iraq at the heart of the Middle East will be a watershed event in the global democratic revolution."[3] The same could be said for Afghanistan. Indeed, if successfully implemented, it may be the watershed geopolitical event in this century. But more must still be done in Iraq and Afghanistan to win the peace.

The international community must stay the course in developing strong central governments in Baghdad and Kabul, supported by competent police forces, capable intelligence units, and sturdy armed forces. Without law and order and stability provided by the police and military, and supported by good intelligence, both countries are liable to return to their troubled pasts. Draw the international community into supporting economic development and civil society in both Afghanistan and Iraq through the provision of economic aid and international loans and grants, the establishment of human rights and democracy institutions, and a free, vibrant press to provide oversight of the government and shed light on corruption. This is particularly important in Afghanistan where resources and economic opportunity are limited. More must be done to beat the drug trade in Afghanistan. The burgeoning Afghan opium trade is funding radicalism and terrorism and polluting societies well beyond Afghanistan. Eradicating poppy production or providing crop substitution will undermine the international heroin trade and cut operational funding to Taliban and al-Qaeda remnants opposing the new Afghan government.

PROMOTE FREEDOM IN THE MUSLIM WORLD

In his 2005 Inaugural address, President George W. Bush said, "There is only one force of history that can break the reign of hatred and resentment, and expose the pretensions of tyrants, and reward the hopes of the decent and tolerant, and that is the force of human freedom. . . . The survival of liberty in our land depends on the success of liberty in other lands." Truer words were, perhaps, never spoken. More specifically focusing in on the

Middle East, in November 2003 in London, President Bush stated, "In the West, there has been a certain skepticism about the capacity or even the desire of the Middle Eastern peoples for self-government. . . . It is not realism to suppose that one-fifth of humanity is unsuited to liberty. It is pessimism and condescension, and we should have none of it."[4] The president is correct again: Freedom and democracy are not Eastern or Western values—they are universal values, and the right of all people.

Bush also rightfully proclaimed that enough is enough—the long-standing Middle Eastern exception to democracy and freedom must end. The region's governments, from Cairo to Tehran, must be persuaded, indeed pressured, to alter their counterproductive political courses away from despotism and toward openness and democracy. "Sixty years of Western nations excusing and accommodating the lack of freedom in the Middle East did nothing to make us safe—because in the long run stability cannot be purchased at the expense of liberty," Bush said.[5] Years of gross political, economic, and social injustice in the Middle East, ignored by many in the name of Persian Gulf stability and, even, access to Middle Eastern oil, led to the horrors of 9/11.

Unless these inequities end, the war on terror is fated to be a permanent fixture of the international political landscape. For without the growth of political freedom and economic liberty in the Middle East, there is not a prayer for ending this reign of Islamic extremism or terrorism. Absent Middle East governments accountable to their people, terrorists will find a welcome mat in Iran, Syria, and Lebanon. Money will flow unabated from Middle Eastern "charities," supporting animosity, violence, and terror around the globe. Weapons of mass destruction will spread from state to state, ultimately falling into the grips of terrorist groups, such as al-Qaeda. The seemingly intractable Israeli-Palestinian conflict will remain insoluble. America, and other open, democratic societies will remain in the crosshairs. These are not the choices the Muslim people would make for themselves if they were, in fact, free to make their own choices.

Some have posited that democracy and the Muslim faith are incompatible, and that the United States' quest for freedom and liberty in the Middle East is a fool's errand. Nonsense. Half of all the world's Muslims already live under democratic rule. In fact, the world's most populous Muslim nation, Indonesia, is secular, tolerant, and democratic. So is Malaysia. This is the same misguided mind-set that said that democracy would not work in post–World War II Japan or Germany—now two of the world's most successful free societies.

The president boldly proposed a "forward strategy of freedom" for the Middle East: a new U.S. policy of persistent, pushy pluralism that would become the Middle East's agent of change, a harbinger of peace and prosperity for the region's people, and a possible death knell for Islamic radicalism. This endeavor has begun with elections and new governments in Iraq and Afghanistan. It has extended to elections for Lebanon, the Palestinian authorities and municipal councils in Saudi Arabia, and even the possibility in the Arab world's largest country, Egypt, for open presidential elections. But it cannot, indeed, it must not end there. Syria, Jordan, Libya, and others in the Muslim world from North Africa to Central and South Asia must open to representative government. America's security, and that of the free world, hinge upon the advance of liberty in this part of the world. Progress has been made, but there's still more to be accomplished to promote democracy in the Muslim world, especially the Middle East.

The international community must push Saudi Arabia to open its political system beyond municipal elections and allow women to vote. Saudi Arabia, one of the Muslim world's most influential nations, and least secular, could encourage other Muslim states to reform their political systems by making changes right at home. Ensure Egypt amends its constitution to open the way for free and fair presidential elections as it has promised. Egypt is the most populous country in the Arab world and one of its leaders. Political progress in Egypt would encourage other Arab nations to follow suit, especially its Muslim neighbors in northern Africa. The Millennium Challenge Account, an innovative U.S. foreign aid program designed to reward political and economic openings in underdeveloped countries, is a good first step. Other international donors should also implement similar programs. In some parts of the Muslim world, education reform must move toward openness and tolerance. The international community, especially the World Bank, must help develop vibrant, tolerant education systems in places like Pakistan and Indonesia to offer alternatives to *madrassas* and *pesantren* that in some cases offer the only opportunity for an education. Building open, just, prosperous societies in the Muslim world will make a tremendous difference in undermining radicalism.

CONTINUE IMPROVING AMERICAN INTELLIGENCE

Intelligence is the first line of defense in the war on terror. Its purpose is to help the president, the National Security Council, and all other government officials who make and carry out U.S. policy by giving them accurate and timely analysis on foreign threats to American national security. There are different types of intelligence that policy-makers need. *Current Intelligence* looks at day-to-day events. *Estimative Intelligence* presents at what might happen in the future. *Warning Intelligence* gives notice to our policy-makers that something critical might happen that will require their immediate attention. There are lots of types of intelligence; the challenge for the intelligence community is to provide good, actionable intelligence to policy-makers and military commanders. Good intelligence provides us an opportunity to understand the events taking place overseas and to see into the future, delineate trends, predict events, and, hopefully, shape events in a fashion advantageous to American interests.

Without solid intelligence, we are deaf, dumb, and blind, attempting to find our way in an exceedingly dangerous world. Although the United States has the world's largest intelligence apparatus, it is incapable of omniscience despite what you might have seen in James Bond movies. It can't—it doesn't—know everything. But one thing is obvious: The incredible intelligence failures of 9/11 and over the existence of Iraqi weapons of mass destruction cannot be repeated. The 9/11 Commission did the country a service in outlining what needs to be done to improve the performance of the fifteen-agency intelligence community. Some of this committee's recommendations have already been implemented to improve the quality of our intelligence. The creation of the Director of National Intelligence (DNI) to oversee the intelligence community and the establishment of a National Counterterrorism Center (NCTC) makes sense. So does increasing the intelligence budget by 25 percent from $30 to $40 billion, although throwing more money at a problem does not always solve it. But besides the DNI, NCTC, and the budget increase, there are still other intelligence matters, including collection and analysis, that need attention.

HUMINT (human intelligence) is one of these areas. HUMINT, that is, espionage using human agents, is critical to winning the war on terror. We need more of it—well-trained experts who understand the Muslim culture and speak languages like Farsi, Arabic, Pashto, Uzbek, and Bahasa Indonesian. A high-tech satellite, as advanced as it might be, may be able to intercept and "geo-locate" the cell phone call of a terrorist operative, but it cannot penetrate a terrorist group like a human operative can. The spy satellite hovering far above the earth's surface cannot sit in on a terrorist cell's safe house meeting, listening to the conversation and noting the body language and the looks on the others' faces as they discuss the intimate details of an upcoming operation. The satellite cannot place a tracking device on a terrorist's car or place a "bug" in the living room of a terrorist's apartment, or recruit a member of the terrorist group's inner circle. Only a human spy can do that. That is why HUMINT is so critical to beating terrorists at their game.

Unfortunately, HUMINT is not like a car in that all you have to do is turn the key and away you go. HUMINT takes time. We must train our own intelligence officers in the tradecraft of espionage, foreign languages, and cultures. It can easily take two to three years just to place someone in the field—without any experience. Once in the field, foreign spies also take time to recruit, sometimes years. Potential foreign spies must be spotted, assessed, developed, and then finally recruited before they provide useful information. Along the way, our intelligence officers must separate good prospects from bad. Some potential agents never pass the test and must be discarded, meaning new prospects must be found. It is dangerous work—an agent's discovery can mean a quick swing in the gallows, after plenty of hours of interrogation and torture, in some countries. The life of an intelligence officer, or an agent, is not for everyone. But we must have more of these people in the field. Today, too many intelligence operations officers are spending their time in Washington and not in the field. You cannot recruit spies or collect intelligence sitting at a desk in Washington. The CIA and the Pentagon must train more operations officers and send them overseas in creative operational covers. The embassy cover routine of the past is just that—passé. Nonofficial covers, placing officers in nongovernmental jobs overseas, must become the rule, not the exception.

Intelligence analysis has been a problem as well. The intelligence community has been accused of "group think" and a "lack of imagination." But as tired as we are of intelligence commissions, that is exactly what we need more of. Ongoing, outside commissions of appropriately cleared experts with unfettered access to all the intelligence can help analysts see what they cannot see looking at the same sort of material day after day. Just like editors do for writers; they help the writer see the things he or she does not see in reviewing and rewriting his or her draft. These "red teams" will help the analysts, including offering "contrarian analysis." A perfect example is Commission to Assess the Ballistic Missile Threat to the United States, headed by Don Rumsfeld in 1998. The commission essentially said that the intelligence community was understating the capability of such countries as North Korea to deploy long-range missiles. Six months later, the North Koreans launched a long-range missile that the intelligence community said would not be ready for testing for years. Commissions that do postmortems on intelligence failure are fine, but commissions that can help prevent intelligence failures are better. Increasing the size of the small congressional oversight committees would also be helpful.

SECURE THE HOMELAND

Protecting fifty states, 95,000 miles of coastline, and 7,500 miles of land border is not easy. And living in a free, open society makes one vulnerable to terrorism—pure and simple. There is no such thing as absolute security in any society. The United States is deeply integrated with the world beyond our borders and, in general, this is to our benefit. Over 300 million visitors come to the United States every year. Nine million seaborne containers enter the United States annually, carrying half of our imports. Many firms in the United States depend on the global market to keep their businesses running and prosperous. Many of our export-related jobs even pay better. Parts of our critical infrastructure, including the Internet, aviation, and energy sectors, are integrated internationally. But this openness and integration has a downside as well, as the 9/11 terrorists entered the United States the same way many harmless tourists or legitimate foreign workers do. The challenge is to protect the United States without disrupting the American way of life or infringing upon our cherished civil liberties.

A tremendous amount is being done to protect the United States from terrorist attack, but more can and should be done. For instance, we should continue pushing our virtual borders out by implementing security measures abroad. Our first defense against terrorism should not come at our shoreline. Cargo containers and airliners should be screened and inspected overseas to American standards before heading off for the United States. Foreign airlines should meet similar security standards as American carriers. Otherwise, an airliner in the wrong hands becomes a weapon. If terrorists hijack an airliner that has left Paris, what can American officials do once it is in the air and headed for New York, especially if the hijacking takes place moments before reaching the Big Apple? If a rogue state sends a nuclear weapon in a cargo container aboard a ship from a Middle Eastern port to Los Angeles, there is not much U.S. authorities can do until it reaches American territorial waters twelve miles offshore. Of course, by then it might be too late. Entry to the United States is a privilege, not a right, and we must ensure that security starts at the beginning, not the end of the journey.

Rigorous oversight of our homeland security policies should also be practiced. Nonpartisan congressionally or executive-mandated commissions, led and staffed by highly qualified people, can be very useful in providing an independent, outside look at the issues at hand as well as helping the administration and Congress see future challenges. They can also help the Congress and White House step back from the day-to-day administration of the government and focus on important, emerging issues, such as terrorism or homeland security, while providing advice about how to implement new policies and best practices, and integrate with state and local authorities.

A fundamental principle of this great country is the protection of civil rights and liberties. Walking the fine line between protecting civil liberties and protecting national security can be challenging. Congress and outside commissions can be helpful in monitoring the preservation of our civil liberties during these extraordinary times. New legal authorities, security methodologies, and new technologies should be assessed to see if they add to our security while not inappropriately infringing on the civil rights of Americans. The FBI must be pushed to embrace the counterterrorism issue as a core FBI issue, and information sharing across government agencies such as the Department of Homeland Security and the FBI and CIA must be dramatically improved.

RECAPITALIZE PUBLIC DIPLOMACY

The legendary British soldier and Arabist T. E. Lawrence (Lawrence of Arabia) once said, "The printing press is the greatest weapon in the armory of the military commander." In the war on terror, this is true for the diplomats as well. Unfortunately, by many accounts, our public diplomacy efforts—of "soft power"—in the Muslim world are troubled. Soft power lies in the ability to attract or persuade people through culture, political ideas, and policies. "Hard power" generally refers to a country's economic and military power. Some of this is understandable. After all, many Muslim countries lack a free press and some governments actively spread misperceptions, while hindering the flow of information from the outside world. However, in some ways, we have exacerbated the problem. Sensing a Cold

War peace dividend, in the 1990s, the U.S. government collapsed the State Department's public diplomacy corps by 40 percent; "face-to-face" foreign exchanges dropped from 45,000 per year to 30,000. The American public relations effort needs to be reinvigorated with more cash and people.

Throughout the world, the United States generates strong emotions, both positive and negative. These public and private attitudes directly affect America's ability to achieve its foreign policy objectives and battle radical anti-Americanism and terrorism. American radio and satellite television broadcasts into the Muslim world, from Southeast Asia to the Middle East to North Africa, will help these people, especially younger generations, better understand America, its policies and people. Equally important, it will counter propaganda, disinformation, and misperceptions about the United States, explaining that there is a better alternative to terrorism. As counterintuitive as it sounds, listening to foreign audiences for understanding is also an important aspect of public diplomacy. Seeing is believing, and promoting international educational and professional exchanges will also communicate America's message of freedom, openness, and tolerance to emerging foreign leaders, experts, students, scholars, and, even, clerics. Taking advantage of the Internet and satellite television (over 100 million satellite dishes in the Middle East), surrogate broadcasting such as the U.S. government's Arabic-language Middle East Television Network (al Hurra) should be expanded to include Farsi (Persian) for broadcast into Iran.

Advancing the Israeli-Palestinian issue toward an equitable resolution would also have a salutary effect on Islamic radicalism and anti-Americanism. One of the most often cited condemnations against the United States is American support for Israel and the lack of progress in the Israeli-Palestinian conflict. In the Arab world, and much of the Muslim world, the issue is not negotiable: Israel and America are wrong—end of discussion. Now this is clearly not the case, there is plenty of blame to go around. But the important thing today is not fixing the blame for the past, but fixing the problem for the future. Fortunately, there is a gleam of hope for progress in this seemingly intractable issue. Though the United States can play an important role, this is an issue for the Israelis and Palestinians to work out ultimately. Greater European involvement could be beneficial, especially in using their strong relationship with the Palestinian side to advance the issue. The positive public diplomacy effect of resolving this issue would be tremendous.

DRY UP TERRORIST FINANCING

Money is the mother's milk of terrorism. Without it, it is difficult for terrorists to recruit, plan, train, and conduct operations, especially on a large scale. The 9/11 attacks cost about $500,000 to execute. Without the availability of this significant sum of money, September 11 may have passed as nothing more than a late summer's day. Unfortunately, it seems that al-Qaeda and other terrorist groups, such as Hezbollah, have way too much "pocket change." Cutting off terrorist financing is no easy task, but it must be done. Terrorist financing follows the path of least resistance. You cut off one source or method of moving money and the terrorists turn to another.

Terrorist-associated Muslim charities here in the United States—and abroad—must be relentlessly hunted and shuttered permanently. *Hawalas*, unmonitored money-transfer businesses, must be regulated widely or shut down to prevent ties with terrorist activities or groups. In addition, we must apply more resources to finding, tracking, and interdicting terrorist cash and more attention to the drug running and gem trading that seems to be funding terrorist activity. In some instances, especially overseas, organizations responsible for stemming terrorist financing are woefully understaffed and undertrained. This must change. So must the political will of countries through which terrorist money moves. As the world's largest international institution, the United Nations should also create organizations for tracking terror financing.

ACT PREEMPTIVELY

Since the threat of losing their own lives is not enough to deter many Islamic terrorists from killing innocent civilians, we must take steps to ensure they never have the opportunity to act out their evil plans. Along with the ideas listed above, a forward-leaning policy of preemption is the right approach to dealing with international terrorism. We must be on the offense. There is no sense in losing an innocent civilian's life or a major American city to a terrorist's nuclear weapon because we did not act quickly or resolutely enough to prevent it from happening in the first place. There is a compelling need to hold open the option of striking terrorists before they strike us. This may mean military operations. It may mean law enforcement. It may mean covert action.

Undoubtedly, there is a risk in these sorts of operations, especially military operations. A suspected terrorist, if arrested unjustly, can be let go. A covert action program can be halted. Military operations, especially those that put U.S. forces in harm's way, can be a matter of life and death for American servicemen and their intended targets. Serious consideration must be given to preemptive military operations because of the potential risks. Good, solid intelligence and the good judgment of policy-makers is critical to undertaking these operations successfully.

Law enforcement is another good option for acting preemptively. Even though it gets much less play in the media, law enforcement agencies around the globe have captured or killed more terrorists than have military operations. This is especially true here in the United States and overseas outside Iraq. In addition, police forces are accepted in most societies as a legitimate tool for addressing terrorism, whereas other instruments, such as the military, especially a foreign military, might be seen as inappropriate in certain circumstances. Covert action (CA), or intelligence influence operations, is another way of acting preemptively. Through the use of information or disinformation, CA may be used to undermine the leadership of terrorist organizations and their popular standing with local communities and supporting governments. CA may also involve combat operations, such as assassinations. Covert action is very sensitive and often requires a presidential finding (i.e., approval) to go forward.

Acting preemptively can also be applied to dealing with weak or failing states. Afghanistan under the Taliban is a stark reminder of a failing state going "bad." The United States can hardly afford to be inattentive to states such as Somalia and Sudan. Identifying and addressing failing states before dramatic intervention is needed is critical. Taking the necessary diplomatic, developmental, and economic action early must be given priority.

ENHANCE INTERNATIONAL COOPERATION

Progress in the war against terrorism depends on strong international partnerships. Terrorism, as witnessed by the last four years, cannot be defeated alone. According to former secretary of homeland security Tom Ridge, "All of our progress, all of our actions, are predicated on the strength we gain by building strong partnerships—global partnerships that build barriers to terrorists, and build bridges to one another."[6] Ridge is right. International cooperation is critical to defeating terrorism. It can come in many forms: asking a country to extradite a particular individual; closing a terrorist train-

ing camp; shutting down a charity funding international terrorism; or collecting and sharing intelligence. Sharing the political and economic costs of
fighting terrorism makes sense, too. For example, several British al-Qaeda
operatives, who were planning attacks in New York City and northern New
Jersey as late as 2004, were arrested in London and indicted in American
courts as the result of an investigation that began in Pakistan. In 2005 a
British court convicted an al-Qaeda-trained Algerian of plans to target London with chemical weapons as well as conventional bombs. The investigation that led to his arrest spanned seventeen countries. It could not have
been done without good international cooperation.

Of course, counterterrorism cooperation is not a one-way street. American teams are also helping international partners build their own capacities
for fighting terror by identifying terrorist vulnerabilities, enhancing military
and police counterterrorism capabilities, sharing intelligence, and cracking
down on terrorist financing. Equally important to the capability to fight terror is the political will to do something about it. Even if you have a gun, it
is of no use unless someone is willing to pull the trigger. A nation's political
leadership must be willing to give the orders to crack down on terror.

Some countries believe that their own risk of terrorism is substantially
less than that of the United States. This is not always accurate and some
countries, such as Saudi Arabia and Indonesia, have learned this the hard
way by becoming the victim of terrorism. No one is immune to the terrorist
plague. As part of diplomatic efforts in the war on terror, new counterterrorist relationships have been built with Russia, China, India, Pakistan, and
the Central Asian republics (i.e., Kyrgyzstan, Tajikistan, Turkmenistan,
Uzbekistan, and Kazakhstan). Collaboration has intensified with such countries as Algeria, Bahrain, Egypt, Morocco, Tunisia, Saudi Arabia, and the
United Arab Emirates, among others, according to the U.S. State Department. Intraregional cooperation is critical as well. For example, critics claim
that more than a year after the 3/11 Madrid train bombing, interstate cooperation on terrorism is stalled, sensitive information is not being shared,
and several security enhancements have not been implemented. Continuing problems along these lines will not prevent the next attack.

The war on terror is not over, as the 2005 London attacks showed. Former Director of Central Intelligence George Tenet said in March 2004, tes-
tifying before the Senate Armed Services Committee, "A spectacular attack
on the U.S. homeland remains the brass ring many strive for with or without al-Qaeda leadership."[7] His successor, Porter Goss, repeated a similar
message in 2005: "Al-Qaeda is intent on finding ways to circumvent U.S.

security enhancements to strike Americans and the homeland." The United States is engaged in a global war against terrorism that will be fought on many fronts, using all the tools of national policy, over an extended period of time in concert with many international partners. In this struggle, we must deal with not only terrorist groups, but also organizations, or governments who support or give them sanctuary. Terrorism is not the work of a religion. It is the political agenda of bloodthirsty Islamic killers bent on changing the world order through violence. We are involved in an epic struggle of good versus evil, which must be won on behalf of the civilized world against those who would destroy it.

NOTES

1. Eric Lichtblau, "Administration Creates Center for Master Terror 'Watch List,'" *New York Times*, September 17, 2003.

2. Senator Bob Graham, interview on "Meet the Press," NBC, July 13, 2003.

3. Graham, interview on "Meet the Press."

4. George Bush, "Global Message" (speech given in London, England, November 19, 2003).

5. Bush, "Global Message."

6. Tom Ridge, Secretary of Homeland Security, "Remarks at the Institute of Defense and Strategic Studies," Singapore, March 6, 2004, http://usinfo.state.gov (accessed March 9, 2004).

7. George Tenet, Testimony before the Senate Armed Services Committee, March 9, 2004, http://www.foxnews.com/story/0,2933,113678,00.html (accessed March 9, 2004).

9

SPREADING SUPER WEAPONS

I . . . find that the proliferation of nuclear, biological, and chemical weapons and of the means of delivering such weapons, constitutes an unusual and extraordinary threat to the national security, foreign policy, and economy of the United States, and hereby declare a national emergency to deal with that threat.

—President Bill Clinton, November 14, 1994

Not willing to be outdone, Pakistan began its nuclear program after its neighbor, and strategic rival, India conducted its first nuclear test in 1974. At that time, an ambitious, young Pakistani metallurgist, Abdul Qadeer (A. Q.) Khan, was working in the Netherlands for a Dutch company called Physics Dynamic Research Laboratory (Urenco), which was involved in manufacturing uranium enrichment equipment for the nuclear power industry. Khan, concerned about the advance in India's relative military power to Pakistan, felt compelled to help his country by stealing the Urenco blueprints for centrifuge technology equipment critical in enriching uranium for nuclear weapons. After spending hours copying the blueprints at home, Khan abruptly left the Netherlands in 1976 just ahead of the Dutch authorities who were hot on his trail.

Upon his return to Pakistan, Khan established A.Q. Khan Research Laboratories (KRL) near the Pakistani capital, Islamabad. At KRL, Khan began to build the Pakistani bomb, often getting supplies and equipment from European companies and China. Under Khan's leadership, Pakistan exploded its first nuclear weapon in 1998, several days after India lit off its own device. Khan became Pakistan's most famous man. At some point in developing Pakistan's first nuclear weapon, he realized that he could share this destructive technology with others for personal financial gain, to advance his own career, and for political purposes.

Armed with nuclear knowledge and a network that spanned Europe, the Middle East, Africa, and Asia, Khan helped several budding nuclear powers. He assisted North Korea with their nuclear weapons program, which, in turn, supplied Pakistan with nuclear-capable North Korean ballistic missiles. For a price, Khan assisted Libya with smuggled nuclear material, technology, and nuclear warhead designs of Chinese origin. Iran was also the beneficiary of Khan's nuclear largesse in the form of uranium enriching equipment, and possibly nuclear warhead designs as well. Some have estimated that the globe-trotting Khan and his cronies may have collected as much as several hundred million dollars or more for their proliferation perfidy. Perhaps most disturbing is that it is not at all clear with whom else Khan's global nuclear network may have shared Pakistan's most prized secrets. Saudi Arabia, Egypt, and Syria are likely candidates. Al-Qaeda is also a possibility due to Khan's strong Islamic religious beliefs and his strong-felt need to bolster the Muslim world. Or with whom else did Khan's clandestine clients, North Korea, Iran, or Libya, share nuclear knowledge? The world may never know as only Pakistanis have been allowed to question Khan. Arguably, Khan's nuclear proliferation activities were the most egregious of any one person in the history of the bomb. For his wickedness, Pakistan's once national hero was pardoned for his wrongdoings, and merely sentenced to house arrest in his Islamabad home. Khan's nuclear genie could not be put back into the bottle.

WMD AND MISSILE PROLIFERATION

The proliferation of weapons of mass destruction (WMD) and the ballistic missiles that carry them is deadly serious business. The prospect of the most destructive weapons ever known coming into the hands of the wrong people is a justifiable cause for insomnia. Without a doubt, the proliferation, or transfer, of WMD and ballistic missiles is one of the greatest challenges facing American—and global—security today. President George W. Bush in an address at the National Defense University in Washington, DC, in February 2004 said that the proliferation of WMD, especially into the hands of a terrorist, poses the most serious danger that Americans face. That's still true today. Their use by an irresponsible rogue state or a deadly terrorist organization could cause unspeakable tragedy for the United States, its interests, and others. As the threat of global world war decreased after the Soviet Union's demise, WMD and ballistic missile proliferation increased. The loss of the Soviet Union as patron state and protector led some of its former protégés such as North Korea to increasingly seek WMD and missiles to ensure their security and increase their strategic influence in relation to their peers and the world's new unrivaled superpower—the United States. Regrettably, the demand for these weapons was matched with an increased supply in the materials and technology required for their development. As Western, developed countries hungered to enter new, previously inaccessible commercial markets, Cold War controls on the high-technology exports were relaxed, allowing it to flow to previously forbidden markets. Moreover, some former Soviet and Eastern Bloc weapons scientists, now out of work, sought employment in new markets abroad, aiding the development of unconventional weapons programs in places like North Korea and Iran. Hoping to enjoy a period of peace and tranquility in the post–Cold War era, the United States instead faces a new host of security challenges and responsibilities as the world's lone superpower.

Today, at least twenty countries possess, or are in the process of developing, WMD and ballistic missiles. For example, in 1998, India and Pakistan joined the nuclear weapons club, previously the exclusive domain of the big five: the United States, Russia, China, Britain, and France. Israel is strongly suspected of being a nuclear state, having as many as one hundred weapons, although it has never tested one so no one can be sure. Iran and North Korea are near nuclear states. Libya was pursuing nuclear status until late in 2003. Some believe that Syria and Saudi Arabia, and perhaps even Egypt, have nuclear aspirations as well. Iran, North Korea, Russia, and Syria, among others, have chemical and biological weapons capability. Although inactive, the former Soviet states of Ukraine, Uzbekistan, and Kazakhstan all have Soviet Union–era facilities that could be reactivated and used once again to produce biological and chemical weapons. On the missile front, North Korea, China, Russia, India, Pakistan, Syria, and Iran all have significant ballistic missile programs, many capable of carrying WMD.

While there are international nonproliferation treaties and regimes that exist to prevent the development and transfer of WMD and ballistic missiles, in some cases they are not effective in stopping the spread of these weapons. Curtailing proliferation is no small challenge, for example, many WMD programs look similar to peaceful, civilian programs in such fields as biotechnology, chemical manufacturing, and civilian nuclear power generation. Further, countries pursuing WMD and ballistic missiles are using sophisticated denial and deception techniques, such as building WMD facilities underground, to keep the international community unaware of their activities. The fact that at least a dozen countries have developed biological weapons since the Biological Weapons Convention came into effect in 1975 is telling. Without some sort of direct intervention or penalty for proliferating these weapons, any country with the political will, financial resources, and scientific-technical industrial base can produce and sell WMD and ballistic missiles today.

Fortunately, the proliferation report card is not all bad. A number of countries have sworn off WMD development and production, most notably in the area of nuclear weapons. Most significant, South Africa is the only country to ever dismantle a nuclear weapons program, ending its program in the early 1990s. The former Soviet states of Belarus, Ukraine, and Kazakhstan returned the Soviet nuclear arsenals located on their soil to Russia after the demise of the USSR. Kazakhstan, for a period, was the world's third largest nuclear power, possessing a nuclear arsenal bigger than Britain and France. In addition, Brazil, Argentina, South Korea, and Taiwan all voluntarily moved back from the nuclear brink and ended their nuclear programs. The decision by a country to forego a WMD program can have significant strategic repercussions due to the threat posed by rivals or neighbors. For instance, Taiwan faces a nuclear-armed China, and South Korea borders a near-nuclear North Korea. But it is likely that due to the advanced state of the scientific and technical capabilities of both of these countries, they could become nuclear weapons states practically overnight.

WMD AND MISSILE DEVELOPMENT

But why pursue WMD and ballistic missiles at all? They are expensive, destabilizing, and broadly condemned by the international community. The primary reasons are quite simple: security, influence, prestige, and nationalism. The possession of the world's most powerful weapons and the means to deliver them provides a country with unparalleled military power on the world stage. Not only can they be used to attack another state, but the ability to retaliate with these powerful weapons is a strong deterrent to attack by others as well. In addition, possessing these weapons ensures that the playing field is quickly leveled with strategic rivals, especially those with larger conventional military forces. This was surely a driving force behind Pakistan's desire to develop nuclear weapons in the face of a superior

Indian conventional military. The development of an asymmetric advantage using WMD and missiles may allow a nation to act outside the norms of the international community without fear of repercussion. The fact that these weapons today cannot be effectively countered only makes them more appealing to ambitious states.

The possession of WMD, especially nuclear weapons, gives a state a strong, influential political voice in the international community. The development of WMD and ballistic missiles may break a country out of the pack from its peers, conferring upon it regional leader status. WMD and missiles also appeal to a state's national ego. Since so few countries have these weapons, especially nuclear weapons, there is a sense of pride that goes along with their possession, in the same sense a space program confers a special status on a nation. For instance, it is widely believed that one of North Korea's major motivators for nuclear weapons is national pride. Pyongyang wants to prove to the world that it is not a poor, undeveloped country, as many might believe, but a highly sophisticated major power, deserving of admiration and respect. Again, clearly, issues of nationalism and pride spurred rivals India and Pakistan toward the nuclear finish line.

Of course, the widespread availability of WMD and ballistic missiles does not guarantee their use, but it may encourage belligerents to use military means rather than diplomacy in settling disputes. The mere fact that a state has WMD may, too, allow it to use blackmail or coercion to achieve its unsanctioned ends, unless the opposing state has a WMD arsenal, too. This sense of vulnerability creates what is commonly known as a security dilemma. The increased military capability of one state may make neighboring states feel increasingly insecure and compel them to increase their own sense of security by procuring counterbalancing capabilities. Basically, this is a military form of "keeping up with the Joneses." In the national security circles it is referred to as an "arms race." At this time, the only real deterrence currently available to the use of WMD by one state is the possession of a similar retaliatory capability by its adversary. For example, during the Cold War, the nuclear weapons arsenals of the United States and the Soviet Union created a countervailing balance of power. Both sides were dissuaded from using these weapons against each other because it was likely that use by either side would lead to mutually assured destruction. There is also a fear that the proliferation of these powerful weapons could lead a state to miscalculate. A nation could undertake ill-advised military actions, believing that its possession of WMD makes it unstoppable. Deposed Iraqi leader Saddam Hussein may have believed this when he invaded Kuwait in 1990, expecting that his possession of WMD meant that his aggression against Kuwait would not be opposed. This belief resulted in an ignominious defeat at the hands of the U.S.-led coalition forces in 1991 during Operation Desert Storm.

PROLIFERATION MOTIVATORS

If the proliferation of WMD and ballistic missiles seems so dangerous, why do countries transfer them? The primary reason is financial. There is considerable money to be made in selling WMD, missiles, or related technology. Of course, bear in mind that much of the technology used in WMD and missiles are of a dual-use nature, that is, applicable to both civilian and military end uses. Therefore, some nations or companies may unwittingly transfer technology and material to foreign WMD or missile programs, believing that they are intended for peaceful civilian use such as producing electricity from nuclear power. Russia, for instance, has built an $800 million nuclear reactor for Iran at Bushehr, which Tehran claims is for the production of civilian nuclear power. Others, including the United States and the European Union, are not so sanguine. In other instances, the transfers of nuclear weapons–related technology and materials are clearly intentional. For example, rogue Pakistani scientist Khan lined his pockets with money from Iran, Libya, North Korea, and possibly others in transferring nuclear weapons technology to them. For North Korea, ballistic missile sales are the main source of foreign hard currency and its chief export. There is also a continuing concern about materials and highly qualified Russian WMD and missile scientists putting themselves on the open market to the highest bidder.

Countries may also share WMD for strategic purposes. China shared nuclear technology with Pakistan to balance China's powerful neighbor, India, which was on the verge of nuclear statehood itself. Pakistan may have shared nuclear technology with North Korea in exchange for missile assistance with its Ghauri-class ballistic missile, which is based on the North Korean No Dong missile. There may be ideological drivers as well. Pakistani scientists may have been willing to sell nuclear secrets to Iran and Libya, not only for money, but because they believed it was their religious duty to supply the Islamic world with the weapons necessary to oppose the West and to prevent American dominance in the Middle East. There are also persistent rumors that Pakistan may have shared nuclear technology with Saudi Arabia for the strategic purposes of balancing its neighbor Iran as well as for financial reasons, arising from Saudi Arabia's vast oil wealth.

WMD AND BALLISTIC MISSILE PROGRAMS

Developing WMD and ballistic missiles is not an easy proposition. It is a complicated undertaking that requires the availability, either domestically or internationally, of sophisticated materials and expertise. WMD and missile programs, especially nuclear programs, can also be very expensive. For a nuclear program, a full-scale nuclear power industry may be required, costing hundreds of millions or even billions of dollars. For example, in the United States a civilian nuclear power plant can easily exceed $1 billion. This does not include the cost of reprocessing facilities needed to develop nuclear materials for weapons use. Alternatively, under the right circumstances, weapons-grade nuclear materials could be bought ready for use in a weapon. The development of a ballistic missile program may, in fact, be the next most challenging. Ballistic missiles require rocket engines, special fuels, airframes, and guidance equipment, much of which is unique. This high-technology equipment is unlikely to be readily available from civilian commercial resources unless a country has an existing space program.

Chemical and biological WMD programs may be the easiest to develop due to their similarity to civilian, commercial biotechnology and chemical industry programs. For the development of biological weapons, there needs to be an initial strain of the organism, accompanied by an appropriate growth medium, and related equipment for manufacturing additional pathogens. For chemical weapons, the compounds can be imported whole, or synthesized in a laboratory from other chemicals. However, additional difficulties do exist for the more complicated biological pathogens and chemical agents as well as placing these materials in weapons such as artillery shells, gravity bombs, or missiles.

Despite the challenges in developing WMD and ballistic missiles, the necessary resources can be found. For instance, the plentiful supplies of WMD and ballistic missile weapons scientists, and the lack of adequate funds to protect stockpiles and research institutes, make Russia an ideal source for the acquisition of materials and know-how for WMD and missile programs. But it does not take sneaking into a Russian WMD facility in the middle of the night to get your hands on the makings of these weapons. A lot of WMD and ballistic missile proliferation occurs from the international communities inability to devise effective strategies to regulate the flow of so-called dual-use items. Dual-use items are equipment or materials that can be used for legitimate, civilian purposes, but can also be put to use in the manufacturing of WMD or missiles. For example, a nuclear centrifuge, such as the one constructed from the parts found on the German freighter *BBC China* intercepted off Taranto, Italy, on its way to Libya in 2003, is a necessary piece of equipment for refining uranium for use as nuclear reactor fuel. However, uranium refined for use as reactor needs only to be enriched a bit further using additional centrifuges to become the highly enriched uranium suitable for nuclear weapons. As such, nuclear centrifuges have both civilian and military applications. Likewise, a country can claim a legitimate need for strains of biological pathogens used in biological weapons in order to do research for their public health system. A country certainly has a right to develop an antidote to deal with a potential outbreak of plague or smallpox. Unfortunately, this same country can also easily develop an offensive military biological weapons capability from the same strains. Chemical weapons can be synthesized from relatively innocuous, civilian chemical compounds. Chlorine gas, a common World War I chemical weapon, is also a common laboratory chemical. Long-range missiles are similar to peaceful, civilian space launch vehicles. Developing plausible deniability for most WMD and ballistic missile programs is quite simple.

Another by-product of the demise of the Soviet Union is the hundreds of thousands of highly trained, but often unemployed, Russian weapons scientists. The Soviet Union had, by far, the largest military industrial complex ever known to mankind, including closed military cities such as Arzamas and Chelyabinsk, dedicated to constructing WMD and ballistic missiles. Today these highly prized weapons skills and expertise can be bought on the world market relatively inexpensively due to the collapse of the Soviet military-industrial complex. Though previously unable to travel outside the Soviet Union due to their sensitive work, today many former Soviet scientists are willing to work abroad for the highest bidder. Since the fall of the Berlin Wall, Russian scientists have aided North Korea's ballistic missile and nuclear programs and China's strategic mobile intercontinental ballistic missile program, to name a few. The widespread use of the Internet means that WMD and missile technical information is more readily available because many scientific publications are now available online. Furthermore, students from rogue or proliferating states can often study at Western universities or work at high-technology firms, allowing the transfer of advanced scientific and technical information to undesirable locations. For instance, Kahn stole uranium enrichment plans from the Dutch firm where he worked before fleeing to Pakistan. Likewise, if some aspect of a WMD or ballistic missile program cannot be accomplished domestically, materials can be acquired on the black market through middlemen, who negotiate their purchase and delivery. The lack of strong export controls in many countries, including Russia and China, make it likely that WMD and ballistic missile exports will occur on the black market. Orders are often routed though front companies, masquerading as legitimate businesses. They are then shipped through a number of countries, using falsified documents and whichever flag of convenience is necessary to throw suspicious customs agents off the trail. The receiving country will also use its diplomatic pouch (i.e., diplomatic courier service), which is immune from inspection under international treaty, to move the shipment to its final destination. North Korea is known to use its overseas embassies for smuggling operations of many kinds, including drugs, counterfeit money, and weapons.

NONPROLIFERATION

There are international arms control treaties (i.e., formal bilateral or multilateral agreements) and regimes (i.e., informal, voluntary arrangements) that are designed to stop the proliferation of WMD and missiles. Unfortunately, their record of success is mixed. Ideally, international nonproliferation treaties and regimes would be binding on the states that agree to them. But in actuality, these treaties can be ineffective in preventing proliferation because there are essentially no enforcement mechanisms, such as punishments for violators. Most everyone agrees that the proliferation of WMD, its related technology, and their delivery systems should be controlled. Unless, of course, a state believes that it is in its national interest to do otherwise, as has been seen so many times over the years. A successful nonproliferation treaty or regime can be a vital security tool, which diminishes international tensions, promotes peace and stability, and nurtures political and economic development. It is even more critical in an age of terrorism. The major nonproliferation treaties in existence today include: the Nuclear Nonproliferation Treaty (NPT), the Biological Weapons Convention (BWC), and the Chemical Weapons Convention (CWC), all falling under the United Nations' rubric. Other smaller, voluntary regimes, which support the treaties, but operate outside the UN framework, include the Nuclear Suppliers Group, the Zangger Committee, the Australia Group, and the Missile Technology Control Regime.

Nonproliferation Treaties

The 1970 NPT, which is the most widely adhered to arms control treaty in history, commits over 180 member states (of 191 UN member states) not to acquire, use, or transfer nuclear capability for other than peaceful purposes. Only Cuba, Israel, India, Pakistan, and North Korea are not members. The treaty prohibits the development, possession, and proliferation of nuclear weapons. However, the United States, China, Russia, Britain, and France, which had preexisting arsenals, are permitted to keep their nuclear weapons. But like the other signatories, these five nuclear powers may not transfer nuclear weapons capability. The treaty mandates that its members be open to inspection by the UN's nuclear watchdog, the International Atomic Energy Agency (IAEA). The inspection regime is intended to deter, and detect, noncompliance and ensure observance with the treaties' tenets. Headquartered in Vienna, Austria, the IAEA negotiates agreements with non-nuclear weapons states to verify their activities at over 900 declared nuclear facilities in over 70 countries.

The 1972 BWC is the first treaty to mandate its over 150 members to eliminate an entire category of weapon from their military arsenals. All members agree not to develop, produce, import, export, or stockpile any biological materials or toxins for other than peaceful or protective purposes. The BWC also prohibits weapons, equipment, and the means of delivery designed for using biological agents for hostile purposes. There is no BWC monitoring agency. The 1993 CWC includes over 160 signatories, all of whom agree to prohibit the development, production, acquisition, stockpiling, transfer, or use of chemical weapons. Aimed at complete disarmament, the treaty requires all chemical weapons and production facilities be destroyed by 2007. This, regrettably, will not be achieved, primarily due to shortages of destruction facilities and cost. In 2005, the United States began the destruction of its CW arsenal at Pine Bluff, Arkansas. The CWC is the most extensive and intrusive arms control treaty in existence, as it not only covers the inspection of government facilities, but civilian ones as well. Its oversight agency is the Organization for the Prohibition of Chemical Weapons, headquartered at The Hague in the Netherlands.

Nonproliferation Regimes

The forty-member Nuclear Suppliers Group is a voluntary agreement exercising control over exports of nuclear material (including dual-use materials), technology, and equipment. The group also requires safeguards and physical protection of all fissile material whether or not are exported. The Zangger Committee is comprised of thirty-five countries, which support NPT safeguards through the monitoring of the export of nuclear materials to non-nuclear weapons states that could be used in a nuclear weapons program. The Australia Group's (AG) thirty-eight members work to support both the CWC and the BWC, by ensuring that industries do not intentionally, or unintentionally, transfer materials to states seeking chemical or biological weapons. The AG began in 1984 as an international response to Iraq's use of chemical weapons against Iran during the 1980–1988 Iran-Iraq war. The Missile Technology Control Regime (MTCR) is an agreement among thirty-seven countries, limiting the transfer of missiles or related technology and equipment, which would support the delivery of WMD. Specifically, the agreement prohibits the transfer of complete missiles capable of delivering a payload of at least 500 kilograms (1,100 lbs.) to a distance of 300 kilometers (180 miles) or more.

Both nonproliferation treaties and regimes are well intentioned, but can fall short of their desired end states due to loopholes, enforcement capabilities, or the absence of restrictions. For instance, some countries continue to produce, proliferate, or buy ballistic missiles, because such practices are not forbidden by arms control treaties and regimes. A perfect example of this was the Spanish navy's attempted interdiction of a shipment of North Korean SCUD missiles to Yemen in 2003. The shipment was ultimately allowed to proceed because there is no international convention banning the transfer of missiles. The MCTR is not an international treaty, but a completely voluntary regime. One of the more troubling aspects of the international community's efforts is the fact that arms control treaties are not much more than international "gentleman's agreements," which depend on the goodwill of the signatories for achieving the stated goals. For example, the NPT contains no automatic penalty for violating, or withdrawing from, the agreement. In fact, a member state can withdraw from the treaty just by giving ninety days notice. North Korea withdrew in 2003 without punishment. India and Pakistan never became party to the treaty and developed nuclear weapons without penalty.

The cooperation of strategic states, such as Russia and China, is vital to the success of arms control treaties and regimes, but they often have not committed themselves to the nonproliferation actions that the United States and other countries believe are necessary to address the issue. In fact, Russia and China are part of the proliferation problem. Economic sanctions, placed on them unilaterally by the United States, have proven to be of limited utility. Broad, multilateral economic sanctions on proliferators would be more painful and prove a greater deterrent to proliferation activity. Loopholes are another problem. For instance, the NPT permits access to dual-use nuclear materials and technology for peaceful nuclear power programs. This same material and equipment also allows a nation to do almost everything required to produce nuclear weapons. Much of the industrial base needed for a peaceful nuclear power program complements a covert nuclear weapons program. Iran's flirtation with nuclear weapons under the guise of pursuing civilian nuclear power is a good example. Iran claims it is developing a peaceful nuclear power program as authorized under the NPT. But there is deep concern that while overtly pursuing nuclear power for civilian purposes, Tehran is simultaneously enriching uranium for nuclear weapons. India's 1974 nuclear test was aided by civilian nuclear power technology from Canada.[1] The same is true for chemical and biological weapons programs.

Finally, arms control can also be expensive, especially for those nations with limited financial resources. The development, implementation, and enforcement of export controls to prevent proliferation can be costly. Some countries have little control over their borders or port facilities through which contraband may pass due to lack of government resources. Local intelligence and law enforcement capabilities may also be a problem. In these instances, paper treaties and regimes fail to slow the growing black market in WMD and missiles. WMD and ballistic missiles allow an adversary to inflict massive damage and suffering. Today, nuclear, chemical, and biological weapons present a gathering danger to America's national security. The threat comes not only from hostile states, but from terrorist organizations, such as al-Qaeda, which view WMD as enhancing their ability to asymmetrically challenge the world's most powerful nations. Preventing WMD and missile proliferation, deterring their use, and defending against their employment must be a central organizing principle of this century's American national security strategy.

NOTES

1. The Associated Press, "Nuclear History in India, Pakistan," *New York Times*, May 28, 1998, http://www.mtholyoke.edu/acad/intrel/nuchist.htm (accessed February 19, 2004).

10

MUSHROOM CLOUDS AND MISSILES

I often remind people that a ballistic missile attack using a weapon of mass destruction from a rogue state is every bit as much [a] threat to our borders now as a Warsaw Pact tank was two decades ago.

—Madeleine Albright, former secretary of state, December 8, 1998

In the seeming blink of an eye, the world added two new members to its exclusive nuclear weapons club. Over just a few days in the spring of 1998, rivals India and Pakistan put the world on Armageddon-like tenterhooks over the possibility of a deadly nuclear exchange between the South Asian giants. Catching the world's intelligence communities completely off guard, through the use of modest, but effective, camouflaging, on May 11, 1998, India became the world's sixth declared nuclear power after simultaneously testing three nuclear weapons at Pokhran in the Rajasthan desert in an operation code named Shakti-1.

Seventeen days later, as widely predicted, Pakistan responded in kind to India's nuclear tests by conducting its own. After a few days of thermonuclear blasting, Islamabad announced that it had successfully conducted six nuclear tests in Baluchistan, including one that yielded an explosion equivalent to forty thousand tons of TNT and generated a seismic tremor registering 5.0 on the Richter scale. For the first time since the fall of the Berlin Wall, the world was once again on a nuclear war footing.

NUCLEAR WEAPONS

Like Clint Eastwood's .357 Magnum in the 1970s blockbuster *Dirty Harry*, in military and political terms, the nuclear weapon is the great equalizer among nations. There is no more powerful military weapon and no blunter instrument of national policy than to use, or threaten to use, a nuclear weapon. Without question, this "wonder" of modern physics is the most devastating weapon known to mankind. The nuke can be used to coerce, compel, deter, or blackmail a potential opponent. The prestige, power, influence, and leverage that come from the possession of these weapons is unparalleled in international politics today. It is no wonder that a number of countries that live outside of international norms and standards of behavior, such as North Korea and Iran, see nuclear weapons as the route to gain respect, legitimacy, and noninterference in their affairs. More frightening, perhaps, is the idea of nuclear weapons in the grips of a blood-thirsty terrorist. An act of nuclear terrorism has the potential to make the tragedy of 9/11 look like a minor event, which it certainly was not. Preventing the proliferation of nuclear weapons to non-nuclear states and nonstate actors alike is a top national security priority.

A nuclear weapon is a weapon of mass destruction (WMD). It uses fissile (i.e., nuclear) material, such as highly enriched uranium (U-235) or plutonium (Pu-239), to create an explosion of enormous magnitude. The tremendous energy released by a nuclear weapon is produced in two ways. One method is by splitting an atom's nucleus. This is also known as nuclear fission. The alternative way to cause a nuclear explosion is combining the nuclei of two atoms. This is referred to as nuclear fusion. The resulting reaction may last as little as a millionth of a second, but will produce exceedingly high temperatures, pressure, and radiation. Modern nuclear weapons may even use a combination of both fission and fusion, resulting in the explosive power of several million tons of TNT. The bomb dropped on Hiroshima that ended World War II destroyed everything within a radius of one mile from the center of the explosion, while nearly everything within a three-mile radius was heavily damaged. Glass was broken up to twelve miles away. That bomb, in comparison to today's weapons, was tiny, packing only 20,000 tons of TNT. Naturally, the explosion of a nuclear weapon causes devastating long-term effects on human and animal life and on the physical environment due to the poisonous effects of the radiation.

THE NUCLEAR CLUB

To date, nine countries have produced nuclear weapons: the United States, Russia, France, Britain, China, India, Pakistan, South Africa (now dismantled), and Israel. As mentioned at the start of the chapter, India and Pakistan are the newest members of the nuclear club, having tested weapons in 1998. Their nuclear breakout came as almost a complete surprise to the international community. All the members of the nuclear club have acknowledged their nuclear power status with the exception of Israel, which is believed to have as many as one hundred such weapons. The United States and Russia are the world's most prodigious nuclear weapons states. The United States has a stockpile of about 6,000 active and inactive strategic nuclear weapons. Russia has a similarly large strategic stockpile of about 5,000 nuclear weapons. These weapons could be used to devastate cities, large military complexes, or land-based, hardened nuclear missile silos. In addition, both countries have large, but publicly unspecified, stockpiles of smaller nuclear weapons for tactical battlefield use. Russia has long been rumored to have small "suitcase" nuclear weapons, being man-portable at one hundred pounds. Russia denies they ever existed. China may have as many as 400 nuclear warheads, while Britain may have as few as 200 and France as little as 100. South Asian rivals India and Pakistan have nuclear arsenals totaling 200 weapons. On the other end of the spectrum from Russia and the United States is North Korea, which in early 2005 claimed it had developed operational nuclear weapons, and may have as many as eight, although this has not been confirmed. Iran appears to be developing nuclear weapons, based on its acknowledged enrichment of uranium. Unchecked by the international community, it is estimated that Iran could join the nuclear club in as little as one to five years. Libya is in the process of dismantling its nuclear program in an effort to shed its pariah status and join the international community. Syria may also be interested in nuclear weapons, as are a number of other Middle Eastern and North African states, including Saudi Arabia and Egypt. The newest concern is Latin America's burgeoning giant, Brazil, which announced in 2004 that it was beginning uranium enrichment activities. Brazil has the world's fifth largest uranium reserves (see Box 10.1).

All told, it is estimated that forty nations have the scientific and technical wherewithal to produce nuclear weapons today.[1] For instance, the former Soviet republics of Ukraine, Belarus, and Kazakhstan—where the USSR

**Box 10.1.   The "Balance of Terror"
(Strategic Nuclear Weapons)**

United States   6,000 nukes
Russia   5,000 nukes
China   400 nukes
Britain   200 nukes
India   150 nukes
France   100 nukes
Israel   100 nukes
Pakistan   50 nukes
North Korea   2–8 nukes (unconfirmed)
Iran   in development

based many of its nuclear warheads—returned their weapons to postcommunist Russia in the 1990s. But all three countries continue to have the scientific expertise to develop these weapons should they decide to do so. The UN's nuclear monitor, the International Atomic Energy Agency, is responsible for overseeing and safeguarding over nine hundred nuclear facilities in over seventy countries, including nuclear hot spots like Iran, Syria, and North Korea (until they were expelled in 2003), to prevent existing nuclear power programs from being used for anything other than peaceful purposes. This is no small task, especially when a country is trying to conceal a nuclear program.

DEVELOPING NUCLEAR WEAPONS

In some ways it is a surprise that there are not more nuclear weapon states today. The scientific knowledge needed to manufacture these weapons is readily available, especially with the advent of the Internet. But even with a head start on research, it is still quite a challenge to become a fully fledged member of the nuclear club. Developing and building a nuclear weapon is difficult for two reasons. The first reason is that the special nuclear materials, such as plutonium or highly enriched uranium, required to create the nuclear explosion are expensive and difficult to produce.

Without question, fissile material production consumes the vast majority of the technical, industrial, and financial resources required to produce nuclear weapons. A significant investment in a nuclear power infrastructure capable of producing fissile material is required. This usually means the construction of nuclear power plants and reprocessing facilities, in addition to the acquisition of nuclear fuel (i.e., uranium) to run the nuclear power plants. Fissile materials for weapons could be purchased or stolen, rather than produced from a nuclear fuel cycle or reprocessed, making the process a bit easier, but not much. The U.S. Department of Energy estimates that four to eight kilograms (ten to twenty lbs.) of fissile material is required to make a small nuclear weapon, although some American scientists believe that one kilogram (2.5 lbs.) of plutonium will suffice. Larger weapons could use much larger amounts of fissile material. The second difficulty in developing a nuclear weapon is the engineering and manufacturing of the bomb itself. It is no small feat to produce a device that will actually create the critical mass needed to initiate a nuclear chain reaction in the bomb's fissile material. Despite these hurdles, experts seem to agree that with the appropriate time, money, and effort even nonstate actors such as terrorist groups could assemble and detonate a crude nuclear device.

EFFECTS OF NUCLEAR WEAPONS

Nuclear weapons have only been used twice in warfare. At the end of World War II in August 1945, the United States dropped a twenty-kiloton uranium atomic bomb on Hiroshima, Japan. Three days later, the United States dropped a hydrogen (plutonium) bomb on Nagasaki, with the explosive force of twenty-two kilotons. The Hiroshima bomb killed 66,000, and injured another 60,000 people, burned victims over a mile away from ground zero (i.e., the point of detonation), and sent flying debris that lacerated victims over two miles away. The Nagasaki bomb killed 39,000, injured 25,000, and burned victims almost three miles away from the blast center.[2] The overpressure from the blast destroyed buildings for miles around. Today, thermonuclear weapons in modern arsenals are up to 1,000 times more powerful than those used in 1945. Depending on the size of the nuclear weapon, the altitude of the nuclear burst above ground, and the topography of the environment, anyone or anything within a several-mile radius of a nuclear explosion is likely to be affected immediately. The overpressure from the blast will kill some. The intense heat generated by the thermal radiation will kill others. Falling buildings, fire, and flying debris will kill more. An electromagnetic pulse will render electronics useless, including computers (or anything that uses even a small computer like cars), communications, and electrical systems such as power grids. Those not killed immediately by the blast may suffer the effects of radiation poisoning from direct exposure to the weapon's toxic radioactive materials, known as fallout. Radiation can be absorbed by the body as happens in an X-ray, or nuclear materials can be ingested as particulate through the skin, lungs, digestive system, or open wounds. Radiation sickness can cause nausea and vomiting in the short term and cancer, birth defects, and death in the long term. Radiation does dissipate over time in a contaminated area. One only has to think back to the 1986 Chernobyl nuclear reactor accident in the former Soviet Union to be reminded of the effects of exposure to nuclear materials.

DIRTY BOMBS

Another frightening weapon that uses nuclear materials is the radiological weapon. Much less powerful than the nuclear weapon, the radiological weapon, or "dirty bomb," is not a nuclear weapon at all. It is not, therefore, a weapon of mass destruction, by definition. The dirty bomb is a conventional explosive that contains nuclear material. The purpose of the radiolog-

---

Box 10.2.   The Effects of One-Megaton* Nuclear Blast

Temporary blindness out to 100 miles from ground zero.

Vaporization of everything up to three miles; spontaneous ignition out to eight miles; severe burns at eight miles and first-degree burns out to twenty miles from ground zero.

Overpressure and 700 mph winds would destroy buildings out to four miles.

Poisonous radioactive fallout will travel for miles from ground zero, depending on wind conditions.

*One Million Tons of TNT

ical weapon is to disperse radioactive materials through a rudimentary conventional explosion, using such materials as TNT or plastic explosives. Radiological weapons do not produce the same physical effects as a nuclear weapon. There is no mushroom cloud, no overpressure, and no fireball normally associated with a nuclear explosion. For instance, at the center of a nuclear explosion temperatures would reach several tens of millions of degrees centigrade, while in a conventional explosion, temperatures at the center of the explosion would only reach a few thousands degrees. This, of course, is of little consolation to the victims of either weapon.

The dirty bomb exposes victims to not only the heat and blast of a conventional explosion, but to life-threatening levels of invisible radioactive material as well. Victims who are not killed by the blast itself could be injured by exposure to the radioactive materials encased in the explosive. These radioactive materials, if ingested, would likely cause illness, and perhaps even death. The effectiveness of a radiological weapon depends on several factors, all of which would affect the dispersal of the material: size of the explosive; amount of radioactive material involved; weather conditions, such as wind; and the topography of the location, including the height of surrounding buildings. People could be exposed to the radioactive materials through proximity to the blast, the radiation cloud, wind movements, or ingesting affected food and water.

Dirty bombs are a credible threat due to their simplicity and to the availability of low-level radioactive materials, such as Cesium-60, Cobalt-137, and Americum, which are stored in thousands of facilities around the United States. These materials could be acquired from unprotected research as well as medical or industrial facilities. Large amounts of radioactive materials are available in scientific laboratories; food irradiation facilities; medical centers that are involved in nuclear medicine; and oil drilling facilities. For example, Cesium-60 and Cobalt-137 are commonly used in medicine in the treatment of cancer. There are a number of cases in the United States of radioactive materials disappearing or being abandoned over the years. Though a dirty bomb would not cause the same number of casualties as a nuclear weapon, it would have a significant effect on the location of the explosion. A dirty bomb could leave tens of blocks of an urban area—such as New York City's Wall Street financial district— uninhabitable. Since it is quite difficult to decontaminate buildings from radioactivity, much, if not all, of the exposed real estate would have to be demolished and carried away. Some have speculated, based on the cost of clean-up following the anthrax attacks in the United States, that it would be cheaper to tear down the U.S. Capitol and rebuild it than decontaminate it if a dirty bomb attack took place.

Of course, it is much easier to disperse nuclear materials through a dirty bomb than it is to detonate a nuclear weapon, due to the complex physics involved in fission or fusion. The low levels of security and porous borders in many places around the world are particularly suited for smuggling nuclear materials for sale to the highest bidder. A dirty bomb could hamper rescue operations, contaminate an area for a long period of time, making it uninhabitable, cause illness, create psychological trauma, and kill those exposed. Because of the simplicity of the radiological weapon, and the availability of low-level radiological materials, it is more likely that the world will see the use of a dirty bomb before the use of a nuclear weapon, especially by a terrorist organization. Nuclear weapons are difficult to develop and deploy, but the incredible destructive power make them attractive instruments of national power for states. For the same reason, they are also attractive to terrorists bent on killing large numbers of people. Fortunately nuclear weapons are much more difficult to acquire for non-state actors. Both of these weapons constitute a credible threat to international security and are worthy of significant attention, including preventive and nonproliferation efforts.

MISSILES

Ballistic and cruise missiles are the weapons of choice for many of today's modern militaries. A missile arsenal provides a nation with a standoff (i.e., from a distance) military strike capability that is, in many cases, indefensible by the opponent. Although there have been advances in missile defenses, the technology is in its early stages of being fielded and is only available to a few nations, including the United States. The fact that missiles are still hard to defend against makes them an attractive weapon. Missiles provide a country with influence, prestige, and national pride, and can serve as a source of income if they are exported as military hardware. Ballistic missiles vary in capability from short range to medium to intermediate and even intercontinental range (see Box 10.3). Cruise missiles, such as the American Tomahawk missile, have shorter ranges, but are even more difficult to detect by radar and defend against because of their small radar profiles and the terrain-hugging low altitudes at which they fly.

Ballistic missiles can be launched from ground-based missile silos or sea-based submarines. Cruise missiles provide even more flexibility. They can be launched from the shore by fixed or mobile batteries, from the sea by surface ships or submarines, or even from the air by large aircraft such as bombers like the American B-52. Both types of missiles can be fitted with conventional high-explosive warheads or with unconventional warheads containing chemical, biological, or nuclear weapons. A radiological weapon is not often discussed as a warhead for missiles, but it is certainly within the realm of possibilities. Long-range ballistic missiles, such as intercontinental ballistic missiles (ICBM) made famous during the Cold War, mated with megaton-like nuclear warheads, are the most destructive and dangerous weapons ever conceived. Capable of destroying large cities, once launched, a target could be attacked without warning by an ICBM within as little as twenty to thirty minutes from the other side of the globe. Today, over thirty nations have some type of ballistic missile. Since 1980, ballistic missiles have been used in six regional conflicts. Perhaps more troubling is that the over twenty countries believed to now possess, or are attempting to acquire, nuclear, biological, and chemical (NBC) weapons, also have ballistic missiles. Some of them, such as Iran and Syria, have strong ties to terrorists.

Missiles are attractive weapons, especially for use with WMD. This is because there are few, if any, means for an attacked country to defend itself. Missiles can also be delivered from great distances, allowing the attacker to keep out of harm's way of the effects of the chemical, biological, or nuclear weapons hurled at the adversary.[3] A missile armed with a WMD warhead could certainly do much more damage than a missile topped with a conventional high-explosive warhead. Because of the expense of a missile (e.g., often exceeding a million dollars), a rogue state—or terrorist organization—would want to do as much damage as possible to its intended tar-

---

Box 10.3.   Missile Types and Ranges

Short-Range Ballistic Missile: less than 1,000 km (600 miles)
Medium-Range Ballistic Missile: 1,000—3,000 km (600—1,800 miles)
Intermediate-Range Ballistic Missile: 3,000—5,500 km (1,800—3,300 miles)
Intercontinental Ballistic Missile: more than 5,500 km (3,300 miles)
Cruise Missiles: 10—3,000 km (6—1,800 miles)

get, leading it to arm the missile with WMD, as opposed to a less destructive conventional warhead, if available.[4]

Ballistic Missiles

The ballistic missile has its origins in Nazi Germany's World War II V-2 rocket project. The militarily ineffective terror weapon was used against Britain, Belgium, the Netherlands, and France before the end of the war. After the end of hostilities, the technology—along with the German scientists who created it—were whisked away to the United States and the Soviet Union, which both went on to develop ballistic missiles with ever-increasing ranges. Eventually, both the Soviet Union and the United States could hold each other's capitals and populations hostage with thousands of nuclear warheads atop intercontinental ballistic missiles. Ballistic missiles are rather simple. They follow a flight pattern having three phases: boost, midcourse, and terminal. In the boost phase, the missile travels upward against the forces of gravity for three to five minutes. The midcourse phase follows, wherein missiles coast or freefall toward their targets for up to twenty minutes. Finally, the missile reaches its terminal phase, wherein it falls to the earth for thirty seconds at speeds of up to 2,000 miles per hour.[5] Modern guidance systems have allowed ballistic missiles to become quite accurate against stationary targets, able to strike within feet of a target using satellite guidance. Ballistic missiles are not effective against moving targets.

Cruise Missiles

While the ballistic missile has been around for over sixty years, the cruise missile is relatively new, coming into operational status in the early 1980s. A cruise missile is an aerial vehicle similar to an airplane, which uses an air-breathing jet engine during its entire flight similar to an airplane to guide itself to a designated target. Cruise missiles fall into two categories: land attack and antishipping. They are highly accurate, jet-powered vehicles programmed to fly at low altitudes into a predetermined stationary or moving target. Like ballistic missiles, cruise missiles follow three flight phases: launch, midcourse, and terminal. Each phase is controlled by an onboard inertial navigation system (e.g., global positioning satellite, or GPS), which is updated during the flight by either radar or satellite-based systems to ensure that they reach and destroy their target.[6] The cruise missile is a very effective weapon and very dangerous in the wrong hands. If you include unmanned aerial vehicles, up to seventy nations have cruise missile capability.

Nations and Missiles

Thirty-five nations are known to field some type of missile. A number of these countries also have the capability to manufacture them, including the United States, Russia, China, Iran, and North Korea. Only five countries currently have missiles with intercontinental ranges: the United States, Russia, China, Britain, and France. Most notably, China is aggressively modernizing its strategic nuclear forces, leading to a several-fold increase in the number of Chinese strategic warheads deployed over the next ten to fifteen years. Both North Korea and Iran are also working on ICBMs to support their nuclear weapons program. It is expected that both Iran and North Korea will have ICBM capability by 2015 according to the CIA. Some experts believe it will be much sooner than 2015. Saudi Arabia, Israel, India, Pakistan, and Iran have MRBMs and most are looking at longer range IRBMs. Another twenty-five countries have short-range missiles, especially upgraded variations of the ubiquitous Soviet-era SCUD missile. North Korea, Russia, and China are the key suppliers of ballistic missiles and related technology to states developing or possessing ballistic missiles. In fact, the Pakistani Ghauri and the Iranian Shahab missiles are both based on the North Korean No-Dong ballistic missile. Russia has a very large ballistic missile weapons research and development program that has proliferated missiles and technology to countries in the Middle East, Eastern Europe, and abroad. China has sold missiles and shared missile technology with a number of countries, including North Korea, Libya, Pakistan, Iran, Saudi Arabia, and probably Syria.

Ballistic missiles have been used several times in regional conflicts.[7] The 1980–1989 Iran-Iraq War saw 600 SCUD short-range missiles fired by both sides, often targeting each other's cities. The Soviets in Afghanistan used over 2,000 SCUDs against the Afghan resistance forces between 1979 and 1989. The Chinese launched short-range ballistic missiles over and around Taiwan in 1996 in an attempt to intimidate the Taiwanese, who were about to hold their first democratic presidential elections. And the Iraqis fired SCUD missiles at Israel and Kuwait during the 1991 Persian Gulf War. Since their advent, cruise missiles have been used as well, perhaps most famously by the United States against Saddam Hussein in Iraq in 1991, the

Taliban and al-Qaeda in Afghanistan in 1998 and 2001, and once more against Iraq in 2003.

The digital age has only increased the distance, accuracy, and lethality of modern missiles. Dozens of nations, many of which are hostile to the United States and its allies, now have these weapons. Terrorist groups may also be seeking these weapons. As a result, the world is a much more dangerous place. Ballistic and cruise missiles, especially in the hands of rogue states, such as North Korea and Iran, will continue to significantly challenge American national security until effective missile defenses are deployed to protect the homeland and our troops overseas.

NOTES

1. Joseph Cirincione, with Jon B. Wolfstahl and Miriam Rajkumar, *Deadly Arsenal: Tracking Weapons of Mass Destruction* (Washington, DC: The Carnegie Endowment for International Peace, 2002), p.35.

2. The Avalon Project at Yale Law School, Chapter 10, http://www.yale.edu/law web/avalon/abomb/mp10.htm (accessed January 26, 2004).

3. Missile Defense Agency, "Ballistic Missile Defense Facts," MDA Link: Making Ballistic Missile Defense a Reality, http://www.acq.osd.mil/bmdo/bmdolink/ html/basics.html (accessed February 11, 2004).

4. Missile Defense Agency, "Ballistic Missile Defense Facts."

5. Missile Defense Agency, "Ballistic Missile Defense Facts."

6. Office of the Under Secretary of Defense for Acquisition, Technology, and Logistics, "Land-Attack Cruise Missiles," http://www.acq.osd.mil/bmdo/bmdolink/ bcmt/lacm_2.htm (accessed February 11, 2004).

7. Missile Defense Agency, "Ballistic Missile Defense Facts."

GAS AND BUGS

We do not need the atomic bomb. We have the dual chemical [weapons]. Whoever threatens us with the atomic bomb, we will annihilate him with the dual chemical [weapons].

—Saddam Hussein, former Iraqi president, April 1990[1]

They did not expect to die this way. They thought they might die of old age or even disease, but never this way. But die they did by the thousands, gasping, wheezing, and vomiting, expiring in clouds of poisonous gas. It wasn't the first time Saddam Hussein used chemical weapons, but this time it was the worst. It was against his own people. Beginning before dawn on March 16, 1988, on what became infamous as "Black Friday," the Kurdish town of Halabja in northern Iraq was viciously attacked by its own government. Iraqi forces rained down chemical weapons on the city of 70,000 for three days. At least 5,000 people died as a result of the mustard, nerve, and cyanide gas attacks. Another 10,000 were injured during the course of the next two days. One woman lost 120 relatives who had come to Halabja to celebrate a wedding. She was the only one to survive. Years after the slaughter, the people of Halabja still suffer from high rates of cancer; skin, blood, and neurological disorders; birth defects; and miscarriages. They will not forget Saddam Hussein's cruelty or "Black Friday" for generations to come.

CHEMICAL WEAPONS

Often referred to as the "Poor Man's nuclear weapon," chemical weapons (CW) are man-made, toxic agents capable of causing widespread injury and death. They can damage the lungs, blister the skin, blind the eyes, or incapacitate the body's central nervous system. Some chemical agents can be lethal if just a few milligrams are ingested. There are thousands of chemicals that could be used as a CW—any poison will do. Further complicating the issue is the fact that many potential chemical agents are dual use—having both civilian and military purposes. Most chemical weapons production follows routine, commercial chemical engineering processes. For example, chlorine gas, which can be used as a CW, can be produced rather routinely and inexpensively. Other CW agents, such as nerve gases, require more sophisticated chemical processes and more complex equipment for production and storage. Although CW production can be simple, effective CW munitions must be mated with a delivery system, such as a bomb or artillery shell, before the weapon is considered ready for use.

Chemical weapons can be grouped into two general types: those that affect the body surfaces they come in contact with (i.e., surface agents) and those that damage the central nervous system (i.e., nerve agents). Surface agents include phosgene gas, chlorine gas, hydrogen cyanide, and mustard gas. Phosgene causes the lungs to fill with water while chlorine gas destroys the respiratory tract lining. Hydrogen cyanide inhibits oxygen from reaching the blood, causing asphyxiation. Finally, mustard gas blisters any surface it contacts, including the skin, eyes, and lungs, and may cause death by respiratory failure. Nerve agents act by interfering with the body's central nervous system, affecting breathing, muscle, and heart function. Nerve agents include sarin, soman, tabun, and VX. Whether inhaled or absorbed through the skin, a single drop of nerve agent can incapacitate the body's central nervous system, causing death within minutes of exposure.

Chemical weapons can be delivered through a variety of means, including bombs, rockets, artillery shells, cruise or ballistic missiles, or aerosol sprayers such as crop dusters. They can be difficult to use because the weather influences their efficiency and effectiveness. For example, winds can blow chemical weapons miles away from an intended target, impacting people and places that the users did not want attacked. Likewise, winds can scatter the agent, reducing its strength or even blowing it back at the attacker. Because of their sensitivity to environmental conditions, CW must often be used in large quantities to be effective. Pound for pound, CW is less deadly than biological weapons.

A Quick History of Chemical Weapons

Chemical weapons have been around for a long time, dating back to the ancient Greeks and Romans. Its first recorded use was in the Greek Peloponnesian Wars (431–404 BC). Back then, armies used smoke and a combination of burning sulfur and pitch resin to create toxic fumes to choke the enemy and obscure their vision. The first use of CW in the modern era came on European battlefields during World War I, when the Germans launched a large-scale chlorine gas attack against French troops at Ypres in 1915. When the wind conditions were just right, the Germans released the yellowish-green-colored vapor from gas cylinders along the front in the direction of the unprotected French troops a few hundred yards away, choking thousands of French soldiers hunkered down in their trenches. The Allies responded with their own chemical weapons when the British reciprocated by using chlorine gas against the Germans at the Battle of Loos in the same year. As the war continued, phosgene, a deadly choking gas, and other chemical weapons were developed and used by combatants on both sides of the bloody conflict. The French were the first to weaponize CW by putting phosgene in an artillery shell and firing it in the enemy's direction. Germany introduced deadly mustard gas in 1917. By the end of the war in November 1918, all the major powers had used chemical weapons, resulting in 100,000 deaths and more than a million casualties, including a young Austrian lance corporal named Adolf Hitler, who was temporarily blinded by a mustard gas attack in Belgium in 1918. In World War I (WWI), CW earned its stripes as a weapon of mass destruction.

The concern over the widespread use of CW in World War I led to an effort to prevent its use in future conflicts. In 1925, the Geneva Protocol prohibited "the use in war of asphyxiating, poisonous or other gases, and of bacteriological methods of warfare." All the major combatants signed the agreement, except Russia. The United States signed with the caveat that it would not be the first to use CW, but reserved the right to do so in retaliation for a CW attack upon itself. Interestingly, the Protocol did not prohibit the manufacturing and stockpiling of these weapons, which many countries did, nor did it ultimately prevent their future use by some nations. Chemical weapons have been used only a few times since WWI, but with deadly results. Italy used chemical arms against Ethiopia in 1936 during the invasion of Abyssinia. Japan employed CW against China in Manchuria in the run up to World War II. Of course, Nazi Germany used poisonous gas to murder millions of innocent civilians in concentration camps during World War II. The Italians, Hungarians, Japanese, French, British, Russians, Germans, and Americans all produced mustard, phosgene, and other agents during World War II, but never used them in combat. Following World War II, the United States used tear gas and several types of defoliants, including Agent Orange, during the Vietnam War. Although not normally considered a CW, some do consider napalm, which was used in Korea and Vietnam, a CW. Egypt used the chemical agents phosgene and mustard against Yemen in their 1963–1967 conflict. Many believe that the Soviets used chemical weapons in Afghanistan during their occupation from 1979–1989, but the accusation has not been proven. Iraq and Iran used CW during their 1980–1988 war, killing tens of thousands of soldiers. Libya may have used CW against Chad in their 1987 conflict. And defectors have accused North Korea of gassing political prisoners and developing untraceable poisons for assassinations.

Types of Chemical Weapons

Chemicals weapons are scientifically characterized as choking, blistering, and nerve or blood agents. Choking agents, such as phosgene, diphosgene, chlorine, and chloropicrin, damage the lungs, causing breathing problems in the victim. When exposed to the agent, the victim's lungs swell, fill with liquid, and begin to dissolve, causing the victim to asphyxiate. Death, depending on exposure levels, can come within several hours. Choking agents are not as effective as other chemical weapons because they disperse rapidly and act slowly, allowing those under attack to take countermeasures, such as donning a gas mask or leaving the affected area in time to save themselves. On the down side, phosgene and chlorine gases are common industrial chemicals and are readily available. Phosgene accounted for 80 percent of the CW casualties in WWI.

Blister, or vesicant, agents include mustard, Lewisite, and phosgene gases, which burn and blister the skin. Exposure can come via liquid or vapor contact with any exposed tissue. Blister agents, namely mustard gas, are absorbed through the skin, eyes, and mucous membranes. These agents are especially damaging to the eyes, air passages, and lungs where they inhibit breathing, often leading to asphyxiation. Blister agents cause blindness, nausea, vomiting, blisters, and death if the agent enters the lungs or bowels. These agents, in addition to producing casualties, also force enemy troops to wear full protective gear, increasing their workload and reducing their fighting effectiveness.

Mustard gases are the most feared CW because of their effectiveness and ease of production. The agent is not commercially available, but its synthesis does not require significant expertise if appropriate instructions are followed. Most of the ingredients are available from the commercial chemical industry. Blood agents, including cyanide and cyanogen chloride gas, can kill a person by disrupting the transport of oxygen through the blood stream, suffocating the brain, causing death. These agents are easy to make. Although they act quickly, they lose their potency as quickly as ten minutes after dispersal.

The development of the most dangerous CW—the nerve agent—dates back to WWII. Nerve agents attack the body's central nervous system, blocking an enzyme that is critical to its functioning. It shuts down the victim's nervous system, affecting basic bodily functions such as respiration and muscle control. Exposure comes through contact with the skin or eyes or through inhalation of the vapor. Both the lungs and the eyes rapidly absorb nerve agents. A deadly dose is normally much smaller than that required for a blistering or choking agent. Death can occur within fifteen minutes of a fatal dose, making these agents especially effective. There are two types of nerve agents. The G-series includes tabun, soman, and sarin. The V-series, which includes VX, is more toxic and longer lasting than the G-series. These agents are not commercially available, and their synthesis requires significant chemical expertise.

States and Chemical Weapons

In an effort to eliminate the threat of CW and strengthen the 1925 Geneva Protocol, the Chemical Weapons Convention (CWC) was drafted by the United Nations during the early 1990s. The CWC bans the development, production, acquisition, stockpiling, retention, and direct or indirect transfer of CW. It also prohibits aiding or abetting anyone else to engage in activities prohibited by the CWC. The CWC became effective in 1997, following ratification by sixty-five countries. One hundred sixty countries have either ratified or acceded to the CWC, including the United States. Nonetheless, a number of nations that have signed the CWC are believed to have chemical weapons. As many as sixteen nations have, or are pursuing, chemical weapons even though most of the world has agreed to destroy their CW by 2007 under the Chemical Weapons Convention. China, North Korea, South Korea, Iran, Syria, Egypt, India, Pakistan, Russia, Libya, Sudan, Israel, Taiwan, Vietnam, Burma, and Saudi Arabia are suspected of having chemical weapons programs at some level. On a positive note, it looks like Libya and Sudan have made the decision to end their CW programs. Iran and Syria are of particular concern because of their state sponsorship of terrorism and ties to Hamas and Hezbollah.

Although Iran is a party to the CWC, it continued to seek CW production technology, training, and expertise from China that could further Tehran's efforts to build a homegrown capability to produce nerve agents. Iran likely has stockpiled blister, blood, choking, and probably nerve agents—and the bombs and artillery shells to deliver them—which it previously had manufactured, according to the CIA's 2004 annual report to Congress.[1] Syria continues to seek CW-related expertise from foreign sources for its CW program due to the limited nature of its chemical industry infrastructure. As a result, Damascus remains dependent on foreign sources for key elements of its CW program, including precursor chemicals (i.e., key chemical ingredients) and critical production equipment. Syria has a stockpile of the nerve agent sarin, but apparently tried to develop more toxic and persistent nerve agents, such as VX. Syria is not a party to the CWC and has never used chemical weapons in a conflict.

North Korea is believed to have a large stockpile of nerve, blister, choking, and blood agents that it would use in the event of a conflict on the Korean Peninsula. North Korea has also weaponized its CW stocks and can deliver it to targets using missiles, aerial bombs, artillery, or special operations forces. Some of North Korea's CW arsenal is believed to be deployed along the demilitarized zone (DMZ) between North and South Korea and within range of the South Korean capital, Seoul. North Korea would likely use CW, especially CW artillery, in a new Korean war against South Korea and the United States. Likely fearful of intrusive international inspections, North Korea is not a member of the CWC. The People's Republic of China is believed to have an advanced CW program, ranging from research and development to production and export. Although China denies having chemical weapons, it is believed to have a well-stocked inventory of choking, blister, blood, and nerve agents, including a wide ability to deliver these weapons to their targets. China's People's Liberation Army routinely conduct military field exercises that involve chemical weapons scenarios to prepare for conflict that would include the use of CW. China is a key supplier of material and technology to states that have chemical weapons programs.

Most troubling, it is believed that Chinese firms have been providing CW-related production equipment and technology to the Iranian CW program.

Russia has the largest stockpile of chemical weapons in the world, involving 40,000 metric tons of CW agent. Its stockpile runs the range of CW types and delivery systems, including artillery shells and truck-mounted aerosol spray tanks. Russia is party to the CWC, but, as a consequence of financial resources and industrial destruction capability problems, it will be impossible for Moscow to destroy its CW arsenal by 2007 as agreed to under the CWC. In addition, there have also been persistent, disturbing rumors of covert Russian CW programs designed to circumvent CWC restrictions. Russia is also a key supplier of dual-use CW equipment, chemicals, and related expertise to such countries as Iran. Russia's well-known expertise in CW and its economic problems make it an attractive target for countries seeking expertise, material, or technological assistance.

BIOLOGICAL WEAPONS

American military personnel have nicknamed them "germs and bugs" and pound for pound, the biological weapon (BW) is the deadliest weapon in existence today. Although it would not cause the same level of physical damage as a nuclear weapon, a virulent biological weapon could easily kill as many—if not more—people as a nuke. Some have argued that an anthrax attack could kill one to three million individuals, the same as a huge one-megaton (i.e., one million tons of TNT) hydrogen bomb.[2] As little as ten grams of anthrax could produce as many casualties as a ton of nerve agent. It should come as no surprise that among counterterrorism officials today, there is no bigger nightmare than the possibility of a terrorist attack in a large city using a biological weapon.

The BW is unique in the field of weaponry because it is composed of living organisms, while the other types of weapons are not. Biological pathogens include bacteria, viruses, fungi, or by-product toxins, which can reproduce and spread clandestinely from victim to victim just like the flu, and are capable of producing disease or death. Once released, the spread of biological pathogens are hard to predict and are often uncontrollable. The victims may never even know they have been infected until they become ill. There are no nuclear fireballs or clouds of noxious gas to indicate a BW attack. It is a silent killer.

Biological weapons offer the military strategist, or terrorist, several advantages over other forms of weapon of mass destruction (WMD). They are quite lethal and relatively inexpensive to produce in comparison with nuclear, chemical, or conventional weapons. A BW is easy to disperse and because some types are contagious, they can claim an increasing number of victims as the pathogen spreads from person to person and from place to place. Because the industrial infrastructure of a biological weapons program often looks similar to legitimate medical, agricultural, or biotechnological endeavors, they are easy to conceal.

A BW program also requires much less industrial infrastructure than a chemical or nuclear weapons program. Deadly amounts of BW could be covertly produced in an area as small as a hospital laboratory. The equipment needed for a BW program is readily available on the international market, too. The rapid advances in biotechnology make the possibility of new, more virulent, vaccine-resistant strains of BW quite likely in the future. The origins of a BW attack are particularly difficult to trace, as evidenced by the unresolved September 2001 anthrax and February 2004 ricin attacks in the United States. BW can be delivered to a target in a number of ways, including artillery shells, rockets, missiles, aerosol sprayer, unmanned aerial vehicle (e.g., a drone), or even aircraft. It can also be dispersed clandestinely through food and water supplies, potentially affecting large numbers of people. For these reasons, many experts agree that biological weapons, especially in the hands of terrorists, are the most dangerous—and likely—threat to American national security today.

Despite its advantages as a weapon, BW has its downsides as well. For instance, where the effects of a nuclear or a chemical weapon are quickly apparent, some biological weapons can take days, or even weeks, to make their victims sick, and, ultimately, may never kill them. Potential victims can also be vaccinated against BW agents, such as smallpox and anthrax, in advance of an attack. Since they are living organisms, BW pathogens are generally more fragile than chemical agents, meaning some might not survive the heat and physical effects of an explosion if delivered by bomb or artillery shell. Lastly, BW has not been used frequently in modern warfare because of its potential for unpredictability, possibly attacking unintended targets or contaminating desirable territory. Of course, this disincentive to the military strategist may suit the objectives of the terrorist perfectly.

A Short History of Biological Weapons

Biological weapons have been used for centuries. In 1500 BC, the Hittites of Asia Minor (modern-day Turkey) sent plague victims into the land of their enemies in hopes of infecting them with the disease. In the fourteenth century, the Mongols catapulted corpses contaminated with the plague over the walls into Kaffa (in modern-day Ukraine), forcing the Genoans to flee the city. Unfortunately, the Genoese ships carried the plague with them back to Europe, unleashing the massive pandemic known as the "Black Death," which killed one-third of Europe's population and caused countless deaths in Asia and Africa, too. In the eighteenth century, the Russians, under Peter the Great, used plague-infected corpses against Sweden's Charles XII in the Great Northern War. Right here in North America, during the French and Indian Wars, the British gave blankets from smallpox hospitals to hostile Indian tribes, intending to infect them with the disease. In the twentieth century, World War I German agents used anthrax and the equine disease, glanders, to infect livestock and feed being shipped from the United States to Allied forces in Europe.

The concern over the widespread use of chemical weapons in World War I led to an effort to prevent the use of both chemical and biological weapons in future conflicts. In 1925, the Geneva Protocol prohibited "the use in war of asphyxiating, poisonous or other gases, and of bacteriological methods of warfare." All the major combatants signed the agreement, except Russia. The United States signed with the proviso that it reserved the right to use these weapons in retaliation for an attack upon itself. Unfortunately, the Protocol did not prohibit the manufacturing and stockpiling of these weapons, which many countries did, nor did the agreement prevent their future use. Following World War I, the only notable biological weapons use was by Japan against China in the late 1930s and early 1940s. In 1937, Japan began a biological weapons research and development program, under the code name Unit 731, in Manchuria in northern China. Over the course of the program, at least 10,000 Chinese prisoners were killed during Japanese BW experiments. In 1940, the Japanese dropped rice and wheat mixed with plague-carrying fleas over China and Manchuria, causing outbreaks of disease. In 1942, the United States began its own biological weapons program at Camp Detrick, Maryland, but unilaterally renounced BW in 1969.

Outside of Japan's use of BW in WWII, the weapon has not been used by a nation-state in warfare. Perhaps this is so out of concern by the belligerents of the unpredictability of the results, including the possibility of a pathogen spreading to its own people or armed forces. On the contrary, Iraq admitted to UN inspectors in 1995 that it equipped shells and warheads during the 1991 Persian Gulf War with anthrax for use against American-led coalition forces. Iraq did not use anthrax during that conflict, most likely due to threats from the United States prior to the war that Iraq's use of WMD would be met with massive retaliation, a not so veiled reference to Washington's use of nuclear weapons in response to Baghdad's use of WMD against American soldiers.

In 1972, in another attempt to strengthen the Geneva Protocol and prevent the use of BW, the Biological Weapons Convention (BWC) was agreed to at the United Nations. This treaty is unique in that it was the first international agreement to ban an entire category of weapons. The BWC bans the development, production, and stockpiling of biological agents or toxins other than those used for prophylactic, protective, or other peaceful purposes. It also covers weapons, equipment, or means of delivery designed to use biological agents for hostile purposes or in armed conflict. This means that a country may not develop an offensive BW program for use in attacking an enemy, but may retain the resources to develop a defensive program, allowing it to develop vaccines and antidotes for BW pathogens. The treaty went into force in 1975 and today has over 150 members. Regrettably, this treaty, unlike the Chemical Weapons Convention, does not have any monitoring or verification procedures, making it ineffective in deterring, preventing, or punishing violators.

But all has not been quiet on the BW front. In an infamous case of Cold War espionage, the Bulgarian security services assassinated Bulgarian dissident Georgi Markov in London with a ricin pellet shot from the tip of an umbrella in 1978. The cause of Markov's death was not discovered until after his demise. In 1979 in the Soviet Union, an accidental release of anthrax from a state BW facility in Sverdlovsk caused an outbreak, which killed at least sixty-six. In a fit of communist secrecy, Russia did not acknowledge the catastrophe until 1992. The only large-scale terrorist attack with a biological weapon occurred in 1984 in the United States in an episode of domestic terrorism. Members of the Rajneesh cult in Oregon placed salmonella bacteria in the salad bars of several local restaurants in an effort to sicken people and prevent them from voting in a referendum that affected the cult's property rights. Although 750 people became ill, none died. In 1995, the Japanese terrorist group and religious cult Aum Shinrikyo (Supreme Truth) unsuccessfully tried to use anthrax and botulinum toxin to attack downtown Tokyo and U.S. military installations in Japan.[3] The group also failed to produce the deadly Ebola virus, an African disease known for causing massive bleeding and the destruction of internal tissues. The group did eventually kill twelve and injure 5,500 in a sarin gas chemical weapons attack in the Tokyo subway that same year. The origins of the 2001 anthrax and 2004 ricin letter attacks in the United States are still a mystery.

Types of Biological Weapons

Biological warfare pathogens include bacteria, viruses, rickettsia, and toxins that can kill or incapacitate. Since they can reproduce, biological agents have the unique potential to make a target environment more dangerous over time. BW may also include dangerous toxins, which are not living organisms, but their by-products. Bacteria are microscopic, free-living organisms, which reproduce by simple division. They are the most common organisms on earth and are intimately connected to the lives of all living beings. Experts assert that hundreds of thousands of bacteria can fit into a space the size of the period at the end of this sentence. They assault living tissue, entering an organism and releasing poisons. Bacterial agents produce such illnesses as anthrax and the plague.

A virus is an infectious agent found in virtually all life forms, including humans, animals, plants, fungi, and bacteria. They are between twenty and one hundred times smaller than bacteria. Viruses are not considered free-living organisms since they cannot reproduce outside of a living cell. They often damage or kill the cells that they infect, causing disease in infected organisms. Smallpox and yellow fever are considered viral agents. Rickettsiae are microorganisms, which have characteristics common to both bacteria and viruses; these include agents such as Q-fever. Toxins are poisonous substances derived from living plants, animals, or microorganisms, but are not living organisms themselves. In this way, they are much more like chemical weapons. Toxins, unlike other living pathogens, cannot reproduce and spread, and therefore are not considered as dangerous as other biological weapons.[4] Botulinum toxin and ricin are two of today's better-known toxins.

States and Biological Weapons

Like chemical weapons programs, it is often difficult to separate a civilian BW program from a military one. As a result, a number of states cheat on their BWC obligations or have never signed the treaty at all. Although he did not specify all the names of all of the countries due to sources and methods, the former director of the CIA, George Tenet, stated publicly in congressional testimony in 2000 that about a dozen states are pursuing BW programs.⁵ That number is still roughly accurate today. Although it appears that Iraq and Libya would not be included on that listing today, it is generally believed that Russia, China, Cuba, Iran, Israel, India, Pakistan, North Korea, Egypt, and Syria are among the others that have offensive BW programs at some level. Iran and Syria are of particular concern because of their ties to terrorism and animosity toward the United States.

Even though Iran has ratified the Biological Weapons Convention, Tehran probably maintains a BW program based on its continued efforts to obtain dual-use bio-technical materials, equipment, and expertise, especially from Russia. While such materials and equipment have legitimate civilian applications, Iran's biological weapons program could be benefiting from its civilian biotechnology industry as well. Iran's BW program reportedly began in the 1980s during the Iran-Iraq war. It is likely that Iran has the capability to produce small quantities of BW agents, but has a limited ability to field them in weapons.

North Korea is a signatory to the BWC as well, but nonetheless has pursued BW capabilities since the 1960s. North Korea is believed to have weaponized its BW agents, including anthrax, cholera, and the plague. It is possible that since North Korean military doctrine still reflects its Soviet origins, Pyongyang would not feel restricted in using BW in a military conflict with South Korean and U.S. military forces. North Korea would almost certainly rely more heavily on CW than BW because of the ability to control CW better.

It is highly probable that Syria also continues to develop an offensive BW capability, despite having signed the BWC. Syria's biotechnology industry has the capability to produce BW, but it is questionable as to whether it has put these biological pathogens into weapons for military use. Damascus would likely require significant foreign assistance to produce BW in large quantities, which may be necessary for a military conflict. Syria's close ties with Palestinian rejectionist groups such as Hamas and Palestinian Islamic Jihad as well as Hezbollah, makes Damascus' BW worth worrying about.

Before its breakup in 1991, the Soviet Union maintained the world's largest BW program, involving as many as 60,000 personnel. The Soviets viewed BW as not only a tactical battlefield weapon, but as an offensive, "deep-strike" strategic weapon for attacking the enemy's large cities, including those in the United States, intending to disrupt life with outbreaks of smallpox, anthrax, and plague. Even though Moscow "formally" shut down its BW program in 1992, there is still deep concern that Russia may have an ongoing BW program in violation of its commitments under the BWC. Russia's well-known biological expertise and dual-use biotechnology equipment makes it a key source of material, equipment, and expertise for countries seeking assistance with their BW programs, including Iran. More worrying, many former Soviet biological weapons scientists are now unemployed, underemployed, or employed outside their specialty and thus may be willing to seek work in BW programs outside Russia. Moreover, many present Russian biological weapons sites have poor security and may be subject to corruption or theft.[6]

China continues to maintain the biological weapons program that it began in the 1950s. China's growing biotechnology sector probably allows it to develop and produce biological agents at will, and its defense industry provides it the ability to weaponize BW. China is a member of the BWC, and although Beijing claims to have no BW program, its declarations under the treaty are believed to be incomplete by the American intelligence community. China's close relationship with North Korea and Iran, and poor export controls, make preventing BW proliferation problematic.

Biological weapons may be the most threatening of all WMD. While nuclear, radiological, and chemical weapons can kill a large number of people without question, biological weapons are the only ones with the potential to grow, spread, and travel on their own, possibly resulting in infections worldwide. Although not a biological weapon, the fact that a worldwide influenza epidemic killed 20 million people, including 500,000 Americans in 1918, is worthy of note—and concern. Pneumonic plague killed 9,300 people in Manchuria in the 1920s. Biological weapons are also among the easiest to covertly produce and disseminate. The rapidly advancing biotechnology field also invites malpractice by those intending to do harm. Other potential biological weapons, such as Ebola, are poorly understood and lack a cure or effective treatment. Because of these factors, BW may indeed be the future weapon of choice.

NOTES

1. Unclassified Report to Congress on the Acquisition of Technology Relating to Weapons of Mass Destruction and Advanced Conventional Weapons. July 1 through December 31, 2003, http://www.cia.gov/cia/reports/index.html (accessed February 15, 2004).

2. Tara O'Toole, "Carnegie International Non-Proliferation Conference 2001,"

Global Epidemiological Monitoring in Response to the BW Threat, June 18, 2001, http://www.ceip.org/files/projects/npp/resources/Conference%202001/panels/bw th reat.htm (accessed February 16, 2004).

3. Harvey G. Kushner, *Encyclopedia of Terrorism* (Thousand Oaks, Calif.: Sage Publications, 2002), p. 75.

4. Joseph Cirincione, Jon B. Wolfsthal, and Miriam Rajkumar, *Deadly Arsenals, Tracking Weapons of Mass Destruction* (Washington, DC: The Carnegie Endowment for International Peace), p. 46.

5. George Tenet, Statement to the Foreign Relations Committee, Worldwide Threat in 2000: Global Realities of Our National Security, March 3, 2000, www.cia .gov/cia/public_affairs/speeches/archives/2000/dci_speech_032100.html (accessed December 12, 2003).

6. Cirincione et al., *Deadly Arsenals*, p. 47.

12

SPECTER OF SUPERTERRORISM

Acquiring [chemical and nuclear] weapons for the defense of Muslims is a religious duty. If I have indeed acquired these weapons, then I thank God for enabling me to do so.

—Osama bin Laden during a January 4, 1999, *Time* magazine interview

Standing in a Bangkok parking lot, the forty-seven-year-old Thai, Narong Penanam, told the prospective buyers he wanted $240,000 for the thirty kilograms. He even told the buyers that his suppliers could get more. Was this just another drug deal involving a Southeast Asian narcotics ring? No, as TIME reported, it was about radioactive materials and terrorists.

Fortunately, the "terrorists" in this case were undercover Thai police, who arrested Narong and seized the radioactive Cesium-137 on that June day in 2003. Narong naturally claimed he was a mere middleman with no clear idea of what he was peddling, and that the material had come from the neighboring country of Laos. Narong later admitted that he intended to sell the material to an unspecified terror group in Thailand—most likely al-Qaeda's Southeast Asia affiliate, Jemaah Islamiya. Cesium-137, a highly radioactive isotope, could be used to make a "dirty bomb"—a conventional explosive packed with radioactive material. Coming just months before twenty-one leaders, including President Bush, would descend upon Bangkok for the Asia-Pacific Economic Cooperation (APEC) forum, security officials on both sides of the Pacific were incredibly worried. The question is, how many nuclear traffickers did not end up in handcuffs like Narong and were able to deliver the materials to the actual buyer?

WEAPON OF MASS DESTRUCTION TERRORISM

The possibility of a terrorist using a weapon of mass destruction (WMD) or radiological weapon against the American homeland is real. Government officials have said so—and—continue to say so. Many even believe that it is only a matter of "when," not "if," such an attack will occur in the United States. FBI director Robert Mueller in his February 2005 testimony before the Senate Select Committee on Intelligence said: "I am also very concerned with the growing body of sensitive reporting that continues to show al-Qaeda's clear intention to obtain and ultimately use some sort of chemical, biological, radiological, nuclear or high-energy explosives (CBRNE) material in its attacks against America."

The thought of a WMD attack perpetrated by terrorists is so horrific that some have dubbed this form of terrorism "superterrorism." But superterrorism is not new. In March 1995, the Japanese terrorist doomsday cult Aum Shinrikyo released sarin nerve agent in Tokyo subway cars, killing 12 people and injuring over 5,000. In its first attack, a refrigerator truck was parked in a secluded parking lot near a residential neighborhood in Matsumoto, Japan, in 1994. Sarin gas was released, creating a cloud that drifted toward houses, apartment buildings, and a dormitory that housed three judges expected to rule against Aum Shinrikyo in an upcoming real estate case. The attack resulted in 7 deaths and 500 injuries.

This incident demonstrated that terrorist groups, right under the noses of highly competent law enforcement authorities, are capable of producing, and using, WMD with significant results. More troubling yet, in the early 1990s, senior Aum Shinrikyo member Kiyohide Hayakawa traveled to Russia numerous times in search of various weapons. It was during these trips that he explored the option of buying a nuclear weapon. Hayakawa's diary, seized by the Tokyo police after the 1995 sarin gas attack, contained the notation "how much is a nuclear warhead?" and listed several prices with the figure of $15 million underlined several times for emphasis.[1] It is not known from where he got that number, whether it was what he was willing to offer or if it was an offer from a potential seller, but it is troubling nonetheless.

Al-Qaeda was involved in basic nuclear research in Afghanistan, and dating from the early 1990s was seeking nuclear materials such as enriched uranium. There is continuing concern that some colleagues of Pakistan's nuclear scientist A.Q. Khan may have been in contact with al-Qaeda in Afghanistan. While many forms of WMD are difficult to manufacture, it is widely believed that a terrorist group with the right motivations, skills, and resources could produce a rudimentary, but functional, nuclear weapon.

Al-Qaeda's core membership had a number of people with scientific backgrounds that could aid a WMD program. Captured senior al-Qaeda members such as Khalid Sheikh Mohammed have confirmed that al-Qaeda's second in command, Egyptian physician Ayman al Zawahiri, is very interested in chemical and biological weapons. Iraq's al-Qaeda lieutenant Abu Musab al Zarqawi is believed to be an expert in chemical weapons. Both are still on the loose. According to the CIA report "Terrorist CBRN: Material and Effects," it is believed that al-Qaeda has been looking to add to its arsenal mustard gas, sarin gas, and VX.[2] A now infamous al-Qaeda video discovered in Afghanistan and aired in 2003 on American TV shows a dog being gassed to death in an al-Qaeda CW experiment. Unfortunately, this only gives an insight into what al-Qaeda may have in store for its future human victims. In April 2004, Jordanian authorities claimed that al-Qaeda planned a chemical weapons attack on Jordan's intelligence headquarters in Amman that could have killed 20,000 people. The attack was thwarted by a series of arrests, and reportedly planned by Abu Musab al Zarqawi. Al-Qaeda operatives arrested in Britain in summer 2004 had been planning CW attacks in New York and New Jersey.

According to the 2005 Presidential Commission on Weapons of Mass Destruction, al-Qaeda made unexpected advances in developing a virulent BW before 9/11 in Afghanistan. The pathogen, only identified as agent "X," could refer to anthrax, which was found in al-Qaeda labs in Afghanistan. The commission believes that al-Qaeda probably developed a small quantity of agent X, and planned to make dispersal devices for it. The program had been underway for several years before the 2001 invasion of Afghanistan. The Senate Office of Majority Leader senator Bill Frist received a ricin-laden letter in February 2004. This incident was the third such incident involving ricin in four months in Washington, DC. In October 2003, postal workers in Greenville, South Carolina, discovered a ricin-contaminated envelope addressed to the U.S. Department of Transportation in the nation's capital. A month later in November, the U.S. Secret Service intercepted a ricin letter addressed to the White House. In other incidences involving ricin, in January 2003, antiterror forces in London found traces of the biological weapon in two apartments occupied by seven al-Qaeda operatives. Further, ricin recipes and traces of the toxin were reportedly found in al-Qaeda hideouts in Afghanistan.

There has already been an anthrax attack in the United States. In September 2001, shortly after 9/11, anthrax-laced letters were sent to the *New York Post*, NBC anchor Tom Brokaw, then Majority Leader senator Tom Daschle, Vermont senator Patrick Leahy, and a Florida newspaper. These letters caused five deaths and twenty-two infections. Publicly available information seems to indicate that a highly trained scientist who likely had previous experience with the bacteria professionally produced the anthrax. The anthrax was very pure and had been refined into fine particles for efficient dispersal. The attack cost the U.S government a reported $125 million dollars to clean up affected public buildings such as the Brentwood Post Office in Washington, DC. It is unclear whether these attacks are related at all to al-Qaeda or 9/11.

In February 2004, in testimony before the Senate Select Committee on Intelligence, former director of central intelligence (DCI) George Tenet said, "I have consistently warned this committee of al-Qaeda's interest in chemical, biological, radiological and nuclear weapons. Acquiring these remains a 'religious obligation' in bin Laden's eyes, and al-Qaeda and more than two dozen other terrorist groups are pursuing CBRN [chemical, biological, radiological, and nuclear] materials."[3] Although Tenet did not further specify the names of the other interested terrorist groups, it is believed that in addition to al-Qaeda, Palestinian terrorist groups such as Hezbollah, Hamas, and Palestinian Islamic Jihad are among those interested in CBRN. Tenet's testimony predicted that poison attacks using simple delivery methods were the most likely threat scenario for the United States, but that the terrorists were looking for more sophisticated ways to deliver CBRN as well. For example, he added that terrorists have widely shared building instructions with one another for an unspecified chemical weapon that could cause a high number of casualties when released in an enclosed space.

On the biological weapons side, the former DCI believed that al-Qaeda is particularly interested in producing and using anthrax as a weapon of mass terror. He did not address the fall 2001 anthrax or the winter 2004 ricin attacks in the United States in the committee's open session, but those unresolved attacks are evidence that a WMD attack is possible here in America. Tenet went on to say that al-Qaeda harbors the desire for nuclear weapons as well and remains interested in radiological weapons, or "dirty bombs." Tenet also opined that the terrorists seem to have a good idea of how these weapons should be employed.

The Director of the Defense Intelligence Agency (DIA), Vice Admiral Lowell Jacoby, U.S. Navy, in his testimony at the same hearing, expressed his mutual concern about al-Qaeda's and other terrorist groups' interest in acquiring CBRN weapons. He stated that the DIA, America's largest military intelligence agency, remained concerned about "rogue scientists and the potential that state actors are providing, or will provide technological assistance to terrorist organizations."[4]

Cofer Black, the former State Department coordinator for counterterrorism, said: "We know beyond a shadow of a doubt that a number of these [terrorist] groups, if they had it [a CBRN weapon], would use it." He continued: "They've got the will. A lot of these guys seek the expertise, and there's a reasonable amount of that out there, but what you're really looking for is the coming together of all the factors: the will, the expertise and the materials."[5] These comments are ominous for the future.

The threat does not seem to have diminished, either. The current DCI, Porter Goss, said in his February 2005 testimony before the same committee: "It may only be a matter of time before al-Qaeda or another group attempts to use chemical, biological, radiological and nuclear weapons." Jim Loy, deputy secretary of the Department of Homeland Security, said in his testimony at the same hearing that, "Al Qaeda leaders and operational planners continue to think about—if not actively plot—the next dramatic attack in the United States . . . [al-Qaeda] will attempt to replicate the 9/11 'model' . . . that cause unprecedented economic damage, mass casualties and physical destruction."

What this means is that there is a continuing belief at senior levels of the U.S. government that some terrorist groups, including al-Qaeda and as many as two dozen others, are inclined to use CBRN weapons, most likely against the United States. Only adding to the concern is that these groups may be receiving, or may receive, support in this wicked endeavor not only from rogue scientists, but from nation-states as well. The fact that the director of the DIA is concerned about states assisting terrorist organizations with acquiring WMD is of particular note and concern, since this is the easiest, shortest, and most direct route for terrorists to acquire and use WMD and radiological weapons.

In 1993, the Office of Technology Assessment, a congressional research arm, estimated that under the right atmospheric conditions, a plane dispersing as little as 220 pounds of anthrax over Washington, DC, could kill three million. So is it only a matter of time before the United States becomes a victim of a terrorist attack involving WMD or a dirty bomb? Is superterrorism the wave of the future? It could very well be, and we should be very concerned.

MOTIVATIONS FOR SUPERTERRORISM

Why would terrorists decide to use these super weapons? There are a number of reasons for them to look for opportunities to use WMD or radiological weapons. Chemical, biological, radiological, and nuclear weapons have some distinct advantages over other conventional weapons that terrorists might find appealing. Motivations for using these weapons as opposed to other types of weapons include: potential casualty rates, economic damage and recovery, and killing efficiency.

Experts believe that terrorists may seek to use CBRN weapons because of the evolving trend in modern terrorism to kill indiscriminately as many people as possible in the most horrific way imaginable in a single act of terror. We saw this in the 9/11 attacks. Many scholars have rightfully argued that since the 1980s, militant religion has replaced politics as the main motivation of terrorist groups. This has led some terrorist groups, such as al-Qaeda, to be less constrained by society's values and more willing to inflict greater levels of violence, including using CBRN weapons, than the more traditional, politically motivated terrorists of the past. For some of today's terrorist groups, the objective of their brand of terrorism is not to persuade the enemy to the group's viewpoint or garner attention to their cause, but to destroy the adversary altogether. Using a CBRN weapon, especially a nuclear device, has the potential to kill large numbers of victims in one fell swoop.

Because CBRN weapons could increase death and destruction multifold, it would be a very effective tool for bringing down an adversarial government. This is certainly the case in some areas of the world where the governments are on shaky ground already with their citizenry, such as Pakistan, Egypt, and Saudi Arabia. Moreover, according to the congressionally mandated Advisory Panel to Assess Domestic Response Capabilities for Terrorism Involving Weapons of Mass Destruction (Gilmore Commission), a superterrorism attack could also exhaust "the capabilities of local authorities rapidly, thus creating panic, instilling widespread fear, and likely undermining confidence in government—perhaps even deliberately provoking counterproductive governmental and law enforcement overreaction."[6] A WMD attack would spell serious trouble for any government, but especially a weak or democratic one, creating opportunities for the terrorists to bring down the government. Furthermore, the Gilmore Commission argues that these weapons have a significant psychological effect even if they may not create mass casualties or destruction. The use of a WMD would surely cause panic among the populace. In fact, some call radiological weapons, which are not WMD per se, "weapons of mass effect" because of the strong psychological impact a dirty bomb would have on the targeted populace. Once again the idea of terrorism is to cause fear in order to reach some sort of outcome desired by the perpetrators.

The result of a significant CBRN event, especially a nuclear or radiological incident, would have a tremendous effect on the economy of a target country, including causing a financial market crash, causing the loss of confidence in the economy, and bringing domestic and international commerce to a catastrophic stand-still. This was clearly an aim of al-Qaeda's 9/11 attacks on the World Trade Center in both 1993 and 2001. The explosion of nuclear weapons in Los Angeles, Chicago, Washington, or New York City would have a devastating effect on the nation's economy. The explosion of a dirty bomb on New York's Wall Street would bring America's—and the world's—financial markets to a grinding halt.

Some types of WMD are relatively inexpensive, but highly potent, making them cost effective weapons. They provide a good bang for the buck. For example, it costs at least $2,000 to decimate one square kilometer with conventional weapons, but only $800 with nuclear weapons, $600 with chemical weapons, and $1 with biological weapons.[7] In terms of potency, a baseball-sized container can hold ten quadrillion deadly bacteria.[8] In addition to low expense and high potency, some WMD are attractive because they can be easily and secretly produced and delivered. Biological weapons can be distributed through aerosol spraying, placed in powder form on the ground for the wind to disperse, dissolved in a food or water supply, or, as is well-known, mailed to an unsuspecting recipient in an envelope.

RESTRAINTS ON SUPERTERRORISM

Just as there are motivations for using CBRN weapons, so are there reasons for restraint on the part of a terrorist group. For instance, the anthrax attacks in the United States killed five people, far fewer than the September 11 attacks on the Pentagon and the World Trade Center did, which used commercial airplanes rather than CBRN. Similarly, the chemical nerve agent attack on the Tokyo subway in 1995 killed far fewer people than the 2005 car bombing at the Hilla medical clinic in Iraq that killed 125. Therefore, some experts have argued that conventional weapons, because of their "success" to date, are of greater concern than WMD. The major reasons that might dissuade terrorist groups from using WMD include: procurement challenges and targeting troubles.

The reason why terrorists would not use WMD is that they are difficult to obtain, especially nuclear weapons. The challenges involved in producing, or procuring, sufficient fissile material and assembling a functional weapon are significant. Basically, splitting the atom is not easy. Weapons-grade nuclear material must be mined, enriched, and meticulously weaponized before it will be able to produce a nuclear explosion. Nuclear weapons, unless used immediately, also need regular maintenance and may not have the appropriate safeguards incorporated into them, which makes them more dangerous to handle. Chemical and biological weapons are easier to produce, but all CBRN have inherent dangers in their handling and could harm the terrorists or other unintended targets even before they are delivered. Members of Aum Shinrikyo are believed to have acquired debilitating diseases from their handling of chemical weapons they produced.[9]

It is hard to be discriminating in your targeting with CBRN weapons. With a nuclear weapon, everyone in the vicinity is likely to be killed or injured. It is not a precise weapon. A nuclear strike could take out supporters or sympathizers as well as an enemy. The same is true with chemical or biological weapons. A terrorist could kill only the people in a hotel lobby with a chemical gas attack, but it is a harder to localize biological weapons. In this highly mobile, globalized world in which we live, it would be difficult to limit the spread of an infectious biological pathogen once it is released into the populace. Just think of how flu viruses spread across town, the country, or even the globe.

Depending on the terrorist's agenda, it might be impossible not to affect those you do not wish to attack. In Israel, for example, Muslim and Jewish populations are closely intermingled, especially in the occupied territories. A WMD attack would undoubtedly affect both groups, even though only one was the target. CBRN weapons may also be unattractive because of the potential long-lasting contamination of the landscape. For instance, would it make sense for a Palestinian group to contaminate with WMD the territory they hope to recover from the Israelis? The answer: Probably not.

Of course, these assumptions do not necessarily apply to all modern Muslim terrorist groups. The aims of these groups can extend beyond the symbolic to the annihilation of any and all perceived enemies. The fact that al-Qaeda has readily attacked Muslims in Saudi Arabia, Morocco, Tunisia, Afghanistan, Turkey, and Iraq, among other places, supports this notion. Would al-Qaeda think twice about using WMD in attacking the United

States, a country it wishes to destroy, but not occupy? The answer may be "no."

WMD ACQUISITION

Terrorist groups seeking WMD capability could develop their own weapons, as did Aum Shinrikyo; recruit unemployed or available WMD scientists; steal materials or weapons; or obtain WMD from a state sponsor. The quickest, most direct route is obviously obtaining WMD off-the-shelf from a state that already has a chemical, biological, or nuclear stockpile.

State Sponsors

Clearly, a terrorist organization could most easily obtain WMD with the help of an industrialized, scientifically advanced state sponsor, especially one with an active WMD program. A state might transfer these weapons to a terrorist organization for military or ideological purposes, allowing the terrorist group to act as a proxy belligerent against another state in much the same way that Iran and Syria attack Israel, using Hamas, Hezbollah, and Palestinian Islamic Jihad. A nation, such as impoverished North Korea, could also transfer weapons for financial reasons. Ballistic missiles already serve as North Korea's major source of foreign hard currency, and there is no reason to believe they could not sell WMD as well to the highest bidding terrorist group.

Though a direct transfer has significant advantages for the terrorist group, there are disadvantages for the states, including the possibility that the weapons may be used against the states themselves at some point. Today's friend could become tomorrow's enemy. The agenda of the terrorist group may change, putting the state in the cross hairs. Alliances shift. The terrorist group could also put the WMD in the hands of a potential enemy state. It is risky business to lose control of WMD.

Smuggling

Smuggling is another method by which a terrorist organization could obtain WMD or radiological weapons. As evidence that smuggling is widespread, the UN's International Atomic Energy Agency reveals that the number of confirmed attempts to smuggle radioactive materials worldwide has doubled over the last five years. Since 1993, 540 confirmed incidents have been recorded in the agency's illicit nuclear material trafficking database. Of these incidents, more than 180 involved nuclear materials; the remaining involved radioactive materials. Smuggling is not only used to move nuclear and radiological materials, it can occur in relation to chemical and biological materials, too.

The materials and equipment needed to produce WMD can be moved through middlemen, including black market arms brokers or organized crime syndicates who negotiate their purchase and shipment on behalf of a client. Orders can be documented with counterfeit paperwork, assisted by corrupt customs officials, routed though front companies masquerading as legitimate businesses and transshipped through several locations before reaching its final destination. To avoid detection, shipments are often routed through countries having lax import-export procedures and enforcement, especially in the Third World.

The demise of the Soviet Union makes its former, and current, WMD facilities and research laboratories particularly susceptible due to inadequate security, graft, and corruption. There have been eighteen seizures of stolen plutonium or highly enriched uranium over the past decade in Russia,[10] and terrorist groups have attempted to acquire nuclear weapons, materials, and expertise as well.[11] There is even concern in the United States about the availability of dangerous material, especially radiological materials from medical waste.

Rogue Scientists

States often pay high wages or provide significant benefits to their WMD scientists because of their highly specialized skills. Some even achieve national hero status, such as A. Q. Khan, father of the Pakistani bomb. These same people, whether a national hero or not, could be persuaded to help others, including terrorist groups, develop or produce WMD or radiological weapons. Kahn sold nuclear information to Iran, North Korea, and Libya for millions of dollars. In the cases of Iran, Khan reportedly provided nuclear secrets to Tehran out of the belief that they had a religious duty to supply Muslim states with nuclear weapons to prevent U.S. dominance in the Middle East. There is a market for the unemployed WMD scientists, such as those displaced from their jobs in the Soviet military-industrial complex precipitated by the end fall of the Soviet Union. For example, it is likely that Russian scientists aided North Korea in its nuclear weapons program. Al-Qaeda reportedly approached Russian nuclear scientists in the 1990s. A terrorist group with financial means such as al-Qaeda could conceivably employ these scientists. Kofi Annan, United Nations Secretary-General, summed it up well at the March 2005 Club of Madrid conference on terrorism: "We live in a world of excess hazardous material and abundant technological know-how, in which some terrorists clearly state their intention to inflict catastrophic casualties."

A TERRORIST NUCLEAR STRIKE

The easiest way for a terrorist to procure a nuclear weapon is to buy or steal one. Once the weapon is in the terrorist's hands, it would have to be moved to the intended target's location. In the case of the United States, it might be moved by merchant ship or airplane into the United States, or it could be trucked over the border in an eighteen-wheeler from Canada or Mexico. If it were moved to the United States by ship, it might be detonated in the port of a large, densely populated city. The weapon could also be unloaded from the ship, trucked to another large urban area, and then detonated.

A radiological attack is perhaps the most likely scenario. This is primarily because radiological materials for a dirty bomb can readily be found in hospitals, industries, and research institutions.[12] While nuclear materials have a rather regimented accounting system in general, there is no concept of the amount of radiological material available worldwide. The situation suffers further from inadequate global regulation regarding the disposal, import, and export of these materials, which are commonly used in medical and industrial processes.

The availability of these materials makes it likely that terrorists will use this weapon before a weapon of mass destruction. A radiological scenario would be similar to a terrorist attack involving conventional explosives. A terrorist carrying it on their person, in a car, or a truck, would deliver a radiological weapon to its designated target. The explosion would seem quite ordinary in terms of blast and shock wave with the exception that poisonous radiological materials would be spread to the environment and people present.

An alternative to detonating a nuclear weapon or dirty bomb is attacking a nuclear power plant. A taped interview of Osama bin Laden in September 2002 on the Arab television station al Jazeera indicates that al-Qaeda planned to attack a nuclear plant as part of its 9/11 attack. Nuclear power plants and spent fuel storage facilities remain tempting targets for terrorists due to the large-scale damage possible from the release of radioactive material into the atmosphere, not to mention the psychological trauma it would sow among the public. Nuclear reactor facilities are in general physically well protected. Therefore, only attacks that apply massive energy to the plant's structure or allow terrorists into the control rooms have a chance of being successful.

For example, an attack using a large passenger aircraft could cause enough damage to a nuclear power plant to cause the drainage of the thousands of gallons of coolant used for the reactor's nuclear core, or spent fuel, resulting in a massive fire and the release of large amounts of radioactive effluent into the atmosphere. Nuclear power plants in the United States are not required by the Nuclear Regulatory Commission to defend against air attacks. It would also be possible to cause a reactor or spent fuel "meltdown" by using an "insider," who would allow terrorists access to a secured area to carry out radiological sabotage.

CHEMICAL TERRORISM

In a chemical weapon scenario, these weapons would likely be deployed in an enclosed, densely populated area such as a movie theater, subway system, train, airplane, or bus. An airplane would be ideal because the air is not filtered or circulated with outside air. It is merely recirculated within the airplane's cabin, meaning the agent would be continuously circulated. Chemical weapons, especially poisons, could also be introduced into a food supply or water system.

Al-Qaeda operatives such as Zacarias Moussaoui made inquiries, before he was arrested, regarding the rental of crop dusters, which could be used with chemical or biological weapons.[13]

Al-Qaeda has also expressed interest in attacking critical infrastructure targets such as chemical plants. Attacking a chemical plant obviates the need to produce, transport, or weaponize a CW. Instead, a terrorist group could attack a chemical plant, spewing toxins into the air, soil, or water. A successful attack could result in severe damage to the surrounding population and the environment as exemplified by the 1984 leak of methyl isocyanate from a Union Carbide factory in Bhopal, India. Long considered the world's worst industrial accident, the deadly gas, which leaked from the American chemical plant, killed over 2,000 people and injured over

200,000 in the vicinity. In the United States alone, there are 66,000 chemical plants. The Department of Homeland Security (DHS), in its 2005 National Planning Scenario report, estimates that blowing up a large, liquid chlorine tank could kill 17,000 and injure more than 100,000 under the right conditions in a highly populated area.

BIOWEAPON ATTACK

Biological weapons are living organisms and, therefore, are mobile and can travel great distances with their host, possibly infecting others along the way. Once again, a highly populated enclosed area would be an ideal deployment point for a biological weapons terrorist attack. An airport, a bus station, a train station, a shopping mall, or a sporting event would be perfect because of the high concentration of people and the possibility that these people would unwittingly carry away the pathogens from the point of attack, possibly infecting others. Arguably, a terrorist's use of spray aerosol devices for disseminating biological warfare agents has the highest potential impact.

In a major metropolitan area this could lead to a major contagion, especially in a highly mobile society such as the United States. The 2002–2003 SARS outbreak in Asia is instructive. As a result of the epidemic that originated with a single person in southern China, there were 916 deaths in 8,422 reported cases in 30 countries, according to the UN's World Health Organization. In 2005 in Angola, an outbreak of Marburg hemorrhagic fever killed over 200. An Ebola-like pathogen, there is no vaccine or cure for Marburg. A virulent, highly contagious, and often deadly strain of airborne pneumonic plague broke out in Congo in 2005, potentially affecting thousands. A BW agent spread in a highly mobile society could easily have the same effect. In its 2005 National Planning Scenario document, DHS speculated that spreading pneumonic plague in the bathrooms of an airport, a sports arena, and a train station could kill 2,500 and sicken 8,000 worldwide.

The problem with a biological weapon attack is that it may initially look like an everyday epidemic, such as the flu, before the true nature of the outbreak is discovered. In the case of anthrax, it may take as long as six days before symptoms become apparent. The challenge for the health surveillance system, including doctors, clinics, hospitals, and national health institutes, is to determine whether the outbreak is a natural outbreak of the flu or another epidemic as quickly as possible. By the time this determination is made, the terrorists may have long fled the scene and the pathogen may well be on its way to the four corners of the country—and the planet. Several biological pathogens, including anthrax, botulinum toxin, ricin, and smallpox, are considered to be the ones most likely to be used by terrorist organizations according to experts. Besides a nuclear weapon, DHS sees an anthrax attack as one of the most devastating. In one possible scenario, an estimated 350,000 people could be exposed to anthrax by terrorists spraying it from a truck driving through five cities in two weeks, ultimately killing 13,000 people.

The potential consequences from any CBRN attack are quite serious. The probability of the use of WMD by a state against the United States is more predictable and less likely today than the likelihood of a superterrorism attack. The American diplomatic, defense, and intelligence agencies are better equipped to predict, deter, or defend against the use of WMD by a state actor than by a terrorist organization. Billions of dollars were spent during the Cold War to deal with the state-driven WMD threat; now appropriate sums must be spent to deal with the terrorist CBRN threat.

Since the use of CBRN by terrorist groups has been quite limited, the motivations and likelihood of terrorists using WMD are not fully understood and, therefore, are more difficult to predict. But the rules of the game have clearly changed. The conventional theory that held for many years was that terrorists were unlikely to use WMD because large numbers of casualties were unnecessary to convey their message. This notion is passé today. It was previously held as "gospel" that mass-casualty attacks would result in the loss of approval and support for the group that the terrorists claimed to represent. This may no longer be true as terrorists look to destroy rather than influence their enemies across international borders. Using WMD as an act of desperation cannot be ruled out either.

While the terrorist's use of nuclear, chemical, biological, and radiological weapons has been scant to date compared to conventional weapons, such as bombings, the growth of the militant fundamentalist terrorist movement combined with the greater availability of the knowledge and means of producing WMD, and the evidence of terrorist group interest in these weapons of mass terror, makes superterrorism attacks a likely possibility.[14]

Former secretary of state Colin Powell said in winter 2004 that the nexus of terrorists and weapons of mass destruction was a new and unique threat, which "comes not with ships and fighters and tanks and divisions, but clandestinely, in the dark of the night."[15] He is right. The threat of superterrorism is real and the consequences of such a threat are so devastating that no U.S. president, or the American people, can afford to ignore the possibility.

NOTES

1. Jess Altschul, "Nuclear Smuggling, a First Step to Nuclear Terrorism," JINSA Online, www.jinsa.org (accessed on April 3, 2004).

2. Terrorist CBRN: Material and Effects, www.cia.gov/cia/reports/terrorist _cbrn/terrorist_CBRN.htm#02 (accessed on February 15, 2004).

3. Central Intelligence Agency, "The Worldwide Threat 2004: Challenges in a Changing Global Context," testimony of Director of Central Intelligence George J. Tenet before the Senate Select Committee on Intelligence, February 24, 2004, www.cia.gov (accessed March 3, 2004), p. 4.

4. Defense Intelligence Agency, "Current and Projected National Security Threats to the United States," Statement for the Record by Vice Admiral Lowell E. Jacoby, U.S. Navy, director, Defense Intelligence Agency, before the Senate Select Committee on Intelligence, February 24, 2004, www.dia.mil (accessed March 3, 2004).

5. Steven Gutkin, "Terrorists Pursuing WMD Capability," Associated Press, February 9, 2004.

6. Advisory Panel to Assess Domestic Response Capabilities for Terrorism Involving Weapons of Mass Destruction [Gilmore Commission], "First Annual Report for the President and the Congress," vol. I, *Assessing the Threat* (Washington, DC: RAND, December 15, 1999), p. 19.

7. Arizona Department of Health Services, "Arizona Department of Health Services: Epidemiology and Surveillance," Definition of Bioterrorism, updated May 5, 2001, www.hs.state.az.us/phs/edc/edrp/es/bthistor1.htm (accessed February 4, 2004).

8. Kathleen C. Bailey, *Doomsday Weapons in the Hands of Many: The Arms Control Challenge of the '90s* (Chicago: University of Illinois Press), pp. 84–90.

9. Jonathan Tucker, *Toxic Terror: Assessing Terrorist Use of Chemical and Biological Weapons*, CNS, Monterey Institute, p. 7.

10. IAEA's Database on Illicit Trafficking of Nuclear and Other Radioactive Materials, "Incidents with Nuclear Material," www-nds.iaea.org/ (accessed January 4, 2004).

11. M. Bunn, A. Weir, and J. P. Holdren, "Controlling Nuclear Warheads and Materials: A Report Card and Action Plan," Belfer Center for Science and International Affairs and commissioned by the Nuclear Threat Initiative, March 2003.

12. Joby Warrick, "Commercial Devices Could Fuel 'Dirty Bombs,'" *Washington Post*, January 16, 2003, p. A14.

13. Judith Miller, "U.S. Has New Concerns about Anthrax Readiness," *New York Times*, December 28, 2003.

14. Audrey Kurth Cronin, "Terrorist Motivations for Chemical and Biological Weapons Use: Placing the Threat in Context," CRS Report RL31831, March 28, 2004, p. 3.

15. Anwar Iqbal, "Powell: Criminalize Nuclear Proliferation," United Press International, March 4, 2004.

13

PREVENTING PROLIFERATION

There is a consensus among nations that proliferation cannot be tolerated. Yet this consensus means little unless it is translated into action.
Every civilized nation has a stake in preventing the spread of weapons
of mass destruction.

—President George W. Bush, February 11, 2004,
National Defense University, Washington, DC

He parked his car below the Waterloo Bridge and climbed the stairs to the
bus line. As Markov neared the bus stop, he felt a sharp pain on the back of
his right thigh. Turning around, Markov saw a man bending over to pick
up an umbrella. He paid little attention and continued on his way to his
London broadcasting job. Although, he was in significant pain, he ignored
it. Three days later, the forty-nine-year-old Markov died in agony in a London hospital of unknown causes. Georgi Markov was no common man. A
prize-winning novelist and playwright, he was arguably Bulgaria's most
famous Cold War dissident. Markov fled Bulgaria in 1969 after a friend
warned him that his latest work, a play entitled "The Man Who Was Me,"
did not sit too well with Bulgaria's communist government. Five years later,
Bulgarian authorities tried him in absentia, sentenced Markov to prison,
and banned his best-selling books. Finally, settling in London, Markov
became an outspoken critic of Bulgaria's communist dictator, Todor Zhivkov, on the BBC's World Service and Radio Free Europe. His words, sent
by shortwave signals into his native Bulgaria, inspired a dissident movement. Not one for taking biting criticism, in July 1977, Bulgaria's strong-

man, Zhivkov, signed a decree proclaiming that any and all measures could be used to deal with pesky émigrés, such as Markov. After two ham-handed assassination attempts on Markov in Germany and Italy, Bulgaria's secret service finally succeeded in September 1978. It took four months for the London coroner to conclude that Markov had been assassinated by 0.45 grams of ricin carried in a small, ball bearings–sized shot from the tip of a Bulgarian agent's umbrella.

THE CHALLENGE OF PROLIFERATION

With the fall of the Soviet Union and the end of the Cold War, America unexpectedly emerged as the world's lone superpower. It continued its ascendance to become history's most powerful nation. As a result, terrorists and rogue states have increasingly sought to obtain even more powerful weapons, including weapons of mass destruction (WMD) and ballistic missiles, to offset—or destroy—America's unparalleled diplomatic, economic, and military might. This has led rogue states and terrorist organizations to no longer consider WMD as weapons of last resort, creating a far more complex and perilous international security environment for all concerned.

In response to these new frightening potentialities, the United States must combat WMD, radiological weapons, and ballistic missile proliferation through not only relying on existing international arms control nonproliferation treaties and regimes, but also taking a more proactive stance through military means and countering proliferation activity in ways not done before. A failure to resolutely address the nonproliferation issue could allow the world's most dangerous weapons to fall into, or remain in, the hands of the world's most despicable regimes and terrorist groups. This could mean future unspeakable tragedies for American military forces overseas and innocent American civilians here at home.

THE PROBLEMS WITH NONPROLIFERATION TREATIES

Nothing is perfect, but this is especially true when it comes to the United Nation's nonproliferation treaties: the Nuclear Nonproliferation Treaty (NPT),[1] the Chemical Weapons Convention (CWC),[2] and the Biological Weapons Convention (BWC).[3] These international nonproliferation accords have shortcomings that undermine their well-intentioned purpose of checking the spread of weapons of mass destruction. Participation in these global agreements is completely voluntary, and there are rarely penalties for noncompliance. The arms control treaties rely on the goodwill and "sound" nonproliferation judgment of the countries that sign them. But the hope that countries will do what is in the best interest of other countries at the expense of what they perceive as their own national interest is often shortsighted and naive. Not surprisingly, countries usually do what is in their own best interest regardless of how it affects others in the international community. In most cases, a nation's sense of international goodwill ends at its own international border.

Another fundamental problem with controlling the spread of WMD is that its preferred delivery method, the ballistic missile, is not prohibited by any international treaty. This makes both WMD and missiles attractive weapons to those who would blackmail, compel, or do us harm. There are other problems with today's UN nonproliferation agreements. Many states, which are party to the international arms control treaties, have yet to fully implement their obligations under these regimes. For instance, some countries, especially poorer ones, are not able to enforce the treaties due to a lack of financial, military, or law enforcement resources.

Accordingly, terrorists and international criminal organizations are becoming increasingly adept at moving WMD contraband through regions with weak governmental controls, such as Southeast Asia, Central Asia, and some of the states of the former Soviet Union. For instance, the centrifuge parts used for enriching uranium intended for Libya's now dismantled nuclear program were manufactured in Malaysia, but were interdicted while being smuggled aboard a merchant vessel making port in Italy. There have also been numerous confirmed reports of radioactive materials being smuggled out of the former Soviet Union in suitcases, car trunks, and, in one case, the pockets of a man's pants. The drug smuggling routes of Central Asia for moving Afghan opium to Russia, especially through Tajikistan, would be idea for smuggling fissile material as well.

Another troubling issue is that current international law does not grant states the right to interdict WMD or missiles in international territory, namely, international airspace and on the high seas. Contraband, which violates national laws, may be seized in sovereign territory such as was done in the Libyan case, but that does not apply to international territory, limiting the ability of the international community to prevent the movement of WMD or WMD materials. Of course, the interdiction of WMD shipments in international territory may be the only method of preventing their delivery.

Verifying regime compliance is another troubling matter. Unlike the CWC, the BWC has no challenge inspection procedures to verify that nations are complying with the treaty. Compliance is completely up to the judgment of each member country. Even with intrusive inspections, any country with even a simple chemical or biotechnology industry could make chemical or biological weapons with limited efforts at concealment. Many industrial processes, such as brewing, used for peaceful purposes can also be employed for weapons production. Because of the dual nature of many chemical and biological materials and technology, it is often difficult to determine whether the transfer of particular materials or technology should be of concern or not, or whether a facility is being used for civilian or military purposes. For instance, an offensive BW program for military purposes would look similar to a defensive BW program used for preventive civilian medical research on the pathogen.

States can also withdraw from these regimes without penalty. Some have done so. North Korea threatened to withdraw from the NPT in 1993 and then actually withdrew in early 2003 after giving the required ninety days' notice. In essence, once withdrawn, a country—without penalty—is no longer required to abide by the treaty. Other countries have simply not joined the arms control treaty. Nuclear weapons states India, Pakistan, and Israel never signed the NPT. Yet others join the treaty, but ignore—or are suspected of ignoring—their restrictions, such as is the case of Iran with the NPT and Syria with the CWC. Another problem is that the cooperation of many strategic states, namely, Russia and China, is vital to the success of arms control treaties and regimes. However, while these states have agreed to control proliferation publicly, they are still considered by American intelligence to be key suppliers of WMD-related materials and technology to countries of concern.

Some of the treaties are not restrictive enough and rife with loopholes. The NPT, for example, allows access to "peaceful" nuclear technology for civilian nuclear power. But in doing so, it allows a country to do almost everything required—all within the bounds of the treaty—to become a nuclear weapons state. This was not the purpose of the NPT. As some states have interpreted the NPT, countries can acquire materials and technologies that bring them to the edge of nuclear weapons statehood without violating the treaty. The Iranian case is instructive. Iran claims it is developing a peaceful, civilian nuclear power capability. Though unlikely, this may be so. Nevertheless, Iran's enrichment of uranium for a civilian nuclear power reactor fuel also will aid Iran in developing and producing nuclear weapons if it should decide to do so.

In all fairness to arms control advocates and aficionados, some nonproliferation treaties have, undoubtedly, played a role in a country's decision to pursue WMD or not. The NPT, in fact, may have actually dissuaded a few states from pursuing nuclear weapons or, even, encouraged the dismantlement of a nuclear weapons program, such as the South African nuclear weapons program in the early 1990s. But it is also fair to say that other reasons such as domestic politics, expense, or a changing security environment weighed more heavily in the decision-making process than concern over contravening an international arms control treaty. Once again, states tend to do what is in their best interest, not what is in the best of the international community—unless they happen to be coincidental.

The ideal end state for American nonproliferation policy is to prevent the spread of WMD and missiles to rogue states and terrorist groups and even roll back troublesome programs in places such as Iran, North Korea, and Syria. Despite the good intentions of the UN's nonproliferation treaties, these agreements need to be strengthened to remain relevant in preventing today's proliferation. Fortunately, there are things that can—and should—be done to stem proliferation and, if necessary, defend against it.

CONTINUE DEPLOYING BALLISTIC MISSILE DEFENSES

One of the reasons that WMD is so frightening is that there is no defense against its delivery by ballistic missiles, especially long-range missiles capable of striking the United States. Contrary to the belief of many Americans, the United States does not currently have a shield against ballistic missiles. Regrettably, should an intercontinental ballistic missile come our way, the only thing that can be done now is "duck and cover." The good news is that we are working on developing a missile defense, and significant progress has been made under the Bush administration. Since 1999, ten missile defense flights have taken place. Today, a rudimentary missile defense system is being installed at Fort Greely, Alaska, and Vandenberg Air Force Base, California, that will defend against a limited attack.

Missile defense has been controversial. Some argue that deploying missile defenses will spur an arms race that will cause potential nuclear adversaries such as China or Russia to do things inherently destabilizing to overcome the new defensive system. Others have argued that it is technologically impossible to defend against certain types of missiles or that such a system would be prohibitively expensive. But the fact is that modern technology is advancing at such an incredibly rapid rate that in the near future it will be possible to do the equivalent of hitting a bullet with a bullet in space. There is no sense in holding ourselves deliberately vulnerable to those, such as North Korea and Iran, or, even, China, that might want to coerce, compel, or blackmail us with WMD and ballistic missiles, if there is an alternative. Missile defense at home and for our troops overseas is one such choice.

Deploying missile defenses would give us a greater range of policy options than just massive retaliation. It would be much better to destroy a rogue state's nuclear-tipped ballistic missile over the ocean than seeing an American city devastated, potentially beginning a nuclear Armageddon. The Cold War strategic paradigm of mutually assured destruction, widely known as MAD, is anachronistic in an age where technology is changing so rapidly that the computer you bought six months ago is already out of date. Technology will be our friend in making missile defenses a reality. In fact, developing a defense against WMD and missiles might dissuade some from pursuing them at all. Lastly, our defense against ballistic missiles must also be extended to defense against cruise missiles.

EXPAND THE PROLIFERATION SECURITY INITIATIVE

Stronger steps need to be taken to counter the spread of WMD and ballistic missiles since nonproliferation regimes do not seem to be an entirely effective prophylactic against proliferation. In May 2003, in Krakow, Poland, the United States and ten other countries—Australia, France, Germany, Italy, Japan, the Netherlands, Poland, Portugal, Spain, and the United Kingdom—rolled out the Proliferation Security Initiative (PSI). The purpose of the new program is to actively counter the proliferation of WMD, ballistic missiles, and related materials between states and to terrorist groups.[4]

The PSI is a growing international partnership, which uses participating nations' own domestic laws to interdict shipments of dangerous technologies and materials at sea, in the air, and on land. For instance, at their own initiative, or at the request of another state, a country's law enforcement or military forces might board and search a vessel located in their internal waters or territorial seas if that vessel is reasonably suspected of transporting WMD or missile contraband. That country may also give others the right to inspect a ship flying under its flag outside of its territorial waters (i.e., twelve miles from shore). A transiting aircraft could also be searched or denied overflight rights if suspected of carrying WMD or missile cargos.

For example, in fall 2003, PSI partners worked together to seize centrifuge equipment for enriching uranium aboard a German-owned ship bound for Libya, making a port call in Italy. Since the ship was in an Italian port, it was subject to search and seizure under Italian national law. (In this case, the German ship owner also gave permission for the Italians to search the vessel.) The PSI requires beefed-up intelligence and law enforcement cooperation, improved export control efforts, expanded use of national sovereignty and laws, and broad agreement on the definition of WMD and missile contraband. The PSI will reinforce, not replace, other nonproliferation mechanisms and is fully consistent with relevant international law and frameworks. The PSI seeks to involve, in some capacity, as many countries as possible. The more countries that participate, the more effective the PSI will be. There are currently over sixty countries involved in the PSI.

As a result, there will be fewer places for proliferators to hide their contraband while it is in transit. The increasingly aggressive efforts by proliferators to circumvent existing nonproliferation treaties require new and stronger actions by the international community. New cooperative, coordinated efforts by PSI-participating countries will give added strength to nonproliferation regimes while helping to address an increasingly important challenge to international security. A National Nonproliferation Center made up of proliferation intelligence analysts should be constituted to support policy-makers and the PSI.

CRIMINALIZE WMD PROLIFERATION

Since there are no real penalties in many countries for companies or individuals that proliferate WMD, for all practical purposes, there is no significant disincentive for not engaging in proliferation, especially if money can be made. This needs to change if we are going to meet the proliferation challenge. WMD proliferation activity should be broadly criminalized. The operative phrase is "broadly," because if it is not done widely, smugglers and proliferators will continue to find and exploit the cracks in the international nonproliferation system. For example, if China and Pakistan do not agree to outlaw proliferation, North Korea could potentially send WMD materials to Iran across Chinese and Pakistani territory. The fact that China and Pakistan border each other and, they, in turn, border North Korea and Iran, provides the proliferators with a seamless air or land bridge across which to transfer WMD and missiles.

To accomplish this, domestic laws and nonproliferation treaties must be strengthened, including seeking all UN states and authorities such as Hong Kong and Macau to criminalize WMD proliferation. States would have to enact strict export controls on WMD-related materials and equipment and secure sensitive radiological materials that may be available at industrial or research sites. Broadening the domain of the Nuclear Suppliers Group for nuclear weapons and the Australia Group for chemical and biological weapons would also help to suture up the proliferation problem. Working to establish and enforce consequences of noncompliance with broadly agreed to international nonproliferation standards is critical to reining in this dangerous trend. The international community should look closely at putting some "teeth" in international nonproliferation regimes by imposing economic sanctions on countries which violate the arms control treaties. The UN's 2005 passage of the Convention on the Suppression of Acts of Nuclear Terrorism is a positive step. It criminalizes the possession of radioactive materials or devices; requires nations to prosecute or extradite those who threaten others while in the possession of such materials; and encourages cooperation among countries on these issues. It is expected to be open for ratification in September 2005.

EXPAND COOPERATIVE THREAT REDUCTION

The most direct way of acquiring WMD, missiles, or radioactive material is to buy it "off the shelf." If you can procure it already fabricated, there is no need to build complex laboratories or gather materials—it is ready to go. So controlling preexisting weaponry is critical. To this end, it makes sense expanding the 1991 Nunn-Lugar Cooperative Threat Reduction (CTR) programs (named after former senator Sam Nunn and current senator Dick Lugar) that finance the elimination or securing of nuclear, chemical, and biological weapons and radioactive materials in the former Soviet Union.[5]

As a consequence of the collapse of the Soviet Union in 1991, in theory, a veritable supermarket of WMD, missiles, and related technology and materials became available to rogue nations and terrorists. The goal of Nunn-Lugar is to lessen the threat posed by weapons of mass destruction and ballistic missiles by deactivating and destroying these weapons, and helping the scientists formerly engaged in research, development, and production of these weapons to remain gainfully employed in work other than WMD or missiles.

Since it inception, the Nunn-Lugar CTR program has deactivated over 6,500 Soviet nuclear warheads and destroyed over 500 ballistic missiles; over 400 ballistic missile silos; over 100 bombers; over 500 submarine-launched missiles; over 400 submarine missile launchers; and over 20 strategic missile submarines. In addition, more than 50,000 former Soviet Union scientists previously employed in WMD programs have been reemployed in other jobs.

The CTR program also removed all of the nuclear weapons from Ukraine, Kazakhstan, and Belarus. When the Soviet Union crumbled, these nations had the third, fourth, and eighth largest nuclear arsenals in the world, meaning Ukraine and Kazakhstan had bigger nuclear arsenals than France, Britain, and China. Other Nunn-Lugar successes include: the 1994 Project Sapphire, which removed 600 kilograms (enough for tens of nuclear weapons) of highly enriched uranium (HEU) from Kazakhstan; and the 1998 Operation Auburn Endeavor that removed eight kilograms of HEU from the former Soviet republic of Georgia.

More still needs to be done. Millions of chemical weapons filled with sarin and VX nerve gas need to be destroyed in Russia. Some shells of the forty-thousand-ton stockpile are small enough to be smuggled out of these facilities in a large briefcase. There are additional concerns about the transparency of Russia's CW program, too. The Russians are not giving access to at least four of their major military biological warfare institutes. Moreover, the activities and the level of security at these sites are unclear. Not all facilities housing nuclear materials in Russia have received security improvements. In addition, as much as 340 tons of Russian fissile material needs to be disposed of or stored securely. At least 70 Russian warhead sites need more protection, and 134 tons of plutonium are not covered by the Nunn-Lugar agreement. Expanding the Nunn-Lugar program in Russia, and in other countries, would further enhance the safety and security of these dangerous weapons. The United States should look to others such as the advanced industrial G-8 countries (i.e., France, Russia, Germany,

Italy Japan, Britain, and Canada) and other international institutions such as the UN to shoulder the load with the United States in accomplishing this important objective. Moscow currently refuses to discuss the subject, but, in addition, the unknown number of Russian tactical nuclear weapons should be brought into the program, too.

CLOSE NPT LOOPHOLES

An agreement cannot be effective if it is full of loopholes. Currently, the NPT allows states such as Iran to produce nuclear material that could be used to build bombs under the cover of a civilian nuclear power program. NPT adherents have the right to pursue peaceful nuclear energy as long as they do not cross over the line into developing nuclear weapons. The problem is that the line between a civilian nuclear power program and a military nuclear weapons program is a very thin one. The nuclear fuel rods used in a civilian nuclear energy program can be reprocessed into fissile material for nuclear weapons.

The point is that, with a finite supply of fossil fuel available and skyrocketing demand in places like India and China, the world must create a system that allows for the fueling of civilian nuclear reactors for the production of energy without increasing the danger of nuclear proliferation. One way of accomplishing this is to ensure that states, which may be pursuing nuclear weapons programs, are not sold nuclear fuel for their reactors or any technology or equipment that can be used to enrich uranium or reprocess plutonium into fissile material for nuclear weapons. In addition, fullscope safeguards must be implemented, and any spent reactor fuel must be returned to the provider. This measure would make it more difficult for countries to develop nuclear weapons under the auspices of a civilian nuclear energy program. In truth, access to legitimate nuclear power technology can be accomplished while limiting the availability of most weapons-related technologies if the international community is willing to work together to closely monitor supply and demand.

EMPOWER THE IAEA

The International Atomic Energy Agency (IAEA) is the UN's nuclear watchdog.[6] Their job is to ensure that the tenets of the NPT are upheld through the monitoring and inspections of the nuclear programs at over 900 facilities in over 140 states. As an international body without any real authority, the IAEA is only as strong as the international community allows it to be. The mission of the nuclear agency is an important one and there are measures that can be taken to strengthen the IAEA's international non-proliferation role.

The international community should support universalizing a more intrusive inspection regime for the IAEA called the Additional Protocol. This new, tougher inspection agreement greatly expands the agency's ability to uncover covert nuclear weapons programs and is a significant step toward exposing NPT "cheaters." The Additional Protocol's essence is the reshaping of the IAEA's safeguards regime from a system focused on accounting for known materials and monitoring declared activities to a system aimed at gathering a more comprehensive picture of a state's nuclear activities. The fundamental shift is from one of accounting for the known to one of uncovering the unknown.

The Additional Protocol improves the IAEA's ability to check for covert nuclear weapon programs and facilities by providing the agency with the additional authority from individual states to poke around their nuclear facilities to see if everything is on the up and up. The Additional Protocol will require NPT states to provide more detailed information about their nuclear programs than before, while allowing inspectors to visit more nuclear–related facilities on "short-notice" visits. "No-notice" visits would obviously be better, especially for countries, such as Iran, where unsanctioned activities are suspected. Lastly, the Additional Protocol gives the agency the right to conduct environmental sampling (e.g., air, water, and soil samples) at sites where tell-tale nuclear particulate might be found, such as downwind from a nuclear facility or in the discharge water downstream from a plant. Currently, NPT members are not required to sign the Additional Protocol, although the IAEA is urging all to do so. The international community should insist that all states sign the accord, but especially countries seeking equipment, technology, materials, and assistance for their "peaceful" nuclear power programs.

Moreover, creating a special committee on the IAEA board of governors to focus on safeguards and treaty verification and compliance will focus the organization's efforts squarely on the issue of nonproliferation as opposed to spreading peaceful nuclear activity cooperation—where it placed its emphasis in recent years. Lastly, countries that are suspected of violating the NPT should be banned from serving on the IAEA's Board of Governors.

CONTROL THE MISSILE TRADE

The proliferation of ballistic missiles and related technologies, materials, and expertise pose increasingly greater risks to American interests as emerging missile states develop more accurate, more capable vehicles. Despite the broad scope of WMD treaties, there is no international treaty limiting the proliferation of ballistic missiles. The current multilateral instrument is the Missile Technology Control Regime (MTCR), which is a group of over thirty nations that voluntarily adhere to a set of principles regarding the transfer of WMD-capable missiles and missile technology. Although the MTCR has had some successes, it has not halted missile proliferation. Countries, such as North Korea (nonmember), China (nonmember), and Russia (member) continue to flout the MTCR's principles for hard currency, technical assistance with military programs, and strategic influence.

Since ballistic missiles are one of the preferred methods of delivering WMD, it is important to limit their proliferation. Reining in the missile trade may undermine the desire of countries to acquire WMD, although ballistic missiles can be very effective with conventional high explosive warheads as well. Unfortunately, checking the missile trade is not easy because there is no international consensus for doing so. The missile trade generates revenue and earns political goodwill for the purveyors. Since the MTCR offers no monetary or other incentives for accepting its guidelines, membership may be financially detrimental to countries that have invested in expensive missile development programs only to find themselves unable to export missile-related equipment and technology.

Limiting missiles is also controversial because any effort to do so is perceived as discriminatory by states that do not have missiles themselves. By definition, any agreement to limit missiles by the missile "haves" discriminates against the missile "have-nots." To satisfy the "have-nots," missiles would have to be eliminated as a class of weapon. Since it is a conventional weapon, an important element of modern conventional warfare, and not a WMD, agreement to eliminate ballistic missiles is unlikely to happen.

Perhaps more promising than eliminating missiles is the 2002 International Code of Conduct against Ballistic Missile Proliferation (ICOC). Its over one hundred members have recognized the threat presented by the proliferation of ballistic missiles and has decided to take action. The ICOC tries to reduce the supply of, and demand for, missiles worldwide by encouraging openness and restraint in developing, testing, and deploying these weapons. Once again this agreement is a political document and is not legally binding upon the members, but the significantly larger membership over the MTCR shows promise. The ICOC should be expanded to include major missile proliferators, such as China and North Korea, portable surface-to-air missiles, cruise missiles, and technology for space-launch vehicles, which are often interchangeable with long-range ballistic missile technology. In the absence of a broad agreement, especially on portable surface-to-air missiles, bilateral agreements such as the 2005 U.S.-Russia agreement should be concluded.

Following conventional terrorism, the most serious and direct threat to American national security comes from the possibility of being attacked at home or abroad by WMD in the hands of rogue regimes or terrorists. Regrettably, current international efforts to stall the proliferation of WMD, radioactive materials, and ballistic missiles, though well-intentioned, are falling short of the mark. These endeavors need to be revised, strengthened, and supplemented by such measures as the PSI in order to meet the challenges of the new international security environment.

In addition, more needs to be done to move the current nonproliferation treaties away from relying only on the international goodwill and self-restraint of individual states. They should move toward multilateral instruments, which take consequential action against violators in concert with other like-minded nations. But while pursuing these objectives, the United States cannot hope that any piece of paper in the form of a nonproliferation agreement will provide the security necessary to thwart potential attacks. Therefore, America must also maintain an active defense posture, including the development of missile defenses. A combination of international diplomacy, counterproliferation, and active defense measures are the best bet for handling today's proliferation threat.

NOTES

1. See www.state.gov/t/np/trty/16281.htm.
2. See www.cwc.gov/.
3. See www.state.gov/t/ac/trt/4718.htm.
4. See www.state.gov/t/np/c10390.htm.
5. See www.nunn-lugar.com/.
6. See www.iaea.org/.

14

IRAN: MULLAHS OF MAYHEM

Our goal is to prevent regimes that sponsor terror from threatening America or our friends and allies with weapons of mass destruction. North Korea is a regime arming with missiles and weapons of mass destruction, while starving its citizens. Iran aggressively pursues these weapons and exports terror, while an unelected few repress the Iranian people's hope for freedom. States like these, and their terrorist allies, constitute an axis of evil, arming to threaten the peace of the world.

—President George W. Bush, State of the
Union Address, January 29, 2002

Some consider the fiery cleric to be the inspiration of modern Islamic terrorism, but he is probably best known as the father of the 1979 Iranian Revolution and the face of Islamic fundamentalism and extremism. Reported to have memorized the entire Koran by the age of six, Ruhollah Khomeini quickly rose to become an Islamic scholar and a high-ranking ayatollah (a senior Islamic cleric, meaning "gift of Allah"). But Khomeini did not come to prominence until the early 1960s, when the Shah of Iran, Reza Pahlavi, introduced the "White Revolution," in which he sought to modernize the Persian nation. He introduced equal rights for women, land reform, and secular education. Some of the reforms undermined the power of the mullahs (religious leaders). This did not sit well with Khomeini, who attacked the Shah's policies from his seminary in Iran's spiritual center, Qom. The Shah imprisoned the ayatollah in 1963, finally exiling him from Iran in 1964. Khomeini settled in the southern Shiite holy city of Najaf,

Iraq, where he proselytized for religious rule in Iran, influencing early members of what would become the Lebanese terrorist group Hezbollah. In 1978, Saddam Hussein expelled him at the request of the Iranian government.

From Paris, Khomeini began calling for the Iranians to overthrow the Shah and his "Great Satan" American supporters, communicating with his followers in Iran through written statements and taped sermons on smuggled audiocassettes. His campaign from abroad instigated widespread riots in late 1978. Reading the handwriting on the wall, the Shah left the country in January 1979 on a "vacation" and never returned. The seventy-eight-year-old Khomeini returned to Iran to throngs of cheering supporters and established an Islamic republic—the first in modern history. The revolution inspired other Muslim extremists and became a model for emulation. In a most "unreligious" fashion, during his first two years in power, Khomeini had most of his secular and religious opponents arrested, tortured, or executed. In the early 1980s, he sent 1,000 Iranian Revolutionary Guards to Lebanon's Bekaa Valley to educate and train young Shiite extremists and mold them into the terrorist group Hezbollah. Until al-Qaeda, Hezbollah was the world's deadliest terrorist group. Iran had gone from the tyranny of the Shah to the tyranny of an aged Muslim cleric. Khomeini died in 1989, leaving Iran a highly repressive Islamic theocracy, in dire economic straits despite its vast oil wealth. To many across the globe, Khomeini came to represent the epitome of darkness and evil—that is until Osama bin Laden burst onto the scene in September 2001.

THE ISLAMIC REPUBLIC OF IRAN

Without question, Iran is the poster child of the *Axis of Evil*. According to the U.S. State Department, it is the most active state sponsor of terrorism in the world today. In the view of the CIA, Iran is the country most actively seeking weapons of mass destruction (WMD), in particular nuclear weapons. There are other good reasons to be concerned as well: Iran's large geographic size (bigger than Alaska and second largest in the Middle East after Saudi Arabia) and substantive population (66 million). It also has great energy wealth with the world's third largest oil and second biggest natural gas reserves and has energy rights in the Caspian Sea. Iran neighbors the new governments in Afghanistan and Iraq, and borders the troubled countries of Pakistan, Central Asia, and the Caucasus. It looms large over the sea-lanes of the strategic Persian Gulf and the narrow Gulf of Hormuz. As an Islamic state, it is a powerful symbol for Muslims the world over, especially the Shia. All this makes Iran a serious player in that part of the world. It is also makes it a troublemaker for American interests in that region as well.

But Iran itself is not without challenges. After twenty-five years, the regime has lost its legitimacy due to poor economic performance and political oppression. Even though it has relatively high energy export revenues from oil and gas of about $25 billion annually (80 percent of total export earnings), Iran continues to struggle economically. Despite having one of the most advanced economies in the Middle East in 1979, today Tehran faces government budgetary problems and significant foreign debt due to expensive state subsidies and a large, inefficient public sector, including state monopolies and a shortage of skilled labor. The heart of the Iranian economy, the oil industry, is old, run-down, and needs foreign direct investment. There is also increasing pressure from young Iranians fed up with a repressive, fundamentalist Islamic government, which promises change, but never delivers it. Iranian moderates and reformers have their proposed changes blocked time and time again by senior religious clerics, who have the final say on all government policies. The increasing discontented young population (60 percent of Iranian are below twenty-five years of age) is also facing high levels of unemployment (20–25 percent), inflation (18–20 percent), poverty, and a lack of opportunity. Economically, the revolution has been an abject failure and much of the country wants change. Unfortunately, the clerics, who benefit from the current arrangement, are not interested in reform.

Iran is also considered a regional outcast because it is ethnically Persian and Shia Muslim, while many of its neighbors are ethnic Arabs and Sunni Muslim. These differences are significant in the eyes of both groups. In addition, Tehran faces international isolation and economic sanctions because of its long-standing support of international terrorism. Its closest ally is Syria, another state sponsor of terrorism and a rogue state all by itself. The fundamentals of Iran's foreign policy consist of spreading its influence in the Middle East; destroying the "Great Satan," the United States, and the "Little Satan," Israel; opposing the Palestinian-Israeli peace process; exporting its fundamentalist brand of Islam abroad; and dominating the Persian Gulf region. There is a fear that if unchecked, Iran may achieve some of these goals.

U.S.-IRANIAN RELATIONS

American interest in the Middle East is actually a recent phenomenon, coming as a by-product of World War II. In fact, prior to the war, it could be argued that American political interest in the Middle East was nonexistent. The Middle, or Near, East was a British concern. But during the war, the American navy, always thirsty for fuel, took notice of the oil reserves available in the region, as did American oil companies, such as Aramco. Iran was also considered strategically important to the United States because it ran along the soft underbelly of the Soviet Union. Furthermore, strategists saw no advantage in ceding large Iranian oil reserves to the Soviet behemoth. Finally, allowing Moscow to get a stranglehold on the oil shipping lanes of the Persian Gulf, accessing a warm water port somewhere in Iran, was believed to be strategic suicide for the West. Despite its strategic significance, before the 1979 Iranian Revolution, few Americans outside the Pentagon, State Department, and the CIA knew much about Iran. In actuality, American involvement in Iran goes back to the early 1950s. In 1953, the CIA, fearing rising Soviet influence in Iran and the nationalization of Iran's oil fields, helped overthrow the militant nationalist Prime Minister Mohammed Mossadeq. In his place monarchist Shah Mohammed Reza Pahlavi took the full reins of power. The Shah's westernization programs, including women's rights, education, and land reform, alienated the Islamic clergy. His authoritarian rule led to massive demonstrations during the late 1970s. The Shah responded with the imposition of martial law in September 1978, using his brutal security police, the SAVAK. This only exacerbated matters.

The Shah and his family ultimately fled Iran in January 1979 in the face of the gathering storm of an Islamic revolution. (He died about one year later in exile in Egypt.) Muslim cleric Ayatollah Ruhollah Khomeini, who had been plotting against the Shah from exile in France, Turkey, and Iraq, returned to establish an Islamic theocracy in Iran. Khomeini proceeded with his plans for revitalizing Islamic traditions, implementing *sharia*, mandating the veiling of women, banning alcohol and Western music, nationalizing the media, closing universities, and eliminating political parties. The Shah's heavy-handedness had been replaced with something as equally repressive—Islamic fundamentalism. Iran would go from ally of the United States to sworn enemy.

Revolutionary militants, demanding the Shah's extradition from the United States to Iran for trial, invaded the American embassy in Tehran on

November 4, 1979, seizing hostage the staff and precipitating an international crisis. Ayatollah Khomeini refused all appeals, even a unanimous vote by the UN Security Council, demanding the immediate release of the American hostages. Washington, under President Jimmy Carter, broke diplomatic relations with Tehran, placed an economic boycott on Iran, and deported large numbers of Iranian students studying in American universities. Ultimately, an aborted American military raid in April 1980 failed to rescue the hostages in Tehran due to a series of aircraft mishaps in the Iranian desert.

As the first anniversary of the embassy seizure neared, Iran insisted on a guarantee by the United States not to interfere in Iran's affairs, the cancellation of U.S. damage claims against Iran, the release of $8 billion in frozen Iranian assets, an apology, and the return of the assets held by the Shah. These conditions were largely met and the fifty-two American hostages were released on January 20, 1981, ending 444 days in captivity. The national humiliation brought on by the hostage situation arguably cost President Jimmy Carter the 1980 election to Republican nominee Ronald Reagan. The Americans and the Iranians crossed swords again in 1987, when the United States began escorting Kuwaiti oil tankers out of the Persian Gulf in the midst of the 1980–1988 Iran-Iraq war to prevent attacks on the ships by either side. The United States and Iran had several minor military clashes during this period.

The relationship between the United States and Iran since the hostage situation in 1979–1981 has generally been one of mutual animus and suspicion. Iran has continued to support terrorism in the Middle East, disrupting the prospects for peace between the Israelis and Palestinians. Its current relationship with the Taliban and al-Qaeda is not completely clear although Iran supported the fundamentalist Taliban's rise to power in the mid-1990s in Afghanistan. The Bush administration aggressively accuses Iran of pursuing an illegal nuclear weapons program; harboring suspected al-Qaeda terrorists; meddling in Iraq, including sending in Iranian Shia clerics, Revolutionary Guards, and intelligence agents; bankrolling radical Iraqi Shia clerics; and allowing foreign fighters and terrorists to enter Iraq through Iran. Now that arch-nemesis Saddam Hussein is gone, Iran is looking to influence Iraq's majority Shia population in a direction favorable to Tehran. Iranian interference in southern Iraq may not be favorable to Washington's interests. Of course, Iran denies involving itself in Iraqi affairs. In early 2005, nervous over American forces in Iraq and the controversy over its nuclear program, Iran promised to rebuff any American attack.

POLITICAL SYSTEM AND HUMAN RIGHTS

Iran is a fundamentalist Islamic republic and has all the trappings of one, including repressive *sharia*. The theocratic government—or "Mullahocracy" as some call it—has both secular and religious leaders, but a council of unelected, senior clerics has the final say on all matters of governance. Reformers have seats in the national assembly, but have gained little traction in getting reforms underway. So, despite the fact that the Iranian president and the members of the national assembly are in theory democratically elected, they have little serious power in effecting change. The current head of state, Ayatollah Seyed Ali Khameini, has direct control over the military, the internal security forces, including the Ministry of Intelligence and Security, the Ministry of Interior, the paramilitary Revolutionary Guards, and the judiciary.

In addition to the government's official internal security forces, there are also volunteer, vigilante gangs sanctioned by the government (*basijis*), which make it their business to harass, intimidate, and mete out street justice to those who oppose government policies or the *basijis'* interpretation of appropriate social behavior. The government's human rights record is dismal at best. In fact, many, including the U.S. State Department's 2004 Country Report on Human Rights, would suggest it has gotten worse as the government wrestles to keep the dissatisfied students under control. Summary executions, stoning, public floggings, disappearances, torture, rape, and arbitrary arrest and incommunicado detention are not uncommon at the hands of the government. Freedoms of speech, assembly, press, political expression, religion, and association are restricted.

WEAPONS OF MASS DESTRUCTION AND MISSILES

Despite signing the Nuclear Nonproliferation Treaty, the Biological Weapons Convention, and the Chemical Weapons Convention, all of which ban weapons of mass destruction, Iran has active WMD programs. In late 2003, Iran revealed to the UN's International Atomic Energy Agency (IAEA) that it had a clandestine nuclear program for almost twenty years. The country has biological and chemical agents, including anthrax and smallpox. Its ballistic missile arsenal is among the largest in the Middle East (Syria has the largest), and missiles with intercontinental range are on the drawing board.

In June 2003, the IAEA criticized Iran's "civilian" nuclear power program, which appeared to be a cover for a nuclear weapons program. In August 2003, the IAEA found traces of highly enriched uranium in a nuclear facility. In the face of this evidence and intense international pressure, Iran gradually admitted that it had a covert uranium enrichment program for twenty or more years. It relented in December 2003 by agreeing to suspend its uranium enrichment program and allow for thorough IAEA inspections. In early 2004, IAEA investigators continued to find anomalies in Iran's declarations about its nuclear program. The IAEA called on Tehran to permit more intrusive inspections of its nuclear sites and cease enriching uranium. Iran has denied using its civilian nuclear resources to develop nuclear weapons, but much of the international community has serious doubts. Among the most skeptical, American officials have projected that within five years Iran will have nuclear weapons if unchecked. Israeli intelligence believes that Iran could become a nuclear weapons state in a much shorter period of time.

A peaceful civilian nuclear power program can provide the necessary nuclear fuel cycle capabilities to produce fissile material for making nuclear weapons. Iran's program is suspicious because Iran, with the world's third largest known reserves of oil (behind Saudi Arabia and Iraq), does not need an expensive nuclear power industry to meets its energy needs. The Russians, Chinese, Pakistanis, and North Koreans have also been involved in the Iranian pursuit of nukes. Russia's building of an $800 million, 1,000-megawatt light water reactor at Bushehr could provide Iran with enough fissile material for 25–30 nuclear weapons a year. Despite Iran's willingness to cooperate with the IAEA and negotiate with the European Union (France, Germany, and Britain), there are reasons to be concerned about Tehran may be stalling for time while it clandestinely develops nuclear weapons. Adding to international suspicion about Iran's nuclear ambitions is Iran's involvement in a sophisticated denial and deception program designed to conceal its nuclear program, including dispersing facilities and placing them near highly populated areas and in underground facilities. These sites are also believed to be ringed by air defenses. According to a number of polls, popular support for Iran's nuclear program is strong, critics often citing American support for a nuclear program under the Shah.

Iran also appears to have an offensive biological weapons (BW) program. The former communist bloc states of Central and Eastern Europe, who learned biological warfare at the knee of the Soviet Union, are a favorite destination for the Iranian BW programs. Although it is believed that Iran has the ability to produce small quantities of biological pathogens, it is not known to what extent they can weaponize them (i.e., place them into weapons for delivery). There is evidence that Iran has developed a chemical weapons (CW) program. Its involvement with Chinese entities is particularly suspicious and has led the American intelligence community to believe that Iran is developing a nerve agent program.[1] It is thought that Iran already has blister, blood, and choking agents and can mate them with delivery systems, such as artillery shells and gravity bombs. It is unclear whether Iran has developed a chemical agent warhead for its ballistic missile arsenal. Tehran is believed to have used CW during its war with Iraq, though this has never been confirmed.

Iran's large ballistic missile arsenal has received help from Russia, North Korea, and China over the years, and is an obvious complement to the Iranian WMD programs. Iran is now self-sufficient in missile production. The core of Iran's existing missile arsenal consists of two to 300 North Korean produced SCUD-B and -C missiles, with ranges of 300–500 km (180–300 miles), 200 or more Chinese CSS-8 missiles, with a 150-km range (90 miles), and, possibly, 30–50 Chinese M-11 missiles with a 300-km range (180 miles.) Iran's short-range missiles can reach major population centers in Iraq, Saudi Arabia, and the smaller Persian Gulf states. The Shahab-3 medium-range ballistic missile, based on the North Korean No Dong missile design, with a range of 1,300 km (780 miles), was declared operational in 2003. It is able to reach Israel and American bases in the region. The 1998 Rumsfeld Commission Report said that Iran has grander plans: "Iran has acquired and is seeking major, advanced missile components that can be combined to produce ballistic missiles with sufficient range to strike the United States."[2] Since the Rumsfeld report, Iran has acknowledged plans to develop missiles with a longer range than the Shahab-3, probably the Shahab-4 (2,000-km range), and space launch vehicles, which serve as the basis for an intercontinental ballistic missile (ICBM) program. The Defense Intelligence Agency assesses that Iran will have the technical capability to develop an ICBM by 2015. This capability could come as soon as the latter part of this decade. In early 2005, Ukraine admitted that it exported a cruise missile with a 2,000-mile range to Iran, which would vastly increase the range of the Shahab-3. There is little doubt that the Iranians intend to make the Shahab missile class nuclear capable.

Iran is not a significant proliferator of WMD, but has the potential to be a troubling source of secondary proliferation in the area of ballistic missiles. Secondary proliferation takes place when a country that previously imported technology and expertise becomes an exporter of these commodities itself. Ballistic missiles and related technology would seem to be a natural export for Iran. If the country were to share or sell technology, its most likely customer would be its closest ally in the region, Syria. Syria is already receiving some assistance with missiles from Iran and North Korea.

CONVENTIONAL MILITARY

Iran has the only regional military that is capable of mounting a credible attack on its neighbors. Since the end of the Iran-Iraq war in 1988, Iran has attempted to rebuild and modernize its armed forces in order to become a regional power. It has, however, had limited success. Its economic woes, limited access to the international arms markets due to economic sanctions, and its costly nuclear program are the chief reasons for the stagnation in Iran's arms modernization program. Lacking the funds to sustain a major, across-the-board military buildup, Iran has had to content itself with selectively enhancing its military capabilities. Recent reporting indicates that Iran may be stepping up military procurement as concern over its nuclear program by the United States and others increases. Iranian military equipment is a combination of (pre-1979) American, Russian, and Chinese origins. The army has about 350,000 personnel and is in poor state of readiness. Tehran can, however, launch limited air strikes against neighboring countries using advanced Russian attack aircraft. The Iranian air force includes some Su-25 FROGFOOT close air support aircraft that defected from Iraq to Iran during the first Gulf War in 1991, and were assimilated into the Iranian inventory. The main conventional Iranian challenge from Iran is the threat to shipping in the Persian Gulf. It has the region's most capable navy. Iran could use its mines, shore-based antiship missiles, patrol boats with Chinese antiship missiles, and Russian-made KILO diesel or North Korean minisubmarines to disrupt maritime traffic in the Persian Gulf and close the Strait of Hormuz for a period. Acts of sabotage against other Persian Gulf oil facilities of other nations are also possible.

TERRORISM

Many consider Iran's religious leaders the founding fathers of modern Islamic terrorism. Since 1979, Iranian-sponsored terrorism has claimed more than 1,000 lives worldwide. A principal patron of Hezbollah, Hamas, and Palestine Islamic Jihad, Iran has also provided support to other terrorist groups in the Persian Gulf, Africa, Europe, and South and Central Asia. The Iranian Islamic Revolutionary Guard Corps (IRGC) and the Ministry of Intelligence and Security (MOIS) are directly involved in funding, arming, planning, protecting, training, and encouraging terrorist groups to pursue their evil goals, including surveillance of American interests abroad. Over the past few years, the FBI has declared several MOIS officers persona non grata for intelligence gathering (i.e., casing) using video cameras to photograph critical infrastructure and iconic buildings in New York City. Iran is especially prominent in aiding and abetting anti-Israel terrorist activities through Hamas, Hezbollah, and Islamic Jihad. Iran's public calls for the destruction of Israel and its proxy terrorist actions supports that rhetoric. The IRGC run terrorist camps in both Iran and Lebanon's Bekaa Valley. Continued support for terrorist groups is sure to undermine hopes for any Middle East peace process.

Iranian-backed terrorist groups focus most of their evil energy on Israel, but have targeted American interests in the past, too. In 1983, Hezbollah truck-bombed the U.S. Marine barracks in Beirut, Lebanon, killing 241. They also bombed the American embassy in Beirut that same year, killing sixty. Hezbollah killed the CIA's Beirut station chief William Buckley. The Iranian government supported the seizing of the American embassy in Tehran in 1979 and is suspected of supporting the bombing of the American Khobar Towers barracks complex in Saudi Arabia in 1996, which killed nineteen American servicemen. Iran has undoubtedly supported terrorist or militant activity in Iraq and Afghanistan in 2004 and 2005.

Iran has also been involved with al-Qaeda. Members of al-Qaeda have transited Iran, including several of the 9/11 hijackers. Iran also approached al-Qaeda after the bombing of the USS *Cole* in Yemen in 2000. Bin Laden rebuffed Tehran for fear of alienating Saudi backers. Abu Musab al Zarqawi, infamous for his murderous reign in Iraq, also found sanctuary in Iran after the American invasion of Afghanistan. Osama bin Laden and his deputy, Ayman al Zawahiri, may have also crossed into Iran after escaping Tora Bora, Afghanistan, in December 2001. Some believe he may be in Iran today. Other al-Qaeda members have operated from Iran, or taken refuge there, including Osama bin Laden's oldest son, Saad bin Laden, operations chief Saif al Adel, and a dozen or so other al-Qaeda operatives. Saif al Adel likely orchestrated a number of al-Qaeda attacks in Saudi Arabia from Iran. Tehran probably also serves as an intermediary for contacts between al-Qaeda, Hezbollah, Hamas, and Palestinian Islamic Jihad.

Thus, the primary threat that Iran poses to U.S. interests comes from the two extremes of the threat spectrum: weapons of mass destruction at one end, and Tehran's support of terrorism at the other. The United States will find both difficult to counter. An Iran armed with WMD would reduce the policy flexibility and freedom of action of the United States and its allies in the Middle East and the Persian Gulf region. Moreover, Tehran has in the past demonstrated its ability to use terrorist surrogates to strike American interests, while obscuring its involvement in such acts in order to escape retribution. Tehran could also be a spoiler for American efforts in Iraq and Afghanistan, which border Iran. Iran may be the most vexing and dangerous challenge in the *Axis of Evil* and is increasingly capable of causing trouble for American interests in its region and beyond.

NOTES

1. Central Intelligence Agency, "Unclassified Report to Congress on the Acquisition of Technology Relating to Weapons of Mass Destruction and Advanced Conventional Munitions" (January 1 to June 30, 2002), www.odci.gov/cia/reports/721_reports/jan_jun2002.html (accessed March 26, 2004).

2. The Commission to Assess the Ballistic Missile Threat to the United States, "Executive Summary of the Report," July 15, 1998. (This is known as the Rumsfeld Commission Report.)

15

NORTH KOREA: NUKES "R" US

The claim that we admitted developing nuclear weapons is an invention fabricated by the U.S. with sinister intentions . . . if the United States evades its responsibility and challenges us, we'll turn the citadel of imperialists into a sea of fire.

—North Korea's government paper, *Rodong Sinmun*, in January 2003

Dictator, *terrorist, playboy, recluse, he is by far the world's most mysterious leader. He may also be the most dangerous and unpredictable. North Korea's "Dear Leader," Kim Jong Il was born on the nation's highest mountain, Mount Paektu, where Korean legend says the country was founded five thousand years ago. According to North Korean history, at the time of Kim's birth, "there were flashes of lightning and claps of thunder. An iceberg in the lake on Mount Paektu emitted a mysterious sound as it broke apart and from it bright double rainbows rose." The truth is that Kim Jong Il was born in 1942 in a refugee camp in the Soviet Union to little or no fanfare. His father, Kim Il Sung, was evading the Japanese for his guerrilla activities, but would become Soviet leader Stalin's choice to lead the North Korean nation after World War II.*

Despite the reality of his humble beginnings, today he commands the world's fourth largest army, which may possess nuclear weapons. Kim inherited from his father an impoverished, hermetically sealed country where Cold War–style brainwashing and the Kim family cult of personality thrive. Enigmatic Kim Jong Il is by far the most interesting aspect of North

Korean life. He is a lover of fast cars, beautiful blonds, expensive brandy and wines, and movies, including James Bond and Rambo. He travels by armored train, wears platform shoes, surfs the Internet endlessly, and moves from palace to palace daily in the event of a coup or American air strike. He has reportedly said that if he did not become North Korea's leader, he would have been a film producer. That may be true: In 1978, he kidnapped a South Korean director and his actress wife to work in his film studios and held them for several years before they escaped. Kim has traveled abroad only a few times (by armored train), is afraid of flying, and rarely meets with foreigners. There is no doubt that he will continue to use his cryptic public persona to play adroitly North Korea's weak hand against more powerful nations such as the United States, Japan, and South Korea.

THE DEMOCRATIC PEOPLE'S REPUBLIC OF NORTH KOREA

A charter member of President George W. Bush's *Axis of Evil*, the Democratic People's Republic of Korea (DPRK), or North Korea, provides U.S. policy-makers with one of their most difficult and intractable foreign policy challenges. Strategically nestled in Northeast Asia at the crossroads of some of the world's greatest powers, including China, Russia, and Japan, Mississippi-sized North Korea is a veritable shrimp in a sea of whales. Long the crossroads of marauding armies, the Korean Peninsula has been invaded over 900 times in just 2,000 years of recorded history (or, on average, a little over 1 invasion every 2 years!). Struggle and strife are in its blood.

Today, Stalinist North Korea remains a museum-like vestige of the Cold War, and a continuing concern for American national security. North Korea has weapons of mass destruction (WMD), including possibly having as few as two operational nuclear weapons and as many as eight. It is also the world's most egregious proliferator of ballistic missiles, especially to the most volatile regions of the world, including South Asia and the Middle East. If that were not enough, the DPRK has one of the world's largest armies, traffics drugs, and counterfeits American currency on the international market.

It is estimated that based on the tremendous military might poised across the misnamed Demilitarized Zone along the 38th Parallel that separates North and South Korea, a million people might perish in just the opening days of a new war between Pyongyang and Seoul. As a defense ally of Seoul since the end of the Korean War, and with 35,000 American troops stationed in South Korea, and another 60,000 in the region at any one time, the United States would be involved in a significant way in another war on the Korean Peninsula.

The situation is not that rosy for the North Korean dictatorship, either. The country's economy is in shambles mostly due to the old-school, Soviet-era, communist collectivist economic policies that are still in place. It is the most centrally planned and internationally isolated country in the world. In the sixty years since their division, South Korea's market free economy has grown to be eighteen times larger than North Korea's. The DPRK may have defaulted on as much as $10–$12 billion worth of international debt since the end of the Cold War, when it lost its Soviet benefactor. In fact, bad economic policies and management have led to a severe famine in North Korea, starving more than 2 million people in a population of 22 million since 1994. With people unwilling or unable to have children in famine conditions, and thousands dying from starvation every year, North Korea actually has a negative annual population growth rate. Bad economic management, and some bad weather, including flooding and drought, means that North Korea has come to rely on millions of tons of international food aid from UN donors every year to feed its people. In essence, the DPRK has become an economic ward of the international community.

This means that an entire generation of North Korean children will grow up malnourished, suffering physical and mental damage from a lack of food throughout their critical formative years. It is believed that due to years of malnutrition the average North Korean soldier is a mere five feet, weighing 100 pounds. Of course, most soldiers, the vanguard of the regime, are well-fed in comparison to their civilian comrades. Tens, maybe hundreds, of thousands of North Koreans have fled the DPRK into an uncertain, but potentially better life as refugees in the hills and towns of northern China, bordering North Korea, where they risk exploitation, internment, and death if they are returned home by Chinese officials.

There are also severe energy shortages. North Korean state-run factories run at a small percentage of their capacity and consumer electricity is in critically short supply. The capital, Pyongyang, goes dark after sundown due to the lack of electricity. A home in a small town may have a single light bulb for lighting. Of course, the shortages do not affect the elite or the military. Current North Korean leader Kim Jong Il reportedly spends $700,000 a year on foreign cognac and brandy alone and on a whim will fly his personal chef out of the country in search of food he may be craving.

To ensure the regime's survival, North Korea's foreign policy is based on opportunism, extortion, and blackmail. Brandishing the Korean People's Army (and possibly nuclear weapons) as its primary instrument of national policy, North Korea gathers international aid for its flagging regime. Once a darling of the Soviet Union, since the end of the Cold War, North Korea has been struggling. China is now North Korea's major benefactor, providing North Korea with enough energy and aid to prevent it from collapsing, sending a torrid flood of refugees into northern China, and disciplining North Korean behavior.

North Korea also wants recognition as something grander than a Third World nation with a large army, WMD, and missiles. It wants respect from the international community for its unique *juche* political system, leaders, and legitimacy as a state. Lastly, it would like to unify South Korea with the North—under Pyongyang's communist leadership, of course. This was the purpose of the 1950–1953 Korean War and would certainly be the purpose of another Korean war. China has a mutual defense treaty with North Korea and is the DPRK's only ally, but a distant one at that. China begrudgingly tolerates neighboring North Korea as an element of its national interests, including keeping American forces south of the 38th Parallel.

U.S.-DPRK RELATIONS

After Japan's surrender at the conclusion of World War II, the Korean Peninsula was partitioned into two occupation zones, along the 38th Parallel. The Soviet Union controlled the northern part of the Korean Peninsula, while the United States took charge of the southern end. In 1948, the division was made permanent with the establishment of North Korea and South Korea. The DPRK was founded on May 1, 1948, with the young communist Kim Il Sung as president.

Hoping to unify the Koreas under a single communist government, and with the support of the Soviet Union, the North launched a surprise invasion of South Korea on June 25, 1950, beginning the Korean War. The UN Security Council condemned the attack and demanded an immediate withdrawal of the North Korean forces. President Harry S. Truman ordered U.S. air and naval units to enforce the UN order. The British government followed suit, and soon a UN multinational command was set up in Japan to aid the South Koreans.

The North Korean invaders swiftly seized the South Korean capital,

Seoul, and pushed American and South Korean forces south toward the southeastern port city, Pusan. In a stroke of military genius, UN commander General Douglas MacArthur ordered an amphibious landing at Inchon west of Seoul in September 1950, landing deep in the enemy's rear area and severing communication and logistic routes. In quick order, the North Korean army collapsed. MacArthur's forces pushed north across the 38th Parallel, quickly approaching the North Korean–Chinese border on the Yalu River.

As UN forces rolled over North Korean forces and approached the Yalu, 200,000 Chinese People's Volunteers entered the war on the North Korean side, driving the UN forces into a retreat south again. Seoul changed hands a couple of times, leaving it a pile of rubble. The war finally stabilized near the 38th Parallel, where it began, but continued on for two more years while cease-fire talks took place. An armistice was finally reached on July 27, 1953. That same year, the United States signed a defense treaty with South Korea and stationed troops there to deter future North Korean aggression.

Tensions on the Korean Peninsula have ebbed and flowed over the years, but in the late 1960s, the situation became particularly strained and moved precipitously toward conflict. In 1968, the North Koreans seized the American spy ship, the USS *Pueblo*, while it was in international waters and held its crew for a year. The following year it ambushed and shot down an American EC-121 reconnaissance aircraft, while it was flying in international airspace off North Korea, killing over thirty navy officers and enlisted men. In the early 1990s, tensions again mounted, this time over North Korea's pursuit of nuclear weapons. Realizing its pursuit of nuclear weapons had been discovered, North Korea threatened to withdraw from the Nuclear Nonproliferation Treaty (NPT) in 1994, including going to war if the international community imposed economic sanctions because of its secession from the UN treaty. Negotiations over the country's suspected nuclear weapons program dragged on until an agreement was reached in June 1994 in Geneva, Switzerland. The Geneva Agreed Framework included provisions for providing North Korea with proliferation-resistant light-water nuclear reactors and fuel oil in exchange for a complete cessation of North Korea's nuclear weapons program. A major crisis had been averted, for the moment.

Always willing to rattle a saber for some attention, in September 1998, North Korea launched a long-range Taepo-Dong ballistic missile over Japan, claiming it was sending a radio satellite into orbit. Fortunately, the missile landed harmlessly in the western Pacific. But the launch alarmed Japan and much of the rest of the world about North Korea's intentions regarding its nuclear weapons program and ballistic missile proliferation behavior. Despite the launch's failure, the North Koreans insisted that their satellite had, indeed, reached orbit and was transmitting patriotic North Korean songs, praising Dear Leader Kim Jong Il.

In early 2002, President Bush described North Korea as part of an "Axis of Evil" during the annual State of the Union address. North Korea was offended by the label, but proved itself worthy of the moniker later in the year. In October 2002, confronted with U.S. intelligence during a meeting in Pyongyang, North Korea admitted that it had violated the 1994 Geneva Agreed Framework. Not willing to leave bad enough alone, in late December 2002, North Korea expelled UN nuclear inspectors from the country and announced it could no longer be party to the NPT. As promised, North Korea gave its treaty-required ninety-day notice and withdrew from the treaty in early 2003. North Korea continued to provoke the international community by reactivating a nuclear power reactor and fissile material reprocessing plant at Yongbyon to convert nuclear fuel into nuclear weapons material. The United States has proposed Six-Party Talks, which include itself, China, North Korea, Japan, Russia, and South Korea, to find a way to completely, irreversibly, and verifiably disarm North Korea of its nuclear weapons programs.

POLITICAL SYSTEM AND HUMAN RIGHTS

North Korea is a one-party Stalinist dictatorship and arguably the most repressive country on earth. It is a complete police state under the absolute rule of "Dear Leader" Kim Jong Il and the Korean Workers' Party (KWP). Fear, intimidation, and propaganda are the motivational drivers in North Korean society. *Juche*, the North Korean revolutionary philosophy of self-reliance and self-sufficiency developed by North Korea's founder Kim Il Sung, is the state theology. *Juche* posits that its adherents can achieve immortality by creating an immortal state in North Korea.

Like many absolute dictators, Kim Jong Il has created a cult of personality around himself and his deceased father, "Great Leader" Kim Il Sung, that is unmatched in recent memory. The Kim persona includes outlandish feats of heroism, bravery, and genius. Every home and office is replete with the pictures of the "Great Leader" and the "Dear Leader." The country is constantly brainwashed about the mythology of the Kim family and it is a capital offense to slander the Kim family or the state. Sitting on a newspaper that has a picture of a Kim is a serious offense.

North Korean society is divided into classes based on perceptions of loyalty to the state from which benefits are doled out accordingly. The government commits human rights abuses against its people on a regular basis. Basic civil rights and liberties, taken for granted in the free world, are seen as a threat to the regime and are, therefore, forbidden. Crimes, including defection, attempted defection, slander against the Korean Worker's Party or DPRK, listening to foreign broadcasts, or reading material from abroad against the revolution, are severely punished. People caught returning from China with food are often sentenced to death. Public executions for crimes against the state are not uncommon, including such crimes as "ideological divergences" and opposing socialism. The DPRK is completely isolated from the outside world. All radios and televisions are hard-wired for government frequencies and cannot be altered. The Internet is reserved for a precious elite few. There is no freedom of speech, press, assembly, religion, or association.

Internal security is handled by the paramilitary Worker-Peasant Red Guards, the People's Security Force, and the Ministry of Public Security— all major human rights abusers. North Korean political repression has extinguished an estimated 400,000 lives over the last thirty years. Today, approximately 200,000 languish in political prison camps throughout the country. Torture and inhumane treatment in North Korean gulags is common. Many die from exposure, starvation, or disease during reeducation through labor. Sometimes entire families, including the children, are sentenced to these penal colonies because of a single family member's offense. Pregnant prisoners often undergo forced abortions or their babies are killed after birth. There are repeated allegations that political prisoners are used as guinea pigs in chemical and biological weapons experiments. Religious activities of any other sort are virtually nonexistent. Government-sponsored religious groups do exist to provide an illusion of religious freedom to the outside world. Suspected members of real underground churches are executed.

WEAPONS OF MASS DESTRUCTION AND MISSILES

North Korea has a full WMD complement, from nuclear to chemical to biological weapons. Most frightening, of course, are nuclear weapons.

North Korea may have as few as two operational nuclear weapons or as many as eight. This is based on the American intelligence community's assessment that North Korea did not declare all of its plutonium produced before the 1994 Geneva Agreed Framework. The spent nuclear fuel rods from the nuclear reactor at Yongbyon, canned in accordance with the 1994 Geneva agreement, contain enough plutonium for several nuclear weapons, and have likely been reprocessed for their plutonium.[1] North Korea's development of nuclear weapons violates four international and bilateral agreements, namely: the 1994 U.S.-DPRK Geneva Agreed Framework, the UN's Nuclear Nonproliferation Treaty, the 1992 North-South Korea Joint Declaration on the Denuclearization of the Korean Peninsula, and the UN's International Atomic Energy Agency (IAEA) safeguards agreement.

American intelligence also believes that North Korea is developing a uranium-based nuclear weapons program. A highly enriched uranium (HEU) nuclear weapons program uses different technology than North Korea's original plutonium-based nuclear weapons program, which was frozen under the 1994 agreement. North Korea has denied the existence of an HEU program, but American accusations have been buttressed by the confessions of wayward Pakistani nuclear scientist A.Q. Khan, who admitted nuclear collaboration with North Korea. It appears that North Korea desired to reap the benefits of international arms control agreements on the one hand, while developing nuclear weapons covertly on the other. The pattern of perfidy makes any agreement on North Korean nuclear weapons problematic and keeps the international community suspicious about others, such as Iranian intentions, regarding nuclear weapons. Using some pretty heated public rhetoric, Pyongyang has threatened to transfer nuclear weapons or nuclear material to groups outside North Korea. Although it is unclear who North Korea had in mind, it did get the attention of the American national security establishment.

North Korea has long-standing chemical (CW) and biological weapons (BW) programs as well. Among its BW are anthrax, cholera, bubonic plague, smallpox, and yellow fever, and other possible pathogens. North Korea can indigenously produce bulk quantities of nerve, blister, choking, and blood chemical agents as well. Pyongyang continues to send its nationals abroad in search of advanced technology and expertise. It is believed that North Korea would use chemical and biological weapons in a conflict on the Korean Peninsula. North Korea has signed the Biological Weapons Convention, but is not party to the Chemical Weapons Convention (CWC). This is not surprising since the CWC requires member nations to open up to inspections of their chemical industry. North Korea is not likely to be open to allowing a bevy of international inspectors to crawl around their chemical plants, civilian or military. The fear that these inspectors might uncover North Korea's chemical weapons program as well as concerns that the inspectors might be involved in espionage are present. Like WMD, paranoia is not in short supply in North Korea.

North Korea has five active ballistic missile programs. It is relatively self-sufficient in missile production, capable of producing around 150 missiles per year.[2] North Korea also continues to procure raw materials and components for its ballistic missile programs from various foreign sources, especially in China. Its arsenal currently tops three hundred ballistic missiles. North Korea can easily strike targets throughout the Korean Peninsula and Japan, including American forces stationed there. The CIA believes that North Korea probably is capable of delivering a light payload to the western United States.[3] A two-stage Taepo Dong ballistic missile (range: 4,000km/2,400 miles) could reach Alaska, Guam, and Hawaii, but its accuracy is suspect. As a follow-on program, the DPRK continues to develop the three-stage Taepo Dong II intercontinental ballistic missile, which is estimated to be able to reach the western continental United States. By some estimates, it could be ready for flight-testing at any time. The DPRK agreed to a voluntary, unilateral missile test moratorium in 1998, but indicated in early 2005 that it would no longer be bound by the self-imposed ban. North Korea is the world's most prolific ballistic missile and related technology salesman. Ballistic missiles are North Korea's most sought after export product by the likes of Iran and Pakistan, providing a significant portion of the country's hard currency export income.

CONVENTIONAL MILITARY

The 38th Parallel, which divides North and South Korea, is the most militarized border in the world. Sixty percent of the Korean People's Army is within 100 km (60 miles) of the Demilitarized Zone (DMZ). This means that nearly two million soldiers face one another across a tiny two-mile wide strip of "No-Man's Land" ready to do battle at a moment's notice. Ten to twelve thousand pieces of North Korean artillery target the South Korean capital of Seoul, just twenty-five miles south of the DMZ. Pyongyang's artillery effectively holds hostage the ten to fifteen million people of Seoul's greater metropolitan area. It is estimated that North Korea could rain down

500,000 rounds of artillery on Seoul in the opening hours of another war, including CW. There is likely to be little warning of an attack by North Korea, but the presence of U.S. forces in South Korea has provided an effective deterrent against North Korea aggression for over fifty years.

North Korea has the fourth largest army in the world with over 1.2 million men and women under arms. It also has the world's largest special operations forces, comprising about 100,000 troops. North Korea spends from 25 to 35 percent of its national budget on the military, under its "military first policy." North Koreans serve in the active reserves until they are forty years of age, and thereafter serve in the Worker-Peasant Red Guard until sixty. Military service is attractive because soldiers receive larger rations, and are less likely to go hungry in comparison with their civilian counterparts.

TERRORISM

North Korea is not an active sponsor of terrorism today, though it remains on the U.S. list of state sponsors due to previous sins. These transgressions include harboring four Japanese Red Army (JRA) faction members, who hijacked a Japanese Airlines flight to North Korea in 1970. Today, only a few of the JRA hijackers remain alive in North Korea, but the DPRK still refuses to extradite them to Japan.

The DPRK's last known terrorist act was in 1987, when its agents blew up South Korean flight KAL 858, killing 115 civilians. In October 1983, North Korean agents attempted to assassinate South Korean president Chun Doo-hwan during his visit to Burma. While the assassination attempt failed, seventeen senior Korean officials, including cabinet members, died. In January 1968, a North Korean commando team sought to blow up the South Korean presidential residence, the Blue House, and the U.S. embassy in Seoul. The plot was foiled and its perpetrators were captured. In addition, since 1953, North Korea has kidnapped over 3,600 South Korean citizens and at least a dozen Japanese citizens during the 1970s and 1980s. The Japanese were kidnapped for the purposes of training North Korean spies in the Japanese language and mannerisms, allowing them to travel to Japan and operate there undetected.

North Korea's egregious behavior is not limited to WMD, terrorism, or human rights violations. North Korea has committed over three hundred provocative acts against its neighbor, South Korea, since 1948.[4] In the 1990s alone, North Korea infiltrated South Korea at least fifteen times, occasionally with embarrassing consequences, like when one of their diesel submarines went aground on the shoals off the South Korean coast during an infiltration operation in 1996.[5] In another incident in 1998, the South Koreans captured a North Korean minisub on an infiltration operation.

Pyongyang is also in the illegal drug business. In order to earn hard currency, North Korea has begun narcotics trafficking, including methamphetamines and heroin. In another get-rich-quick scheme, the North Koreans produce an outstanding counterfeit American $100 bill. The North Korean "Super K" was such a fine imitation of the U.S. note that it caused the U.S. Treasury Department to redesign the American $100 bill.

North Korea's troublesome behavior at home and abroad is a significant challenge to American interests and international peace, stability, and security. Its policies are designed to ensure the survival of one of the world's last communist dictatorships and most repressive governments. North Korea is using nuclear weapons, and the missiles to deliver them, much less as an instrument of military power than as a tool of desperation, coercion, and blackmail aimed at achieving legitimacy and influence within the international community.

It is not clear whether North Korea's leader Kim Jong Il is in complete control of his faculties. Considering the destructive power in his hands, this is cause for concern. People who have met him say that he is articulate, bright, and logical. This may be so, but it is clear that the prism of reality that he looks at the world through is different from the one the rest of us see the world through. Seeing the outside world through a glass darkly makes the chances of North Korean misperception and miscalculation much more likely and the regime that much more unpredictable and dangerous.

NOTES

1. Central Intelligence Agency, "Unclassified Report to Congress on the Acquisition of Technology Relating to Weapons of Mass Destruction and Advanced Conventional Munitions," January 3, 2003, www.cia.gov/cia/publications/bian/bian _jan_2003.htm.

2. Jack Spencer, *The Ballistic Missile Threat Handbook* (Washington, DC: The Heritage Foundation, 2000).

3. Central Intelligence Agency, "Foreign Missile Developments and the Ballistic Missile Threat through 2015," September 1999.

4. Balbina Hwang, "North Korea Deserves to Remain on U.S. List of Sponsors of Terrorism," Heritage Foundation Backgrounder no. 1503, November 19, 2001.

5. Hwang, "North Korea Deserves to Remain on U.S. List."

16

SYRIA: BAATHISTS BEHAVING BADLY

Syria's interest is to see the invaders defeated in Iraq.

—Farouk al Sharaa, Syrian foreign minister, 2003

The president was dead and an emergency session of the parliament was needed to amend the constitution. A Syrian president could be no younger than forty years of age and Bashar al Assad, son of deceased president Hafez al Assad, was only thirty-four. But constitutional details such as this are not a problem in a one-party state. Within days of his father's death on June 10, 2000, Bashar al Assad was elected secretary-general of the Baath Party. Shortly thereafter, the constitution was amended and, running unopposed, he won the presidency with 97 percent of the vote. No primaries, no stump speeches, no passing the hat—it is good to be a dictator's son.

In spite of the lack of transparency and openness in the process, many inside and outside Syria hoped that the young, British-educated eye doctor with the British-born Syrian wife would be a breed apart from his strongman father. Syria was living in the 1970s in many respects and desperately needed reform and modernization. A Western-looking technocrat was exactly what was needed to bring Syria out of the authoritarian dark and into the light of democracy and economic reform. But, alas, it was not to be. The Baathist old guard quickly regrouped and quashed any talk of change. They had benefited from the current system for too long. Even early cooperation with the United States on al-Qaeda in the war on terror turned to providing weaponry to Iraqi forces, allowing foreign fighters to transit

Syria to fight coalition forces during Operation Iraqi Freedom, and harboring insurgency organizers. The mild-mannered, mustached Syrian leader had earned his own place in the rogue's gallery.

THE SYRIAN ARAB REPUBLIC

The Syrian Arab Republic continues to chafe away at international good will. Ignoring complaints and warnings from a sizeable portion of the international community, Syria continues to sponsor international terrorism, develop weapons of mass destruction, and repress it own people. Its proxy attacks on Israel, using the terrorist groups Hamas, Palestinian Islamic Jihad, and Hezbollah, create an interminable cycle of violence that undermines the festering Middle East peace process. Syria willfully serves as a conduit for terrorist money, operatives, and munitions from Iran to Lebanon and Palestine. Not content with ruling Syria, Damascus ran Lebanon from 1976 until 2005. Moreover, Syria represses its own people and allows insurgents, foreign fighters, and terrorists to plot and seep across its borders into Iraq, sowing death and destruction in the new Iraqi state. Even though Syria is not yet in the same disrepute as Iran, its leaders seem to be racing the mullahs to succeed Saddam Hussein's Iraq as the Middle East's most vile regime. Not yet a card-carrying member of the *Axis of Evil*, Syria is certainly knocking at the club door.

Despite its success in the evil arts, or perhaps because of it, Syria has fallen on tough times politically and economically. The statist economy is corrupt, stagnant, and desperately needs liberalization and restructuring. The standard of living for the average Syrian is declining and unemployment is out of sight at 20 percent. The young people are restless, looking at Iraq and wondering about more freedom and regime change at home. The regime is under pressure to reform from within and from without. The democratization of Iraq altered Syria's strategic position in the Middle East. The United States is right next door with tens of thousands of battle-hardened American GIs—not to mention that Washington is seething at Damascus. The regime change in Iraq means that Damascus has lost access to, and the income from, black market Iraqi oil that circumvented UN sanctions. Even Lebanon, long considered a friendly window to the outside world, looks less hospitable and more uncertain toward Syria. Instead of turning toward reform, Syria is retrenching and turning to the likes of Iran for partnership.

U.S.-SYRIAN BILATERAL RELATIONS

Long the domain of the French, Syria came to America's attention in the late 1960s during the 1967 Arab-Israeli Six-Day War. Israel quickly vanquished the Syrian army in battle. But before accepting a UN-sponsored cease-fire, Israeli forces took control of Syria's fortified Golan Heights. Because of American support for Israel, Damascus broke off diplomatic relations with Washington. In November 1970, General Hafez al Assad, father of Syria's current leader Bashar al Assad, seized power in a bloodless coup from the civilian government. Assad became president in March 1971. He formed a new cabinet in December 1972, giving the pan-Arab Syrian Socialist Resurrection, or Baathist Party, more than half the cabinet posts. From that time on, the Baathists would never relinquish power. Like Assad, many of the new members of the government belonged to Syria's minority Alawite Islamic sect (12 percent of Syria's population.)

Smarting from the last defeat by the Israelis and eager to regain the Golan Heights, Syria joined Egypt in attacking Israel in October 1973 in the fourth Arab-Israeli war, widely known as the Yom Kippur War. In the latest effort to settle the score with Israel, Syria not only failed to regain the Golan Heights, it lost more territory. At one point, Israel advanced to within twenty miles of Damascus, the Syrian capital. Henry Kissinger, the U.S. secretary of state, brokered a peace settlement among the parties, allowing Damascus and Washington to resume diplomatic relations.

Looking to influence its western neighbor, in 1976, Syria sent some 20,000 troops to Lebanon to support Lebanese Muslims in their struggle with Lebanese Christians during the civil war there. Israel, supporting the Lebanese Christians and concerned about a hostile state to its north, invaded southern Lebanon in 1982 and clashed with the Syrian troops already deployed across large swaths of the country. In the mid-1980s, Syria began to be singled out by the international community, including the United States, for supporting Middle Eastern terrorism. U.S.-Syrian relations became particularly tense when U.S. Marines were attacked in 1983 while serving as peacekeepers in Beirut during Lebanon's civil war. The attack on the U.S. Marine Barracks by Lebanon-based, Syrian-supported Hezbollah killed 241 marines and navy sailors.

Syria also has had a long and troubled history with its neighbor, Iraq. Fearful of being dominated by a powerful, hegemonic Iraq, Syria was one of the few Arab nations to support Iran during the 1980–1988 Iran-Iraq war. In fact, after Iraq invaded Kuwait in August 1990, Syria sent 20,000 troops to Saudi Arabia to defend the Saudis. It later joined the U.S.-led coalition in the first Persian Gulf War against Saddam Hussein. Syria's participation in the multinational coalition both helped improve its relations with the Arab world and the United States and undermined the Iraqi threat.

In October 1991, Syria and several other Arab nations entered into U.S.-sponsored peace negotiations with Israel. Syria's chief concern, of course as one would expect, was the return of the Golan Heights from Israeli occupation. Little progress was made on this issue, in part because Israel was involved in negotiations with its longtime nemesis, the Palestine Liberation Organization (PLO), headed by the nettlesome, late Yassir Arafat. In September 1993, Israel and the PLO signed a landmark peace accord, the Oslo Accords, in Washington, DC. Having been left out of the negotiations, which did not address the Golan Heights, Assad expressed serious reservations about the agreement. Understanding the importance of Syria to Middle East peace, in January 1994, President Hafez al Assad met with President Bill Clinton in Geneva, Switzerland, regarding opening peace negotiations with Israel, in the first meeting of the two nation's heads of state since 1977.

Ever an opportunist power, Syria underwent a wholesale reconfiguration of its foreign policy strategy after the fall of its patron and protector, the Soviet Union, in the early 1990s. Facing a steadily strengthening strategic partnership between Israel and Syria's Muslim neighbor to the north, Turkey, Syria took steps to construct a countervailing alliance by improving relations with Iraq, including siphoning off $2 billion a year in oil sales by helping Baghdad evade UN sanctions from the first Persian Gulf War. It also took steps to strengthen ties with Iran and collaborate more closely with oil-giant Saudi Arabia.

In June 2000, President Hafez al Assad—one of the longest serving Middle Eastern heads of state—died at age seventy. His son, and successor, Bashar al Assad, a London-trained ophthalmologist, succeeded him, running unopposed in rigged elections after a minor, rapid adjustment to the country's constitution to make his succession "legal." The younger Assad has emulated his father's autocratic rule. Although there was some hope early on that there would be a relaxation of the everyday restrictions of Syrian life. In a positive development, in the summer of 2001, Syria withdrew nearly all of its 25,000 troops from the Lebanese capital, Beirut. As many as 20,000 Syrian soldiers, however, remained in the Lebanese countryside.

Out of the tragedy of September 11 came a warming in Syrian-American relations. Al-Qaeda's allies, the radical Syrian Muslim Brotherhood, were no fans of Syria's secular government. Damascus calculated that a crackdown on the Brotherhood and cooperation with the Americans could prove mutually beneficial in fighting Islamic extremism. Syria also hoped that this cooperation would get the Americans to overlook Damascus' continuing military presence in Lebanon and their support for Lebanese and Palestinian terrorist groups, such as Hezbollah and Hamas.

Syria opposed the 2003 war against Iraq's Saddam Hussein, mostly because it was making easy money off the UN sanctions imposed upon its neighbor. Damascus let Saddam illegally truck as much as 150,000 barrels a day of Iraqi oil to Syria for export abroad in violation of the UN's Oil-for-Food program. The benefit to Saddam Hussein: $2 million a day. No doubt Syria also realized that the 2003 war was not going to end like it did in 1991 with Saddam still in power. The Iraqi dictator was going to be ousted and the Americans at least temporarily would be Syria's new neighbors. In spring 2003, shortly after major combat operations in Iraq wound down, the Bush administration turned its ire on Syria, accusing Damascus of transferring military equipment, including night-vision goggles, to Iraqi forces during Operation Iraqi Freedom; harboring members of Saddam Hussein's deposed regime; allowing insurgents, foreign fighters, and al-Qaeda terrorists to transit Syria into Iraq; and holding up to $2 billion in Saddam Hussein's riches in Syrian banks. There was even an assumption in some quarters that Iraq has relocated its weapons of mass destruction (WMD) to Syria. Relations, which started on a brighter note after 9/11 when the Syrians cooperated against al-Qaeda, had turned markedly sour. In fact, President George W. Bush signed the Syrian Accountability Act of 2004 and subsequently implemented a number of economic sanctions on Damascus. In early 2005, Syria came under renewed pressure from the international community after Damascus was accused of involvement in the assassination of popular former Lebanese prime minister Rafik Hariri in Beirut. The outcry led to the withdrawal of Syrian troops, but probably not influence, from Lebanon.

Syria's foreign policy is best described as opportunistic. With a population of 18 million, Syria has never been the most powerful country in the region. It has spent a good deal of its history looking for other Middle East-

ern partners and others, such as the former Soviet Union, to help ensure
its security. Beyond continued existence as a state, Syrian objectives include
preserving the primacy of the regime and leading the Arab world; wresting
the strategic, water-rich Golan Heights back from Israel; preventing Lebanon and Iraq from becoming adversaries; and re-creating Greater Syria,
which included Lebanon, Jordan, and Israel before it was carved up by the
French and the British in a confidential agreement in 1916. In fact, in 1958,
Syria unified with Gamal Abdel Nasser's Egypt under a federation called
the United Arab Republic (UAR) in an effort at pan-Arabism. Syria later
changed its mind, and seceded from the UAR in 1961 after a coup in
Damascus.

Syria and Iran are now key allies in the Middle East. Damascus has
allowed Tehran to use it as a transit point for resupplying terrorist groups,
primarily Hezbollah, in Lebanon. Damascus has not always been adverse
to al-Qaeda. Damascus has been implicated in assisting al-Qaeda and Hezbollah in the attack against the Khobar Towers in 1996 in Saudi Arabia,
killing nineteen American servicemen, although it remains unclear to what
extent Damascus directly supported al-Qaeda in the attack. In early 2004,
Iran and Syria signed a bilateral defense agreement intended to boost
security cooperation. In early 2005, after meeting with Syrian prime minister Naji al Otari, Iranian vice president Mohammad Reza Aref said: "We
are ready to help Syria on all grounds to confront threats." No doubt the
vice president was referring to the United States.

Syria, which held broad sway over Lebanon for almost thirty years, maintained 15,000 troops until 2005 when it began a phased draw down. The
Arab League originally legitimized Syrian troop deployments to Lebanon
during Lebanon's civil war. The 1989 Taif Accord, which ended the Lebanese civil war and provided a roadmap for national reconciliation, allowed
for continuing Syrian occupation. Damascus justified its military presence
in Lebanon by citing Beirut's requests for Syrian support. It also noted the
Lebanese government's failure to implement all of the constitutional
reforms in the Taif Accord, especially as related to more equitable power-
sharing between Lebanese Christians and Muslims. Israel's withdrawal
from its security zone in southern Lebanon in May 2000, however, embold-
ened some Lebanese Christians to demand that Syria withdraw its forces
as well. Many Lebanese Christians resent Syria for its role in imposing a
settlement that ended the civil war, and diminished the traditional political
power of Christians in favor of the country's Muslim majority. (Syria is 75

percent Muslim; 15 percent Christian; and 10 percent Jewish.) Even after the withdrawal of Syrian troops, questions remain about the influence of its intelligence and security forces, which have been so influential in Lebanon in the past.

POLITICAL CONDITIONS AND HUMAN RIGHTS

Syria is a totalitarian state, but not to the same extent as Iran or North Korea. It is a secular military republic under the absolute authority of the Arab Baath Socialist Party. The president and a small circle of "old guard" personal advisers make key decisions regarding foreign policy, national security, internal politics, and the economy. This style of decision-making has not always been beneficial to Syria, especially considering its record of failed economic policies. In fact, just to make sure the Baath Party continues to reign supreme, its primacy is mandated in the Syrian constitution. The Syrian parliament is essentially powerless.

The powerful, prolific role of the Syrian security services extends beyond strictly law enforcement and security to all matters of state. This is due to the ostensible "state of emergency," which has been in place since 1963. The Syrian government justifies the ongoing martial law because of its state of war with Israel and past threats against the state from radical groups such as the Muslim Brotherhood. To ensure tranquility at home and ensure no open criticism of the government, Syria employs thirteen different intelligence and security services, allowing the Baathist regime to rule with an iron hand.

Overall, the Syrian government's human rights record remains poor, and members of the security forces commit numerous, serious human rights abuses. There is no political opposition to the Baath Party and continuing serious abuses included the use of torture, arbitrary arrest and detention, and "kangaroo courts" for security-related matters. The government restricts freedom of speech and the press, although satellite television dishes and the Internet are allowed. Freedom of assembly does not exist under the law, and the government restricts freedom of association. The government does not officially allow independent domestic human rights groups to exist; however, it has permitted periodic meetings of unlicensed civil society forums. The Syrian government places some limits on freedom of religion and freedom of movement as well.

WEAPONS OF MASS DESTRUCTION AND MISSILES

Since losing the support of the Soviet Union at the end of the Cold War, Syria has looked to WMD and ballistic missiles as a source of strategic deterrence against its ever-changing adversaries, including Israel. It has increasingly viewed to these unconventional weapons as a means of countering Israel's superior conventional forces. Syria has one of the most advanced chemical weapons capabilities in the Arab world, and is believed to have an offensive biological weapons program, too. Its nuclear program is the least well developed of its WMD programs. Damascus is a member of the Nuclear Nonproliferation program, but has a 30-kilowatt Chinese-supplied nuclear research center at Dayr al Hajar, which has raised suspicions about Syrian intentions regarding nuclear weapons. Russia and Syria have continued their long-standing agreements on cooperation regarding nuclear energy, including the production of a nuclear power plant, although specific assistance has not yet materialized. Construction of a Russian nuclear reactor in Syria could start Syria down the slippery slope toward nuclear weapon state status just like the reactor at Bushehr has done for Iran. Russia also constructed North Korea's original nuclear reactor at Yongbyon. Concerns were raised recently when it was discovered that rogue Pakistani nuclear scientist A. Q. Khan made offers of nuclear weapon technology to Syria. Damascus, fortunately, did not take Khan up on his offer, believing it was a scam.

Syria's interest in chemical weapons (CW) goes back to the 1970s, and Damascus continues to seek CW assistance from abroad. Syria has stockpiled the nerve agent sarin, but apparently has looked at more deadly agents, such as VX.[1] Fortunately, Syria remains dependent on foreign sources for important elements of its CW program, including precursor chemicals and key production equipment. It has not signed the Chemical Weapons Convention.

Although it has signed the Biological Weapons Convention, it is highly probable that Syria also continues to develop an offensive biological weapons (BW) capability.[2] The BW program is probably capable of supporting limited biological pathogen production. There have also been persistent rumors that Iraq's WMD stockpiles from before the 2003 war were spirited across the Iraqi border into Syria. If true, Iraqi materials could boost Syria's own programs—or be passed along (with the middleman's "fingerprints" carefully wiped off) to its terrorist acolytes for use in Iraq, Israel, or elsewhere by Hamas or Hezbollah.

Syrian policy considers ballistic missiles an important military weapon, especially for possible use against Israeli military bases and cities during any future conflict. Damascus has the largest missile arsenal in the Middle East, including several hundred Soviet and North Korean–origin SCUD and SS-21 ballistic missiles with ranges of two to three hundred miles. This makes Syria capable of striking Israel, Jordan, Turkey, and Iraq from well inside its borders. Damascus continues to develop its missile capabilities, including extending the range of its arsenal, primarily with the help of North Korean, Iranian, and Russian concerns. Syria is believed to have weaponized chemical weapons for use on the SCUD missiles.

CONVENTIONAL MILITARY

Syria's military modernization has slowed since it lost its Soviet patronage. The cost of its military deployment in Lebanon, on top of a faltering economy at home, has hampered Syria's ability to replace its aging Soviet-era equipment. Although it did receive an infusion of cash after the 1991 Gulf War from Persian Gulf states for siding against Iraq's invasion of Kuwait, it had little effect on improving Syria's military capabilities over the ensuing ten years. Nevertheless, Syria remains one of the largest and most capable militaries in the Middle East with over 300,000 soldiers under arms in the Syrian Arab Army. To broad disappointment, Russia agreed in February 2005, just a few days after Hariri's assassination, to sell Syria an unspecified number of advanced SA-18 surface-to-air missiles, despite American and Israeli objections and Russia's commitment under the Helsinki Agreement not to support terrorist regimes. There is a strong concern that these weapons will find their way to terrorist groups such as Hezbollah, Hamas, and Palestinian Islamic Jihad, or even to the insurgents and al-Qaeda for use in Iraq. Damascus has transferred Russian-made weapons, especially small arms, to Syrian-aligned groups in the past. In addition to terrorist groups, Syrian ally Iran may also be a beneficiary of Russian arms sales to Syria. This sale may not be the end of Syrian-Russian arms deals, as Moscow also announced the canceling of three-fourths of Syria's $13 billion defense debt to Russia.

TERRORISM

Syria is the world's second most active state sponsor of terrorism—after Iran. It provides support to a number of Lebanese and Palestinian terrorist groups, including allowing them to maintain "offices" in Damascus. Syria, of course, claims that the Damascus offices are for political and informational activities and that terrorist activities are not planned or supported out of Syria. This is untrue. Damascus has been supporting, funding, training, and arming these groups for years. In 2003, the Israeli air force bombed training bases in Syria used by Hamas, Palestinian Islamic Jihad (PIJ), and the Popular Front for the Liberation of Palestine (PFLP) after nineteen Israelis were killed in a Palestinian Islamic Jihad suicide strike in the northern city of Haifa.

The most notable Palestinian terrorist groups supported by Syria include the PFLP, the Popular Front for the Liberation of Palestine-General Command (PFLP-GC), the PIJ, and Hamas. Syria has taken a leading role in promoting the view that Palestinian and Lebanese terrorist groups fighting Israel are not terrorists, but freedom fighters. One of the world's deadliest terrorist groups, Hezbollah, operates among Syrian military, intelligence, and security forces in southern Lebanon and the Bekaa Valley. Syrian support for these groups will undoubtedly continue whether Syrian forces remain in Lebanon or not. Nonetheless, the Syrian government has not been implicated directly in an act of terrorism since 1986. Many believe that Syria played an indirect role with Hezbollah and al-Qaeda in the 1996 bombing of the American military barracks at Khobar Towers in Saudi Arabia. In addition, it is likely that Syrian security forces were intimately involved in Hariri's assassination, and other recent killings.

According to the U.S. government, Syria has cooperated significantly with the United States and other foreign governments against al-Qaeda and the Taliban. It also has discouraged any signs of public support for al-Qaeda, including in the media and at mosques.[3] Syria's initial helpfulness with al-Qaeda was probably due to its own concern about being targeted by the group itself, since it is a secular, non-Islamic government in a predominately Muslim country. But Syria's anti-al-Qaeda stance may have changed since the 2003 Iraq war. Hezbollah and Hamas may have trained, and be training, al-Qaeda recruits in Palestinian refugee camps and in the Bekaa Valley in Lebanon with Syria's knowledge. In addition, there are persistent reports that al-Qaeda personnel have come to Syria and settled there with government knowledge and support, using Syria as a hub for moving Islamic extremists and money into Iraq. Perhaps Syria has come to a new accommodation with al-Qaeda-associated groups in order to counterbalance the new American presence in Iraq and Lebanon. It is not uncommon for Syria to quickly change alliances in the face of a new challenge to its security. Although fundamentalist al-Qaeda and secular Syria are not natural allies, their mutual disdain for the United States and Israel and the changes in Iraq could drive them together. A Syrian "alliance of convenience" with al-Qaeda could ultimately lead to big trouble for the Assad regime.

The Bush administration says that despite promises to close the spigot, insurgents, foreign jihadists, and al-Qaeda terrorists continue to flow largely unimpeded across the porous Syrian border into Iraq, resulting in the deaths of American and coalition soldiers, Iraqis, and international civil servants. Indeed, Syrians are so common among captured militants that some coalition military commanders collectively have called foreign radicals "The Syrians." Syria could continue to be a real spoiler for American efforts in establishing peace and stability in Iraq if it continues to serve as an outpost for insurgents and terrorists. Damascus could also undermine the nascent Israeli-Palestinian peace process by unleashing its terrorist allies. Finally, Syria could seriously destabilize Lebanon using its security forces and Hezbollah, despite the absence of its military forces.

The strategic landscape of the Middle East has changed forever with the removal of Saddam Hussein from power in Iraq. For Syria, surrounded by Turkey, against which Syria supported the Kurdish terrorist group, the PKK; Israel, against which it fought several wars; a restless Lebanon, which Syria had occupied for almost thirty years; and now a free Iraq, Syria's future is an open question. The country's fluid, opportunistic foreign policy has served it well in the past, but with fewer alternatives, those days may be past.

Damascus can do the right thing. Syria supported the 1991 Gulf War and signed onto the UN's November 2002 Security Council Resolution 1441, which paved the way for UN inspectors to return to Iraq. But today Syria must make a fundamental choice between joining the *Axis of Evil* and standing with those who oppose it. Assad is facing arguably the most critical decisions of his young presidency—choices that will prove fateful for Syria's eighteen million people. Isolated in the region, overshadowed by powerful neighbors, and bridled with a flagging economy, Syria is out in the cold. Its prospects do not look good unless the regime changes course.

NOTES

1. Office of the Secretary of Defense, "Proliferation: Threat and Response," January 2001, p. 45.

2. Central Intelligence Agency, "Unclassified Report to Congress on the Acquisition of Technology Relating to Weapons of Mass Destruction and Advanced Conventional Munitions 1 January through 30 June 2003," www.cia.gov (accessed March 2, 2004).

3. "Patterns of Global Terrorism 2002," U.S. Department of State, Washington, DC, www.state.gov/s/ct/rls/pgtrpt/2002/pdf/ (accessed January 5, 2004).

17

ROLLING BACK ROGUES

Diplomacy and defense are not substitutes for one another. Either alone would fail.

—President John F. Kennedy

THE ROGUE CHALLENGE

Dealing with rogue states is challenging at best. It is nightmarish at worst. The stakes, which often involve authoritarian governments, weapons of mass destruction (WMD), terrorism, and anti-Americanism are exceedingly high for American national security and international peace and stability. Rogue states' behavior often lies way outside of well-established international norms and generally accepted standards of global conduct. In some cases, their actions are seemingly inexplicable, irrational, or even erratic. Their leadership is often reclusive, inaccessible, and unsusceptible to international public opinion or pressure. The rogues' decision-making processes are frequently byzantine, dictatorial, and opaque to the outside world. In no way does this make the development of substantive policies for handling this unique set of international actors easy. In fact, in some ways, it is akin to Winston Churchill's description of the Soviet Union when he said: "I cannot forecast to you the action of Russia. It is a riddle wrapped in a mystery inside an enigma."

Regrettably, there is no "cookie-cutter" approach to foreign policy, and there certainly is not a "one-size-fits-all" policy formula for dealing with rogue states. Policies that advance American interests with one state may not work at all with another. Each country is different based on its language, history, geography, and culture. Moreover, each international situation is unique, requiring each rogue state to be dealt with in its own way. But in each case, it is important to ensure that the rogue states fully understand what is considered to be unacceptable behavior.

The international community, including the United Nations, can best influence the rogues if they present them with clear choices and a united front on such issues as terrorism, WMD, and human rights. If achievable, this prevents the rogues from playing one state off another in an effort to outflank attempts to modify or punish their behavior. Unfortunately, getting the international community, especially the UN, to work together at times can be somewhat similar to "herding cats." In spite of this challenge, this cannot deter us from tackling the rogue state challenge. We should also do our best to keep rogue states from working together and to eliminate their patrons' support for their untoward activities. The problems of rogue states will not go away on their own. We ignore them and their activities at our peril.

LIBYA: A ROGUE COMES IN FROM THE COLD

Libya may have had the dubious honor of being the first rogue state, having been branded an outlaw by President Ronald Reagan in the early 1980s—and rightfully so. But despite its evil legacy, Libya has shown that even a rogue state can change its wicked ways. In December 2003, Libya, a pariah state for thirty some years under the erratic leadership of Colonel Moammar Qaddafi, decided to join the international community as a responsible state. Libya actively repressed its people, supported international terrorism, aggressed against its neighbors, and pursued WMD. But it seems that even the most evil among us can have a change of heart.

In an effort to improve the standard of living in the oil-rich, yet unnecessarily impoverished, North African nation, Libya agreed in late 2003 to change course after thirty years of economic sanctions. Tripoli consented to give up its WMD arsenal and eliminate missile programs covered by the Missile Technology Control Regime, which included nuclear weapons development, swore off sponsoring international terrorism, and settled with the international community on the December 1988 Pan Am 103 bombing over Lockerbie, Scotland (killing 259 people on the plane and 11 people on the ground). In return, the international community, led by the United States and Britain, is taking incremental steps to reintegrate Libya into the international community by lifting economic sanctions and reestablishing full diplomatic relations with Libya, beginning with liaison offices in Tripoli.

The reintegration process is based on Libya's progress in dismantling its WMD programs and addressing past acts of terrorism, including compensating the victims' families. It may be too early to really understand what sort of "epiphany" brought Qaddafi around to changing his longstanding national policy, but there are some initial lessons learned from Libya's monumental decision. First, the broad, multilateral economic sanctions against Libya by the international community made life painful enough for Qaddafi's regime that a new path for Tripoli's international relations was in order. The absence of a Libyan patron state capable of making up for short-falls in international commerce and hard currency income probably helped convince Qaddafi of the hopelessness of the situation. It is also likely that the threat of involuntary regime change, like Afghanistan and Iraq, also helped convince Qaddafi his days as a despot might be numbered. Among the rogue states, Libya, along with Syria, are the two regimes most susceptible to outside intervention due to their relative weakness. Among the rogue states, Libya and Syria are some of the "lowest hanging fruit."

Most interestingly, the evolving Libyan situation provides an important alternative path for rogue states to choose. They can remain international pariahs, impoverishing their people and living under one political or economic sanction regime after another. Alternatively, they can follow the "Libyan Model," unshackling themselves from the trappings of "rogue-dom," allowing their nation and people to achieve their potential as a state, become prosperous, and contribute to the international community—all without changing the regime. In some cases, changing the regime's behavior is more important than changing the regime's leadership. No doubt Tehran, Pyongyang, and Damascus are closely watching the Tripoli transformation.

DEALING WITH IRAN

Unquestionably, Iran is one of the most troubling countries in the international community today. It is certainly the Middle East's "enfant terrible." Tehran actively sponsors international terrorism. It has chemical and biological weapons and is vigorously pursuing nuclear weapons. The Iranian government harshly represses its people under fundamentalist Islamic rule. Moreover, Tehran has the potential to destabilize the new governments in neighboring Iraq and Afghanistan, attain hegemony over the Middle East, and dominate the oil transit lanes of the Persian Gulf, through which much of the world's oil flows. With its tremendous oil wealth and nuclear weapons, Iran is a potential regional superpower. Iran could be a real danger for American interests in that part of the world.

Iranian Goals

Iran is interested in increasing its influence and prestige in the Middle East and throughout the Muslim world while decreasing American influence in the region, especially in the Persian Gulf. Tehran would like to see friendly governments in Iraq, Pakistan, and Afghanistan, and will work at cross-purposes with the United States to prevent the establishment of open, democratic societies in these bordering states. Tehran's preference, of course, is that these governments embrace a fundamentalist Islamic ideology similar to its own. Tehran also does not support Israel's right to exist, and looks to undermine any prospects of a Middle East peace process. It will continue to look for opportunities to export its brand of Islamic fundamentalism, foment trouble in nearby Muslim Central Asia, and deepen its relationship with Syria and, perhaps, North Korea on missiles and nuclear weapons technology.

U.S. Goals

The United States seeks peace and stability in the Middle East and Persian Gulf regions, continued access to its petroleum reserves and the region's commercial markets, the success of the new democracies in Iraq and Afghanistan, and the spread of freedom in the region. To this end, the United States would like to see a cessation of Iran's support for international terrorism, especially as it concerns undermining the Israeli-Palestinian peace process through the activities of Hamas, Hezbollah, and

Palestinian Islamic Jihad sponsorship and aiding or abetting al-Qaeda. Washington would like to see a termination to the Iranian nuclear, chemical, biological, and long-range missile programs, and destabilizing conventional military developments. Iranian support for a just, comprehensive, and lasting peace between Israel and the Palestinians, and noninterference in the development of civil societies in Afghanistan and Iraq would also be welcomed. Further, the Iranian people should have the right to choose all of their governing leaders through democratic elections, and be afforded greater civil liberties.

Policy Prescriptions

Dealing with Iran is no small challenge, especially because of its oil and gas wealth, which, not surprisingly, attracts many willing international partners interested in Iranian energy. But there are ways to influence its behavior in a direction more in line with the desires of the United States and the broader international community.

Promote Internal Change

Perhaps the best way for the United States to promote democratic change in Iran is by seeking to influence Iran's younger generation, 60 percent of whom are under twenty-five years of age. Giving the younger audiences access to alternative ideas other than the Iranian state-controlled media could influence change from the inside. Through increasing radio and satellite television broadcasts and Persian Internet websites, young Iranians could be fed a diet of news and views of free, open societies. Supporting democracy in the surrounding countries of the region, such as Iraq, Afghanistan, and Pakistan, would also be influential and leave the people of Iran asking why they do not have greater levels of freedom themselves. Democracy in Iraq and Afghanistan would undermine the argument promoted by many in the Muslim world, especially the Middle East, that liberal democracy and Islam are incompatible.

Generate International Pressure

Iran interacts diplomatically and economically with a number of powerful international partners, including Russia, China, Japan, India, and members of the European Union (EU) such as France and Germany. The

United States must seek to have these countries pressure Iran to conform more closely to international standards of behavior. Improving Iran's domestic and international deportment is not only the responsibility of the United States; it is an international community concern. Perhaps the best way of disciplining Iranian behavior is through limiting trade.

Despite its great oil and gas wealth, Iran's highly centralized economy is in dire straits due to mismanagement and corruption. Tehran is already under a host of U.S. economic sanctions, dating from the 1979 Iranian Revolution and the seizure of the American embassy and its staff, and it can ill-afford additional multilateral sanctions. However, Iran does significant business with other trading partners, including Germany, France, Italy, Switzerland, and South Korea.[1] The EU, for instance, is pursuing a trade and cooperation pact with Iran. France, Japan, Malaysia, and China have signed oil and gas deals with Tehran worth billions of dollars.

Iran's economy is highly centralized, meaning that its trade profits are going directly into the pockets of the central government. This, in turn, funds Iran's WMD programs, international terrorism, military modernization, and the repression of the Iranian people. Until Iran swears off these activities, additional multilateral economic pressure, including economic disengagement by other nations, should be brought to bear on the Iranian government. Full-scale economic relations with Iran give the appearance of approval of Tehran's troubling activities. Certainly not all nations will follow America's lead on this matter such as China, but nations concerned about Iranian activities should be persuaded to pressure Iran using economic disengagement. Positive inducements might also be used to ameliorate Iranian behavior, such as lifting American sanctions, normalizing diplomatic relations, or supporting Iran's bid to join the World Trade Organization.

Counter Proliferation

Without a doubt, the United States and the international community have no interest in seeing Iran develop a nuclear weapons capability. It would destabilize the military balance in the region and set off a nuclear arms race with its neighbors, including Saudi Arabia, which fears Iranian hegemony in the Persian Gulf. Therefore, it makes sense that Iran be a target of the forward-leaning, multinational Proliferation Security Initiative (PSI). The United States should also support a vigorous International Atomic Energy Agency (IAEA) effort to expose Iranian violations of the

Nuclear Nonproliferation Treaty (NPT). If violations are found, these transgressions should be reported to the UN Security Council for action, including the imposition of multilateral economic sanctions. The United States should also support the European Union's efforts to arrange a complete and verifiable dismantlement of Iran's nuclear program, making it clear that Washington expects the EU to support tougher measures should their diplomatic efforts fail. The military option of striking Iranian nuclear sites to destroy or delay Tehran's nuclear program should remain a viable, but last, option since a military strike against Iran will likely result in terrorist or Iranian military strikes against the U.S., Iraq, or even Israel.

Ensure a Robust Military Presence

The U.S. military should maintain a distinct military presence, including naval assets, in the Persian Gulf to balance Iranian military power, discourage Iranian adventurism in Afghanistan or Iraq, and keep the Persian Gulf sea lanes open. Washington should also look to improve military relations with the states which ring the Persian Gulf, Gulf of Oman, and northern Arabian Sea. Because of Iran's growing missile capability, the United States should deploy land-based and sea-based missile defenses to the region, including Iraq and Afghanistan, when available. Military containment of Iran is also an option.

DEALING WITH NORTH KOREA

North Korea is the most dangerous of the rogue states in terms of its pure destructive power. It has an exceedingly large conventional military and possesses WMD, including as few as two, and as many as eight, nuclear weapons. The 1.2 million-soldier North Korean People's Army is precipitously positioned forward along the Demilitarized Zone (DMZ) separating North and South Korea and ready to spring into action at a moment's notice. Almost without warning, Pyongyang could send hundreds of thousands of soldiers south across the DMZ and unleash a 10,000 artillery piece fusillade on the South Korean capital of Seoul of a magnitude never before seen in modern military history. North Korea's use of chemical weapons in a new Korean war is highly likely. Biological weapons are a possibility. How Pyongyang might employ its likely nuclear arsenal in a conflict is anyone's guess, although it is clear that it could use it against South Korea or Japan, including American forces stationed in both places. In the future, North Korea might be able to use nukes against the United States itself. Less threatening, but thoroughly disturbing, North Korea also counterfeits currency and traffics narcotics.

North Korean Goals

Considering that the regime is theoretically on the brink of collapse, Pyongyang's basic goal is to survive another year. China, its patron state, is likely to ensure that North Korea does not implode for fear of civil war or massive refugee flows across the border into northern China. Chinese aid, added to irregular assistance from South Korea and other international donors, will likely allow North Korea to muddle through for the foreseeable future. But North Korea's relative weakness, in contrast to South Korea and the United States, will not allow it to achieve its ultimate goal of reuniting the Korean Peninsula under its red and blue communist flag. Brandishing nuclear weapons and a top-notch ballistic missile program, Pyongyang will try to compete for a position of respect and acknowledgment among the other powers in the region and in the international community at large. Based on recent history, it may try to do this through provocative acts such as long-range missile testing. A nuclear test, though risky politically, is also possible.

U.S. Goals

American objectives regarding North Korea run the gamut of international relations challenges. The United States seeks continued peace and stability on the Korean Peninsula and supports the aspirations of the people of North and South Korea to be peacefully reconciled and reunited at some point in the future. Understanding that the reunification objective may take some time, the United States will maintain its military presence on the Korean Peninsula, and in the region, to ensure that the North does not aggress against the South once again like it did in June 1950. Washington would like to see Pyongyang give up its WMD and ballistic missile programs and proliferation once and for all. Lastly, North Korea should liberalize its economic and political systems away from being one of the world's last, and most repressive, communist dictatorships. Changes in North Korea's Stalinist political system would certainly enhance the prospects of

North-South reunification. Regime change is extremely unlikely, but changes in regime behavior, although remote, are possible.

Policy Prescriptions

North Korea is a particularly vexing problem for American policy-makers, but one too dangerous to ignore. At a minimum, North Korea's irresponsible international behavior should be confined to the Korean Peninsula.

Eliminate the Nuclear Program

The United States and the international community must insist on the complete, verifiable, and irreversible dismantlement of all of North Korea's nuclear programs, including both its plutonium- and uranium-based nuclear weapons programs. The international community must not be forced again to revisit the possibility of a nuclear North Korea should some future disarmament agreement be achieved. Unfortunately, the international community has the right to be skeptical of North Korean promises. In 1994, Pyongyang agreed to halt a nuclear program in exchange for energy aid only to be discovered to have begun another nuclear weapons program clandestinely in about 1998. If an agreement is reached, it must be structured so that North Korea cannot resume a nuclear weapons program and blackmail the international community with it once again. The United States should also be firm in getting North Korea to return to the NPT, from which it withdrew in early 2003. This is important to the future viability of the NPT and other UN nonproliferation treaties.

Engage Multilaterally

The North Korean problem is not a bilateral issue between Washington and Pyongyang as many have suggested. It is a regional issue, whose outcome deeply affects the security of China, Russia, Japan, and South Korea. It is also a broad challenge to the UN's global nonproliferation treaties, especially the NPT. The U.S. bilateral effort to address the North Korean nuclear problem, resulting in the 1994 Agreed Framework, was well-intentioned, but less than successful due to Pyongyang's perfidy. Quite simply, other concerned parties must bring their influence to bear to get North Korea to change a wide range of destructive policies and behaviors. Only a united front, including some of its biggest patrons such as China, has any chance of success in dealing with the recalcitrant North Koreans. The question is whether China, the country with the most influence in Pyongyang, is willing to pull the North Korean regime back from the abyss.

Maintain Military Deterrence

North Korea must never again believe that it can resolve the division of the Korean Peninsula through force of arms. Pyongyang, which lacks political or economic clout, embraces the Maoist ideology that political power comes from the barrel of a gun. Maintaining a strong U.S. military deterrent in South Korea will persuade North Korea of the futility of opening another Korean war. To do this, the United States, along with its South Korean ally, must ensure that the most advanced military technology is devoted to the defense of South Korea, including land-based and sea-based missile defenses. The United States will spend upwards of $4 billion on upgrading U.S. forces in Korea over the next decade.

Encourage Economic Reform

North Korea has become a ward of the international community because of a devastating ten-year famine, which has claimed the lives of as many as 2 million (of 22 million) North Koreans. Some of this is a result of bad weather such as floods and drought, but the bulk of famine comes from disastrous economic policies and management, dating back to the Soviet collectivist era. The northern part of the Korean Peninsula has never been the peninsula's "breadbasket," but Pyongyang can do much more to feed itself if it changes its economic and agricultural policies. The international community, especially the UN's World Food Program, has made a tremendous effort to partially overcome shortfalls in food production in North Korea.

The problem is that the North Korean government has not done enough itself to address the famine, such as changing its agricultural policies and practices. Despite North Korean stubbornness regarding change, food aid should continue because it is not the people of North Korea who have created this situation, but the Stalinist government. As President Ronald Reagan was famous for saying: Starving people have no politics. In this case, the people of North Korea are the victims of their own government and should not be punished. The international community should insist that, as part of the food assistance program, North Korea do its part to improve the situation by changing its agricultural and economic policy and practices. Currently the world's most closed economy, North Korea would greatly benefit from increased interaction with the world's markets.[2] North Korean labor rates would likely be lower than China's, and if the political conditions were right, foreign direct investment would flock to the cheap labor supply in the DPRK. Economic liberalization and the influx of Western ideals might very well lead to some political liberalization of the regime as well. Of course, this is exactly what the regime fears most.

Counter Proliferation

Based on new information, in early 2005, North Korea was implicated in aiding Libya's nuclear program before Tripoli decided to dismantle its program. Using the PSI, the United States and its international partners must prevent further North Korean WMD and ballistic missile proliferation off the Korean Peninsula. This would support international nonproliferation goals, while having the added benefit of preventing North Korea from profiting from the ill-gotten gains of weapons proliferation, which fund Pyongyang's military, WMD programs, and political repression at home. Pyongyang must understand that any proliferation of nuclear capability to terrorist groups will not be tolerated and would meet serious, but unspecified, actions.

DEALING WITH SYRIA

Not intending to understate in any way its potential for troublemaking and mischief, Syria is the least dangerous of the three rogue states. However, Syria does hold hostage one of the world's seemingly most intractable foreign policy challenges through its sponsorship of Middle Eastern terrorist groups: the Israeli-Palestinian conflict. Syria's ability to destabilize the new Iraq should not be underestimated either. If that is not enough incentive to address the Syria question, Damascus may also be looking toward WMD as a means to offset the conventional military strength of neighbors such as Turkey, and Israel, and possibly Iraq who look increasingly unfavorably on Syrian destabilizing policies.

The Arab-style socialist, Alawite minority government is under increasing pressure from Syrian young people to open up the repressive political system and liberalize its limping economy. Syria's young leader, Bashar al Assad, had promised political and economic reforms, but these changes have been put on the shelf by his father's "old guard," who fear losing influence and position under the heir's new regime. That noted, Syria is the most likely rogue state to change its behavior peacefully if exposed to the right leverage from the international community.

Syrian Goals

Syria's regional goals are practical and modest in comparison with Iran and North Korea, which both aspire to dominate their respective corners of the globe. Syria, surrounded by larger powers, seeks security, the return of the strategic Golan Heights currently held by Israel, internal stability, regime survival, the protection of Syrian interests in Lebanon, and a friendly, or weak, Iraqi neighbor. If possible, it would like to assume a position of leadership in the Arab and Muslim world and develop allies, who will support its national objectives. To this end, Syria has developed close ties with Iran.

U.S. Goals

Ending Syria's state sponsorship of terrorism must surely top America's wish list for Damascus. Syrian support of anti-Israeli terrorism has a negative effect on the Middle East peace process. Resolving the Israeli-Palestinian struggle in a comprehensive and just manner would have a positive effect not only on peace and security in the Middle East, but also on the war on terror. Many Muslims consider the Israeli-Palestinian conflict and perceived American support for Israel as a legitimate basis for Muslim rage, violence, and terrorism. There is no question that solving this problem would undermine the radicals' arguments for violence and jihad. Beyond terrorism, Washington would like to see Damascus give up its WMD programs, swear off its perceived nuclear aspirations, and end its support for destabilizing Iraq. Finally, the United States would welcome an opening up of its economic system and authoritarian political system in favor of greater pluralism.

Policy Prescriptions

As a small, secular state, Syria is, perhaps, the most susceptible to international pressure to reform. Syria is increasingly isolated in the Middle East by countries unsympathetic to its "bad-boy" agenda, including Turkey, the new Iraq, and Israel. Iraq is the latest country to look askance at Syria's roguish behavior, including its support of the Iraqi insurgency. Syria has limited economic and military resources to buck the international community's calls for change. But one should not forget Syria's intimate relationship with terrorist groups, including Hamas and Hezbollah, and how they might respond to international pressure on Damascus.

Use Economic Pressure

Syria's economy is in desperate need of restructuring and liberalization, and suffers from high levels of corruption and unemployment.[3] Syria is already experiencing 20 percent unemployment among its young people. Though Syria is already heavily sanctioned by the United States, economic pressure could be broadened to include Germany, Italy, France, and Turkey, which are major trading partners. Broader economic pressure could pose a threat to Syria's internal stability, hinder its WMD programs, and undermine its support for terror. In addition, limiting Syria's economic integration with oil-rich Iraq, including a Syrian-Iraqi oil pipeline, which conveyed seventy thousand barrels a day of oil to Syria for export, could encourage Damascus to make promised economic and political reforms.

Counter Proliferation

The United States, in concert with others, should ensure that Russia does not aid Syrian aspirations for nuclear weapons by supplying Damascus with nuclear know-how or technology. Iran is also suspected of collaborating with the Syrians on nuclear issues. Syria is unlikely to swear off the nuclear option while Israel is in possession of a nuclear arsenal, but may reconsider should a peace deal be reached with the Israelis over the Golan Heights. In the meantime, all means, including the PSI, should be used to thwart the advancement of Syrian ballistic missile and WMD programs.

End Support for Terrorism and Iraqi Insurgency

Make it clear to Damascus that the return of the Golan Heights is not a possibility as long as Syria sponsors terrorism or the Iraq insurgency. There should be no negotiations regarding this issue until Syria has demonstrated that it has permanently closed terrorist offices in Damascus and ended its support for Palestinian and Lebanese rejectionist groups and Iraqi insurgents. This must include not allowing Iran to use Syria as a conduit for supplying terrorist groups such as Hezbollah and Hamas in Lebanon and Israel and al-Qaeda in Iraq. If Syria ends its support for terrorism and the insurgency, it could deepen its economic engagement with the international community. It might open the possibility of aid and assistance from the United States, which ended in 1981, by being removed from the U.S. State Department's State Sponsors of Terrorism List. Military strikes against Iraqi former regime elements in Syria should be considered if they can be located.

CONCLUSION

There will always be states that live outside the international community. Dealing with rogue states is never easy, but it is necessary. Rarely does a problem get better or resolve itself. Challenges must be faced squarely. Fortunately, the Libyan model may provide a new paradigm for the peaceful evolution of these rogue states from poor pariahs to prosperous, participating members of the international community. Finally, international politics is tough business, dynamic, and often unpredictable. Developing and implementing foreign policy is difficult work. Today's sound policies may be outdated by sunrise tomorrow. One policy solution will not address all rogue states.

As political scientist Hans Morgenthau once observed: Good foreign policy is nothing but good common sense, and good common sense generally makes good foreign policy. So, despite the complexities of dealing with rogue states in an increasingly challenging and dangerous world, Morgenthau's guidance serves as a good point of departure for dealing with these nettlesome international problems.

NOTES

1. The Heritage Foundation and *Wall Street Journal, 2005 Index of Economic Freedom*, Washington, DC: The Heritage Foundation and Dow Jones & Company, 2005, available at www.heritage.org.

2. *2005 Index of Economic Freedom*.

3. *2005 Index of Economic Freedom*.

CONCLUSION

The only thing necessary for the triumph of evil is for good men to do nothing.

—Edmund Burke (1729–1797), Irish philosopher and statesman

The end of the Cold War in 1991 brought a fundamental change in the international security environment. The good news was that the superpower rivalry between the United States and NATO on one side and the Soviet Union and the Warsaw Pact on the other had ended without a single shot being fired; a nuclear Armageddon had been averted.

The bad news is that with the fall of the Berlin Wall, the threats to international peace and security became less predictable and more diverse. No longer was there a single, well-defined enemy like the Soviet Union. The rise of international Islamic terrorism, the proliferation of weapons of mass destruction (WMD), and troubling rogue states replaced the U.S.-Soviet superpower rivalry as the central organizing theme of the new national security environment. The idea of a post–Cold War "peace dividend," consisting of years of international tranquility, stability, and prosperity, were dashed forever on a warm, sunny September 11 morning four years ago. Unpredictable adversaries posing multiple threats on many fronts replaced Cold War threats. Former director of central intelligence James Woolsey, who served in the post from 1993 to 1995, described the change in the security environment: "If we were struggling with a large dragon for 45 years, killed it, and then found ourselves in a jungle full of poisonous snakes—and the snakes are much harder to keep track of than the dragon ever was."

The burning question is, what should America do about these new security challenges? One obvious, though ill-advised, option is to withdraw from the international security arena. The United States could seal its borders and hide behind the two large oceans that have insulated us from so much danger for so long. We could create a "fortress America." However, considering how integrated we are politically, economically, and socially with the world today, and how isolation would affect our quality of life, such a decision would be foolhardy. In the modern era, whole-hearted attempts at isolationism during international crises have never succeeded anyway. And that is exactly what the enemies of peace and freedom want us to do. The United States cannot, and should not, retreat from full engagement in world affairs.

The United States, as the leader of the free world, is the biggest obstacle to the evil plans of the terrorists and the rogue states for changing the international order to their liking. It is not the American way to cower to the demands of international outlaws. We ignore the gathering storm of terrorism, WMD, and rogue states at our peril. This struggle is not "over there." It is here and now. The United States can face these threats squarely and emerge victorious if we have the will and resolve to carry it through. Weapons proliferation can be curtailed. Rogue states can be fenced in. Terrorists can be out of business.

To win the war on terror, we must help the successful transition of Iraq and Afghanistan to open, free, and tolerant societies. More freedom must be injected into the Islamic world, giving the Muslim people democracy and basic civil liberties that they have long been denied. Our intelligence must be the best possible to predict and prevent attacks before they begin. We must also continue to work to secure the homeland, while maintaining civil liberties and our way of life.

America's image is often distorted overseas and enhancing our reputation by improving our public diplomacy efforts is important. Taking steps to keep money out of the hands of terrorists will make it harder for them to recruit, train, and operate. We should have no quarrel with striking terrorists before they strike us. Lastly, America must continue to look for new ways to cooperate internationally on intelligence, law enforcement, financial operations, and military matters. We are all in this fight together.

To limit the effects of the proliferation of weapons of mass destruction and ballistic missiles, the United States must first take steps to undermine the utility of these weapons by deploying a missile defense at home and with our troops overseas. We must also implement the proactive Proliferation Security Initiative, which is using innovative ways to stop the trafficking of WMD and ballistic missiles. The United Nations should criminalize WMD proliferation to provide a strong disincentive for the transfer of these horrific weapons.

Led by the United States, the international community can also take steps to strengthen controls on WMD in places like Russia, and look to close loopholes in the Nuclear Nonproliferation Treaty, which allows states to pursue nuclear weapons under the guise of a civilian nuclear power program. The UN should readjust the focus of its International Atomic Energy Agency to ensure that it concentrates on preventing proliferation, not just spreading peaceful nuclear energy. Lastly, the international community should take a crack at controlling the ballistic and cruise missile, and surface-to-air missile (SAM), trade to discourage states from being tempted to mate those missiles with WMD, or allow SAMs to fall into the hands of terrorists.

In handling perilous rogue states, the Libyan transformation provides an interesting opportunity. Should the Libyan model prove successful, it should be thrown up to the rogues as a unique opportunity to change their ways once and for all. In Iran, we should promote internal change from within by encouraging reform-minded, young Iranians, while generating broad international pressure from without by limiting economic engagement. We should not accept any Iranian proliferation activities. To contain Iranian aspirations for domination in the Persian Gulf, we should ensure a robust American military presence in that part of the world.

Regarding nettlesome North Korea, the United States and its international partners must strive to eliminate Pyongyang's nuclear program once and for all by insisting on a complete, verifiable, and irreversible disarmament. Along with our South Korean allies, we must ensure that our military might is robust enough to discourage another North Korean attack. Lastly, North Korea must do more to feed its people, and internal economic reform should be part of any international food aid program. When dealing with the slippery Syrians, we should use economic pressure to guide the regime away from its bad behavior, such as supporting terrorism, destabilizing Iraq and the Middle East peace process, and pursuing WMD.

The great American president Theodore Roosevelt summed it up well when he said, "We are face-to-face with our destiny and we must meet it with a high and resolute courage." He was right then; it is true today, too. The United States is in a Herculean struggle in the defense of freedom and our way of life. Public debate is important, but our national security quibbles should end at our water's edge. A failure to meet these security challenges head on could lead to an incident that would make the unspeakable horrors of 9/11 seem like a minor tragedy. Besides Islamic terrorism, WMD proliferation, and rogue states, our next greatest challenge is remaining vigilant. As Secretary of Homeland Security Michael Chertoff so aptly put it at his swearing-in in early 2005: "We cannot afford to become complacent."

With resolve, determination, constancy to purpose, and a willingness to lead, America will successfully meet these challenges, prevailing over a Devil's Triangle.

INDEX

ABOUT THE AUTHOR

Peter Brookes is a Senior Fellow for National Security Affairs at the Heritage Foundation, a Washington, DC–based think tank. He also writes a weekly column for the *New York Post* and appears regularly on TV news networks such as FOX, CNN, MSNBC, and CNBC. Prior to joining Heritage, Brookes was deputy assistant secretary of defense at the Pentagon, senior staffer with the Committee on International Relations in the House of Representatives, operations officer with the CIA, adviser with the State Department, and served on active duty with the U.S. Navy. He is a graduate of the U.S. Naval Academy, the Defense Language Institute, the Naval War College, and Johns Hopkins University and has received a number of military decorations.